# Acknowledgments

To have my name alone listed as author on the front of this book is somewhat misleading. It would have been impossible to assemble this book without the abundant and generous help of many colleagues, who are also friends. Further, without the good fortune of many firms and institutions who preserved the photographs presented herein, as well as the supporting documentation, the history of the M3 would have been lost. A debt of gratitude is owed to all who through the past 75+ years have said, "I think I'll save that" – rather than consigning a document or photo to a landfill, which is where so much history has been deposited.

I, unknowingly, began gathering the material for this book 20 years ago, when I stumbled across a captivating album of photos. At the time, I had some interest in the M3 tank, but a great deal of interest in steam locomotives, and the crossover between the two caught my attention.

Through the years, I occasionally would find more material of interest, or someone would point something out to me, until finally five years ago work on this volume aggressively began. Five years may seem like a long time to put into a project which yielded such relatively modest results, but a great deal of time is spent turning over every stone (sometimes driving hundreds of miles to do so), and often finding nothing beneath those stones.

Throughout this half-decade, Joe DeMarco has given selflessly of the material he has located, and even more selflessly of his time in correspondence, telephone calls and face to face visits.

Kurt Laughlin, arguably one of the most analytical of modern day tank historians also gave generously of his time, and materials that he had accumulated and organized over many years.

Tom Kailbourn lent his keen analysis of photos. Mack Bell, and his father, Dana, along with Jim Gilmore, kept me from having to make even more trips to the National Archives by generously scanning documents for me

that either forgot, ran out of time to get, or could not find during the many trips Denise and I made to the Archives.

Brandt Rosenbush and Danielle Szostak-Viers with Chrysler, and Larry Kinsel and Christo Datini of General Motors all were generous with their time and dug out material that had not been seen for decades. Beyond photos, much of the documentation of the history of the production of these tanks came from the archives that these four individuals maintain.

Dr. Rachael Johnstone and Randy Talbot of TACOM provided large pieces of the intricate puzzle that was the workings of Chrysler's Detroit Tank Arsenal.

Noted authors and historians Steve Zaloga and David Fletcher were quick to respond to my queries, eagerly sharing their knowledge and materials. Rob Ervin spent most of a day in my office, helping sort through the mountain of accumulated material, helping organize it and helping sift the gold from the tailings.

Shane Lovell kindly provided literally thousands of pages of material documenting the British side of the M3 story.

Mike Kalbfeisch tracked down an elusive cache of material for

me, and Scott Taylor not only provided imagery from his own collection, but proofread the entire book – twice.

The team at AFV Modeller not only were enthusiastic about this project, and worked diligently at presenting the material in a clear, crisp manner, they also tolerated innumerable delays and set backs that none of us could have foreseen.

Even with all the tremendous help from those named above, this book would not have been possible without the loving support of my amazing wife Denise. Denise took in stride the various trips seeking long-lost archives, some in areas that were far from being postcard destinations. Once at these points, she threw herself into digging through files and scanning materials, knowing full well that likely only 10% of the material would ultimately be incorporated into the manuscript. She also tolerated weeks of 18-hour work days, where the burden of the entire household fell on her as I stared at a computer screen while surrounded by boxes of musty materials. Most importantly, her love and support were a source of encouragement during difficult days (and nights) of this labor.

David Doyle
October 2019
Memphis, TN

**Above:** *The very first M3, Rock Island Arsenal-built W-304191, is demonstrated on a course simulating rugged terrain before an assembled group. Often criticized, the M3 laid a firm foundation not only for wartime US medium tanks, but the entire US tank industry for decades thereafter.*

# Table of Contents

# Introduction

It is often said that during WWII, the United States was the Arsenal of Democracy. The nation, thankfully removed from aerial attack and combat in the streets, and blessed with abundant resources and industry geared toward mass production, certainly lived up to the moniker. However, before the gears of industry can begin to churn out armaments, the decision has to be made what was going to be made, and by whom. Reaching these decisions were not always linear processes.

In the years immediately following WWI, the United States Army tank units were primarily equipped with two types of tanks. The most numerous were the M1917 6-ton light tank which was derived from the famed French FT-17. These were augmented by one hundred Mark VIII 40-ton heavy tanks produced by Rock Island Arsenal, where were similar in design to British tanks.

The US Army Ordnance Department desired a medium tank, with far greater mobility than either of the two existent types. Two styles of medium tank were proposed, a so-called convertible type, advocated by J. Walter Christie, which could operate on its tracks, or with the tracks removed, could be driven more rapidly on improved roads, riding directly on its road wheels. The second type of medium tank, advocated by the Ordnance Department, was a conventional type fully track laying vehicle.

With the limited funding available to the postwar army a successive series of experimental and trial tanks of both styles were procured from the 1920s through the mid-1930s.

The T4 and T4E1 convertible tanks were recommended for standardization in February 1936. In 1939 the vehicles were classified as Medium Tank, M1, Limited Standard. The 18 examples produced were reclassified as obsolete in March 1940.

The conventional type tanks advocated by Ordnance gained favor through the T1 and T2 series vehicles, as well as the M1921 and M1922 vehicles. All of these vehicles, however, suffered from being underpowered.

By 1936 the stage had been set for the direct path of development of what would be the US Army's medium tank program of WWII.

**Above:** In this volume we examine the M3 medium tank from bottom to top. This early M3 has side doors, thus no bottom escape hatch, thus only the stiffeners interrupting the flat bottom surface.

# Chapter 1
# Setting the stage, the T5/M2

In 1936 efforts began to develop a new medium tank to meet the requirements set forth by the Infantry Board. The Ordnance Committee recommended the development of the vehicle on 21 May 1936. The tank itself, which was designated Medium Tank T5, was derived from the M2 light tank, albeit with heavier armament and armor. The armor, however, was somewhat restricted due to the weight limit, which had been established at 15 tons. This low weight was based on the prevailing bridge capacity in rural America. Although the decision had been made that this was to be a conventional tank, rather than a convertible tank, the matter of armament remained to be settled. Some advocated turret-mounted main armament, as had been seen on the T4 medium

tank, while others favored sponson-mounted guns. Ultimately, the decision was made to go with both. Atop the tank was a turret, capable of 360-degree rotation, designed to mount the new 37mm high velocity antitank gun then under development. Additionally, four machine guns were mounted in sponsons on each of the four corners of the hull. Additionally, a pair of fixed .30 caliber machine guns were installed in the front of the hull. One example of the machine was built, designated T5 phase 1, and assigned Army registration number W-30369. The vehicle was completed before the high velocity 37mm gun was perfected, and as an interim a pair of 37mm M2A1 guns were mounted instead. The vehicle, which survives to this day, is still armed with the interim weapons.

**Above:** *Although the U.S. Army tested several new medium tanks in the 1920s and 1930s, the direct ancestor of the Medium Tank M3 was the Medium Tank T5, of which two variants, the Phase I and the Phase III, were produced (there was no T5, Phase II). The Phase 1 had a 15-ton weight limit, to enable the vehicle to operate on primary highway bridges in the United States. The vehicle, as shown in a photo dated 24 February 1938, was assigned registration number W-30369 and began testing in November 1937. It was constructed of mild steel and was equipped with a turret with a dummy 37mm high-velocity gun; four .30-caliber machine guns in flexible mounts in the sponsons; two .30-caliber machine guns on the glacis; and two removable .30-caliber antiaircraft machine guns. Steve Zaloga collection*

**Above:** *The two bow machine guns are visible in this left-front view of Medium Tank T5, Phase I, on 24 February 1938. A crew door with a small vision port was on the left and the right sponsons; two vision slots were over each door, and vision ports were on the turret. The driver's compartment had hinged doors on the front and sides, shown in the raised positions. Steve Zaloga collection*

The tank, which carried a five-man crew, was powered by a Continental R-670 7-cylinder air-cooled radial aircraft engine. Although aircraft and tanks are very different types of equipment, in terms of powerplant they share requirements of high horsepower, light weight and compact size. Even today, the M1 Abrams is powered by an AGT1500 turbine powerplant derived from an engine originally used to power helicopters.

The engine of the T5 was mounted in the rear, with the transmission mounted at the front of the vehicle. A long driveshaft at the bottom of the fighting compartment connected the two. The suspension system consisted of three two-wheel vertical volute suspension bogies mounted on each side of the tank, with a return idler at the rear.

The tank, known as the T5 Phase I, was tested at Aberdeen Proving Ground as well as by the Infantry Board at Fort Benning. With several minor modification, the tank was recommended for Standardization as the M2 on 2 June 1935, which was approved shortly thereafter.

While Phase II did not leave the drawing board, by winter 1938 the T5, Phase III was undergoing testing. The Phase III machine upped the weight limit to 20 tons, which allowed an improvement in armor.

Additionally, the suspension bogies were

redesigned, with the return roller now centered over the support casting. The driver's position was relocated to the left front of the superstructure, and the vehicle was armed with the new 37mm high velocity antitank gun, mounted in cast armor turret. One of the biggest improvements was the result of an engine change, with the Wright R-975 being the engine of choice. Also a radial, air-cooled aircraft engine, this nine-cylinder engine would go on to power many further types of American tanks.

However, the T5 Phase III was built during the early development of the engine, which although rated at 400 horsepower for this application, was shown to only develop 346 horsepower during testing. As a result of the increased weight, and despite the increase in horsepower, the Phase III had a top speed of 32.9 MPH, only about a 2 MPH increase over the Phase I.

Diesel engines had begun to attract the attention of the army, and the T5 Phase III was rebuilt with a Guiberson 9-cylinder air-cooled radial Diesel engine. In September 1938, the tank was redesignated T5E1, reflecting the change in powerplant.

Concurrently with this, the T5 Phase I was standardized as the M2 Medium Tank, and funds were allocated to produce 18 of the vehicles at Rock Island Arsenal during fiscal year 1939, and a further 54 in the following fiscal year. The

production vehicles would differ somewhat from the T5 in that they were equipped with the high velocity 37mm antitank gun and were powered by the Wright engine as used in the Phase III vehicle.

Even as the M2 was going into production, the T5 Phase III was further modified, with a new, smaller turret mounting a machine gun replacing the 37mm-armed turret originally installed. Even more radical, the hull was modified such that a 75mm howitzer M1A1 was installed in the right front of the hull. So configured, the vehicle was redesignated the T5E2. The modified tank underwent testing, lasting nearly a year, beginning in April 1939.

Through service testing of the M2, the need for some improvements became evident, especially with regard to the turret design. A new turret, with nearly vertical sides, was designed, increasing space inside the turret, and an improved recoil system for the main gun was engineered, reducing the interior space requirements, both resulting in a roomier turret. The armor thickness was increased to 1 ¼-inches on all vertical surfaces. To help overcome the weight increase, the track width was increased 1-inch, to 14-1/4 inches, which reduced ground pressure to 15.3 psi, and a more powerful engine fitted. The new engine, the Wright R-975-EC2, developed 400 horsepower at 2,400 RPM.

The improvements were significant enough that the improved vehicle, designated Medium Tank M2A1, was slated to replace the M2 in the planned 1940 procurement.

The outbreak of war in Europe, and specifically the rapid advances made by German Panzer divisions, triggered sweeping changes in the US Army. It was clear that many more tanks were needed, far more than the Army could produce in their own Rock Island Arsenal. To use these tanks, a separate Armored Force was formed on 10 July 1940, with Major General Adna Chaffee commanding.

The Rock Island Arsenal order for M2A1 tanks was increased to 126 units, which was acknowledged to be woefully inadequate for the growing army. Nevertheless, production of those tanks began in December 1940, and would continue until August 1941.

Strategic planning at the time had held that the prime contractors for mass tank production would be locomotive and railway equipment manufacturers. Locomotive manufacturers were equipped to and acquainted with working with large steel assemblies and castings – the engine bed of a steam locomotive was often a single piece steel casting weighing 20 tons and over 50-feet long.

**Above:** *By the time this photo was taken, on 3 June 1938, the dummy long-barreled 37mm gun had been replaced by twin 37mm Guns M2A1 in a Mount T10. This vehicle survives in the collection of the National Armor and Cavalry Museum. The plates shaped somewhat like quarter-circles on the rear corners of the hull are bullet deflectors, to allow the two rear sponson machine guns to at least attempt to hit enemy troops who were in the blind spot near the rear of the tank, or that were in trenches that the tank was crossing. Note the mufflers on the engine deck to the rear of the turret. Steve Zaloga collection*

**Above:** *The Medium Tank T5, Phase I, as armed with the twin 37mm guns is viewed from the left rear, with the turret traversed to the left and the guns slightly depressed. Details of the rear of the superstructure are in view, including two vision slots and two vision ports. The two mufflers on the engine deck were oriented in opposite directions. A curved shield was between the front muffler and the superstructure. Steve Zaloga collection*

**Right**: *An Aberdeen Proving Ground photograph dated March 27, 1947, shows the Medium Tank T5, Phase I, registration number W-30369, on outdoor display. The weapons, headlights, and other accessories had been removed. In some of the frontal photos of this vehicle, such as this one, the vertical fins on the final-drive assembly are visible. The T5, Phase I, used 12-tooth sprockets. TACOM LCMC History Office*

Accordingly, contract 670 ORD 434 was placed with Baldwin Locomotive Works in June 1940. In the company-produced booklet, American Locomotive Went to War, it is noted that Alco began the process of building tanks in July 1940, with the formal contract not being issued until November. While the details of this contract have not yet surfaced, it is likely that both of these contracts were initially let for the production of M2A1 medium tanks.

Also in June 1940 came what would become one of the most influential decisions in the US tank program for years to come – the involvement of the Chrysler Corporation.

**Above:** *The Medium Tank T5, Phase III, registration number W-30443, varied in several respects from the T5, Phase I, including the use of armor instead of mild steel; replacement of the Continental R-670-3 seven-cylinder engine, rated at 260 horsepower, for the Wright R-975 nine-cylinder Whirlwind engine, rated at 346 horsepower; and shifting the driver's compartment more to the left, due to changes in the drive train, making for an asymmetrical layout for the front of the vehicle. The T5, Phase III, is shown on November 15, 1938, with a soldier standing next to it for scale. Steve Zaloga collection*

**Above:** *A left rear view of the Medium Tank T5, Phase III, provides details of the rear of the hull, which did not have an overhang and was equipped with two engine-access doors. The mufflers were moved to the rear of the bullet deflectors. Brackets extended from the tops of the center and rear bogie assemblies to the sponsons, for extra support. The front bogies lacked brackets on this vehicle. Note the .30-caliber machine gun on a pintle mount the on left side of the turret. Steve Zaloga collection*

**Above:** *The arrangement of the pioneer tools on the right side of the T5, Phase III, is displayed. A machine-gun tripod is strapped to the fender to the rear of the headlight. A small placard with crossed cavalry sabers is above the door on the sponson, and a .30-caliber machine gun on a pintle mount is on the side of the turret. Although a support bracket was not attached to the front bogie assembly, three bolt holes for attaching a bracket were tapped near the top of that assembly, as these bogie assemblies were interchangeable. Keith Buckley collection*

**Above:** *Details of the suspension, the end connectors of the track, and the midsection and rear of the right side of the hull of Medium Tank M2 registration number W-30447 are displayed in a photo taken by Rock Island Arsenal on 3 November 1939. The photo illustrated the method of loading the tank in a railroad boxcar designed for transporting automobiles. 30-caliber machine gun on the right-rear sponson mount. National Archives*

**Left:** *In order to test the concept of a self-propelled howitzer on a medium-tank chassis, the Army ordered a pilot vehicle with a 75mm Howitzer M1A1 mounted on a modified Field Carriage M3A1 in the right sponson of the remodeled Medium Tank T5, Phase III. The result was designated the Medium Tank T5E2. The original turret was removed, and a smaller turret with a range finder and a .30-caliber machine gun on the front was installed atop the superstructure. The Medium Tank T5E2 underwent testing at Aberdeen from April 1939 to February 1940, and, although the vehicle wasn't selected for production, it was considered a satisfactory design, and it provided the U.S. Army valuable lessons for the future development of self-propelled guns and howitzers. Steve Zaloga collection*

**Above:** *The second production Medium Tank M2, registration number W-30445, is viewed from the front right during tests at Aberdeen Proving Ground in August 1939. The main armament was the high-velocity, long- barreled 37mm Gun M3, with a dome-shaped gun shield or mantlet similar to the one that would appear on the Light Tank M3. The Medium Tank M2 retained the sponson machine guns and the two bow machine guns. The structure of the vehicle was of face-hardened armor. Power was supplied by a Wright 350-horsepower radial engine. The tracks were 13.25 inches wide. Note the small, horizontal ribs on the outer faces of the bogie brackets, the large castings holding the bogie wheels and suspension arms. On the left side of the final-drive assembly is cast the part number, 5E814381.*
*TACOM LCMC History Office*

**Left:** *Following satisfactory tests of the Medium Tank T5, Phase I, at Aberdeen Proving Ground and Fort Benning, the Ordnance Committee recommended the vehicle for standardization as the Medium Tank M2 on 2 June 1938. In the foreground in this photo is the prototype Medium Tank M2 under construction at the Rock Island Arsenal, in Illinois, on August 1, 1940. Light Tanks M1A1 are being assembled in the background. A 13-tooth sprocket assembly is lying on the floor next to the front bogie assembly. A view is available of the engine compartment and of the design of the two hatches on the roof of the fighting compartment. Note that the right hatch door is hinged at the front, while the left hatch door is hinged at the rear. Patton Museum*

**Left:** *The wooden mockup of the Medium Tank M2A1 was photographed at the Dodge Conant Avenue plant on 21 July 1940, on the occasion of an official visit by William Knudsen, formerly president of Chevrolet and, later, of GM and now a member of the advisory commission to the Council of National Defense. Knudsen's visit was for the twin purposes of inspecting the mockup and reviewing plans for the layouts of tank-manufacturing plants. The principal external difference of the M2A1 compared with the M2 was the vertical, instead of sloped, plates of the turret, except for the front plate. Military History Institute*

**Above:** *Above the engine deck of the Medium Tank M2 armed with the Flamethrower E2 were three compressed-nitrogen cylinders and related plumbing, for pressurizing the flamethrower. Mufflers and their shields and bullet deflectors are on the rear of the hull. The photo was taken at Fort Knox on 11 June 1941. In addition to the registration number, on the rear part of the sponson is a number 2 and a triangle with a numeral 1. These figures are also partially visible on the hull to the front of the nitrogen tanks. Patton Museum*

**left:** *The U.S. Army's Chemical Warfare Service, in its quest for self-propelled flamethrower tanks, experimented with a Flamethrower E2 mounted in the turret of the eighth Medium Tank M2, registration number W-30451. The vehicle is shown during tests for the Armored Force Board at Fort Knox, Kentucky, on 11 June 11 1941. The flamethrower head was on the end of a long extension that protruded from the gun shield. The recoil cylinder of the gun mount remained in place; it is the short cylinder to the front of the gun shield. Tests of the vehicle disclosed that the length of the flamethrower made it vulnerable when operating in woodlands. Patton Museum*

**Above:** *The Flamethrower E2 on Medium Tank M2 W-30251 is firing directly to the front during evaluations at Fort Knox on 11 June 1941. Patton Museum*

**Above:** *Another photo of the Flamethrower E2 on the Medium Tank M2 at Fort Knox on 11 June 1941, shows the devastating effect of the flame with the turret traversed directly to the left. Because of mechanical problems encountered during testing, this vehicle was not approved for series production. Patton Museum*

# Chapter 2
# Preparing for war

"Big Bill" Knudsen, more formally William S. Knudsen had come to America from Denmark as a 21 year-old in 1900. A bicycle mechanic in Denmark, once in the US he worked in shipyards and then the shop of the Erie Railroad until gaining employment with the John R. Keim Mills of Buffalo, NY in 1902. Keim manufactured bicycles, and when that business was slow, also produced metal components for other manufacturers. One of those was Ford Motor Company. By 1908 Knudsen was superintendent of the Keim plant, which was making Model T mufflers, fuel tanks and axle housings.

In January 1911 Ford purchased Keim, and in 1913 relocated much of the plant and 62 key men to Highland Park, Michigan. One of the men hired was Knudsen, who remained in Buffalo with his new wife Clara.

Knudsen's new job with Ford did not require him to live in the Detroit area, as he was charged with establishing 14 additional Ford assembly plants in the US, as well as three in Europe. Working with Albert Kahn, the two men revolutionized plant design by planning the work flow first, and then creating a structure to house it, rather than the

**Right:** *Although often overlooked, the impact of William S. Knudsen on the US armament program of WWII cannot be overstated. Knudsen, former president of General Motors, in 1940 resigned his position at GM to lead the nation's arms program for $1 per year, first serving as Commissioner of Industrial Production and later commissioned as a Lieutenant General. In these roles, Knudsen brought the automobile industry into tank manufacturing. General Motors LLC*

previous convention of adapting the work flow to fit the building.

By 1914 Knudsen had become a US citizen, and along with his family had relocated to the Detroit area, where beginning in 1915 he oversaw all Ford branch assembly plants, as well as the Highland Park plant. At that time he was earning $25,000 per year plus a 15% bonus.

In 1919, following a confrontation with Charles Sorensen, then the number 2 man in Ford manufacturing operations, Knudsen began to see his directives overruled by Henry Ford, in favor of Sorensen. Knudsen left Ford on 1 April 1921.

On 12 February 1922 Knudsen went to work for General Motors. During the interview, reportedly GM Vice-President Alfred P. Sloan, Jr. asked

Knudsen, "How much shall we pay you?" Knudsen gave the stunning reply, "Anything you like. I am not here to set a figure. I seek an opportunity."

Knudsen was hired at $30,000 annually, but within three weeks, Pierre. S. du Pont, GM President, promoted Knudsen to Vice-President of Chevrolet at $50,000 per year.

On 15 January 1924, Knudsen moved up to Vice President and director of General Motors itself, as well as President and general manager of Chevrolet. In 1933 he rose again to Executive Vice President of GM, and was over all vehicle operations in the US and Canada. Chevrolet production by itself had overtaken that of Ford, with Chevy production rising from 75,700 in 1921 to 1,001,680 in 1927.

Yet another promotion came in 1937, when Knudsen replaced Sloan as President of General Motors, with a salary of over $500,000 per year. By 1940 General Motors was firmly dug in as the nation's biggest automaker, and arguably the largest corporation. It was from the position of president of the company that Knudsen resigned in 1940. In May, President Roosevelt had asked Knudsen to be one of seven men serving on the National Defense Advisory Commission as Commissioner of Industrial Production – at a pay rate of $1.00 annually.

Knudsen's Division controlled contracts valued at a half-million dollars or more, and was responsible for Army ordnance and aircraft among other things. Chief among his responsibilities was obtaining the fullest use of all manufacturing facilities, and when necessary, providing additional facilities. Once approved by the Production Division, the Army or Navy could then award a contract based on the usual considerations of price speed, quality, etc. By virtue of his position as Industrial Production Commissioner, Knudsen also served on the War Priorities Board.

Knudsen, would find, however, that there was too much politics involved in enforcing the Advisory Commissions findings, and in 1942 accepted an Army commission as Lt. General, although his responsibilities remained much the same.

While the imposing (6'2") Bill Knudsen was moving up the GM ranks, across town Kaufman Thuma (K.T.) Keller was rising in the Chrysler organization. Keller had come to Chrysler from GM in 1926.

Keller, the son of poor farmer, had grown up on a farm in Lancaster County, Pennsylvania. Keller had only a modest education before becoming an apprentice at the Westinghouse plant in Pittsburgh. Keller impressed works manager Henry L. Barton with his work ethic, inquisitiveness, ability to learn and frugality. In time, Barton came to work for General Motors, and brought Keller with him. There, Keller worked for Walter P. Chrysler, who was president of Buick. Chrysler would leave General Motors in 1919, ultimately forming the company that bares his name two years later. The same year that Chrysler organized his company, Keller was named Vice-President of Chevrolet.

In April 1926, Chrysler hired his old protégé Keller, becoming general manager in charge of production. In 1929 Keller was promoted to President of the Dodge Division. On 22 July 1935, Keller had been named president of the Chrysler Corporation.

Keller, who is sometimes criticized as being an autocratic leader, had a considerable tendency to think big. Among the projects undertaken by Keller was the construction of the Albert Kahn-designed Dodge truck plant at 21500 Mound Road near Warren, Michigan. The plant, which was initially set up to build 5,000 trucks per week, plus spare parts equal to an additional 1,000 trucks per week, opened in 1938. This facility, erected in rural Macomb County, would produce Dodge trucks for the US military in WWII and beyond.

When William Knudsen took up his National Defense Advisory Commission duties in May, one of the first things he examined were the War Department's plans on tank production. Having previously worked for the Erie Railroad, he knew full well that the proposed railway equipment manufacturing firms had the facilities to build tanks, and the equipment and experience to work with large, heavy components. He also knew that these firms were not accustomed to mass production on the scale that was to be needed by the War Department. He knew, however, that the automotive industry was well acquainted with true mass production, but lacked the facilities to build tanks in the numbers needed.

On Friday, 7 June 1940, Knudsen picked up the telephone in his Washington office and called Keller asking if Chrysler would be interested in building tanks for the government. The two men agreed to meet in Knudsen's summer home at Grosse Ile, near Detroit on Sunday to discuss this in greater depth.

**Above:** *Development of the Medium Tank M3 was underway by the summer of 1940, with design work continuing through that fall. A wooden mockup of the tank is on the shop floor at Aberdeen Proving Ground on 4 October 1940. The guns—.30-caliber in the cupola, 37mm in the turret, and 75mm in the sponson—are all set at maximum elevation. At this stage the details of the mockup were rough, and a pronounced ledge was incorporated in the left side of the turret to support the cupola. Military History Institute*

While during that meeting Keller expressed on behalf of the Chrysler organization a desire to consider this, he admitted that no one in his organization were knowledgeable on this subject.

On Tuesday 11 June, Keller, along with Bernard Edwin (better known as B.E.) Hutchinson, Vice President and Chairman of the Chrysler Finance Committee, C.E. Bleicher, Vice-President of the Desoto Division, Edward J. Hunt, Staff Master Mechanic, and Nicholas Kelley, Vice-President and general counsel, descended on the massive Munitions Building at the foot of the Washington Monument, in Washington, DC.

The men were there to discuss in greater detail what the government's requirements were, and to hopefully secure the specifications. The Chrysler delegation first met with Major General Charles Wesson, Chief of Ordnance, who K.T. Keller in

1965 reminisced, "...did not think an automobile company could make tanks. He gave a contract to Baldwin and American Locomotive."

General Wesson turned the group over to Colonel Alexander G. Gillespie, who provided additional details. From E.J. Hunt's notes, we know specifically what Gillespie outlined: That the Army was about to order 1,600 tanks. While the drawings were available for a 20-ton tank (less armament) – the M2A1 – the army envisioned this increasing to 25-tons, less armament. The Chrysler men were told to they should make their bid based on the smaller tank, and once the new design was finalized, a supplemental contract would be issued for the changes, assuming that the Chrysler bid was accepted. Gillespie further opined that the government was actually apt to purchase 5,000 tanks, and that it would take 750 days to complete the 1,600-tank order.

**Above:** *The three moveable gun mounts on the wooden mockup are pointed at different angles, as seen from the front. On the lower right corner of the glacis are representations of two gun muzzles; these pertained to two Browning .30-caliber M1919A4 machine guns that were to be installed on mounts to the left of the driver's station. Note the finned final-drive assemblies, of the type used on the Medium Tanks M2 and M2A1. Military History Institute*

The Chrysler men had hoped to see a tank in Washington, but none were available.

The next day, Wednesday 12 June, Hunt, along with the rest of the Chrysler Corporation Master Mechanic staff, arrived at Rock Island Arsenal, Illinois. They were accompanied by L.A. Moehring, Chrysler Corporation Comptroller, W.J. O'Neil, president of the Dodge Division, his vice-president, F.L. Lamborn, A. P. Rascall, Purchasing Agent, and Robert T. Keller. Robert, or R.T., the son of K.T. Keller, was on Mr. Hunt's staff at the time of the visit, and would play a significant role in Chrysler's tank production for over a decade.

After a greeting from Colonel Ramsey, commanding officer, the group was turned over to Captain Pinkerton, who briefed the group concerning the tank manufacturing process.

The next day the men were joined by K.T. Keller and B.E. Hutchinson, who had just arrived from Washington. The group were given a demonstration of a light tank, and toured the shop floor where the pilot M2A1 medium tanks were being assembled.

On Thursday most of the Chrysler men departed, except for Hunt, R.T. Keller and a few more staff who stayed to further observe the manufacturing process and to arrange to get copies of the blueprints so to prepare a bid to produce the

vehicles. When this group left for Detroit later that day they left with a roll of assembly drawings and a partial set of specifications. A complete set of blueprints were being packed for shipment to Detroit. These drawings arrived at Chrysler at 5:00 PM on Monday 17 June. Immediately 197 men set to work estimating the production cost of the vehicle.

On 1 July Mr. Hunt returned to Rock Island for further discussions with Colonel Ramsey. During the meeting Hunt expressed some concern about the considerable expense Chrysler was facing in preparing the estimate on the M2A1. Colonel Ramsey responded by reminding Hunt that this contract would be issued on a bid basis, and estimated that the initial order would be for 752 tanks, possibly to be increased to 2,584.

By 17 July, four and one half weeks after starting, the Herculean task of producing the estimates had been completed. The 197 men tasked with this process had worked 7 days per week, until 7 PM weekdays and 5 PM weekends, to accomplish this. The team also constructed a wooden mockup, in order to confirm the fit of the components.

With this information in hand, K.T. Keller along with B. E. Hutchinson, Nicholas Kelley, and L.A. Moehring went to see W.S. Knudsen and his deputy, John David Biggers, who was on leave from his usual job as president of the Libby-

Owens-Ford Company. The Chrysler men told the Defense men that they had a handle on fundamental production and equipment costs, and that "...discussions of rate of production and quantities were in order."

Mr. Knudsen asked for an estimate on 2,000 tanks at a rate of 5 per day, working one shift, while Mr. Biggers asked for pricing on ten tanks per day, again working one shift.

The Chrysler team, sans Kelley, next visited Major General Wesson and Colonel Burton Lewis.

Keller, following up on discussions that he and Knudsen had had previously, advocated that a dedicated Tank Arsenal be constructed, which could be used not only for the production of the currently contemplated order, but also future orders as well as experimental development of tanks.

**Above:** *By the time this photo was taken at Aberdeen Proving Ground, the wooden mockup of the M3 had been equipped with a representation of the suspension and tracks. Details that would appear on the early-production M3s included vision ports on each side of the cupola, pistol ports with Protectoscopes—indirect viewing devices—on the right rear quarter of the turret and on the right side of the rear plate of the fighting compartment, and exhaust pipes and mufflers under the rear overhang of the hull. TACOM LCMC History Office*

With this information, Wesson and Lewis then asked Chrysler to submit an estimate for producing tanks, and a separate estimate to build and equip the Tank Arsenal.

Two days later K.T. Keller, along with Hutchinson, Moehring and Kelley, returned to Knudsen's office, and presented to Knudsen and Biggers two proposals.

One proposal would have the tank plant amortized, becoming Chrysler's property, and the other would have the plant a Government Owned, Contractor Operated facility.

Bill Knudsen as well as Biggers both saw advantages to the latter arrangement, and all further discussions on plant planning centered on that plan. With regard to tank production, the Chrysler men were advised that the currently available funding would only allow consideration of the production of 1,000 tanks, not the 2,000 discussed two days prior.

The Chrysler team again next went to Major General Wesson and Colonel Burton O. Lewis, who were joined by Brigadier General Charles T.

Harris, Jr. The three Ordnance officers then began negotiating the tank contract. Not surprisingly, the Army was interested in lowest possible price of the tanks. Chrysler's men explained that the "staring load" of the project had a significant impact on the unit cost of the tanks. Specifically, that the reduction in quantity from 2,000 to 1,000 had the effect of raising the unit cost of the tanks from $31,500 each to $34,500 each, sans government supplied equipment such as weapons.

Colonel Levin H. Campbell was then called into the meeting to outline the proper procedure for arrangement of the construction and fitting out of the Tank Arsenal. Colonel Campbell, incidentally, three months later was promoted two grades and made temporary Brigadier General and given responsibility for building government owned, contractor operated production facilities. By spring of 1942 his rank was made permanent, and he was named Chief of Ordnance.

On 21 July William Knudsen visited the Dodge Conant Avenue plant to inspect the tank mockup as well as to review proposed plant layouts of the Tank Arsenal.

**Above:** *A crewman is standing in the cupola of the M3 wooden mockup on 23 December 1940. A taillight assembly is attached to each side of the overhang on the rear of the hull. The tilted antenna bracket as seen here would not carry over to production M3s. Military History Institute*

**Below:** *In a frontal view of the mockup of the M3 taken at Aberdeen on 23 December 1940, crewmen are standing in the hatches on the cupola and on the hull. Since October 1940, the Medium Tank M2-style final drive assembly had been replaced by a representation of the three-piece bolted final drive that would be incorporated in production M3s. Patton Museum*

Two days later a Chrysler delegation consisting of Hutchinson, Kelley, and Hunt met with Colonels Lewis and Campbell in Washington in order to report that as expected, no suitable existing facilities for the Tank Arsenal were available in the Detroit area.

More importantly, the Chrysler men advised the officers that under standard War Department contract procedures, it would not be possible to meet the various deadlines set forth by the Army in prior discussions. It was decided to seek help from Biggers and the National Defense Advisory Commission in resolving this.

On 26 July a large meeting was held at the office of Mr. Biggers. Attending from Chrysler were K.T.

Keller, along with Hutchinson, Kelley, Hunt, along with H.S Wells, staff plant engineer and Frederick M. Zeder, Chrysler chief engineer. On the government side were John Biggers, Major General Wesson, Major General Edmund Gregory, Quartermaster General, Colonel Campbell, Brigadier General George E. Hartman and representatives of the Advocate General.

Mr. Biggers told the assembled group that a working arrangement had been arrived at between the Ordnance and Quartermaster branches which would solve the practical problems in executing an arrangement with Chrysler to build tanks, with the Quartermaster assisting in the construction of the tank plant.

K.T. Keller, speaking for Chrysler, advocated engaging noted industrial architectural firm of Albert Kahn Associated Architects and Engineers to design the plant, and General Hartman readily agreed. It was further agreed that a Detroit firm be used as construction contractors.

The meeting concluded with an agreement that the appropriate contracts would be drawn up at once.

On 16 August various Chrysler officials met with Ordnance officers at Chrysler's Highland Park (Michigan) plant to discuss the purchase of a site for the Tank Arsenal. The site agreed upon was a 113-acre tract between 11 and 12 Mile roads, bordered by Van Dyke Ave on the east, and the Michigan Central tracks on the west. The area was being used to grow corn, onions and buckwheat, and several small farm buildings dotted the parcel. Colonel Campbell also recommended the purchase of a 40-acre plot adjacent to the 113 acres. This site was 4 miles north of the massive, recently constructed Dodge Mound Road truck plant.

On 15 August 1940, Chrysler and the Army signed a contract calling for the production of 1,000 M2A1 medium tanks, as well as buying the land, constructing the Tank Arsenal, equipping the Arsenal, operation of the Arsenal by Chrysler.

Chrysler was to purchase the 113-acre plot and sell it to the Government at cost. The tanks were

$33,500 each on a fixed price contract, the 700,000 square foot plant and its equipment were to be charged at cost plus a fixed fee, the latter totaling about $20 million. Chrysler would then lease the plant from the government for $1 per year.

The tanks were to be delivered in the following manner:

3 tanks – 12th month after approval
25 tanks – 13th month after approval
75 tanks – 14th month after approval
100 per month thru the 22nd month
97 tanks – in the 24rd month.

Chrysler began ordering equipment to outfit the plant on 26 August.
Only two days later however, the contract was modified, calling for production of the new M3 medium tank rather than the obsolescent M2A1. Chrysler's team of engineers, while not completely reinventing the wheel, nevertheless had a vast amount of work to redo – but the rework could not begin until Ordnance finalized the drawings.

The new tank, designated the M3, was a further development of both the T5E2 and M2A1. At the same time that the US Army had quietly contracted with Baldwin and Alco, and had undertaken the extensive negotiations with Chrysler detailed above, British forces had taken a tremendous pounding. That nation, rallying in an effort to save France, had lost much of its mechanized force.

**Above:** *Part of the interior of the turret of the wooden mockup of the M3 at Aberdeen is viewed from the left side in a 23 December 1940, photo. In view are the elevating hand wheel, part of the gun and gun mount, and stored 37mm ammunition. Military History Institute*

**Above:** *In an 4 October 1940, view of the interior of the wooden mockup through the right side door, to the left is the turret basket, at the center is the driver's station, and to the right are the 75mm gun and its recoil shield. Military History Institute*

**Above:** *The turret of the wooden mockup of the Medium Tank M3 is observed through the left side door. At the bottom, on the floor of the turret basket, is the Logansport hydraulic-traverse motor and pump. To the left is the driver's compartment. Military History Institute*

In July 1940 the British sent a delegation, headed by Michael Bruce Urquhart Dewar and including Major General Douglas Pratt, Deputy Director of British Ministry of Supply Mission and previous commander of the 1st Army Tank Brigade. Dewar, chairman of British Timken, was well connected with US industry through his associates in the US firm Timken Roller Bearing Company of Canton, Ohio. The Ohio firm owned a substantial interest in British Timken.

Beyond his strong ties to American manufacturers, Dewar was well suited for this role. Educated as an engineer, he had served with the Royal Engineers, and during WWI had been posted to the Ministry of Munitions. Shortly thereafter Dewar was made Director of National Projectile Factories and Assistant Controller of Shell Manufacture.

Originally intending to operate from New York offices, Dewar quickly realized that a Washington office was needed, and prevailed on his friend Frederick V. Geier the president of the Cincinnati Milling Machine Company to allow the use of his suite at the Carlton Hotel.

Once in DC, Dewar then set out to arrange for production of the British tank designs. Very soon, however, he ran headlong into the very straight talking William S. Knudsen. Dewar was "plainly informed that purely British designs of war material would not be permitted to be manufactured in the United States."

The Americans had several concerns – first that there were not sufficient manufacturing resources to support two parallel programs. Further, in the event of collapse, the US government did not want US manufacturers saddled with in process materials that were only usable in what the Army considered to be inferior British designs.

Equally strongly, the British felt that they had the superior designs, and the planned US tanks were inferior.

The British delegation, in addition to being shown the inferior M2, and having described for them the forthcoming M3, was provided a list of potential manufacturers. On August 20, the British Purchasing Commission made their initial selection, and asked that Ordnance provide the chosen potential manufacturers assembly drawings so that estimates could be prepared.

**Above:** *An officer is standing by the turret intended for use on the tanks ordered by the British, which would be referred to officially as the Cruiser Tank General Grant I. For experimental purposes, a mockup of the British turret was installed on a Medium Tank M2A1, and this combination is shown in a shop at Aberdeen Proving Ground on 7 November 1940. Two steel beams had been riveted to the roof to strengthen it to hold the weight of the turret, and this was a feature that also was employed on the Medium Tank M3. Patton Museum*

**Above:** *The mockup of the Grant turret on the Medium Tank M2A1 is seen from the left side. The production turrets would have a pistol port with a Protectoscope on the forward part of the left side of the turret. A large, round opening for a hatch ring was on the left side of the roof. The bustle on the rear of the turret was large enough to hold the vehicle's wireless equipment. Patton Museum*

**Left:** *The Grant turret mockup is seen from the front in a shop at Aberdeen Proving Ground on 7 November 1940, showing the opening for the 37mm gun mount. The Grant turret was designed by L. E. Carr. CECOM History Office*

Those manufacturers were:

- American Car and Foundry Company
- American Locomotive Company
- Baldwin Locomotive Works
- Pullman Standard Car Company
- St. Louis Car Company
- American Bridge Company

Added to this, in November 1939 the Ministry of Supply had estimated the cost of tank acquisition would be £1,100,000. However, most of the potential manufacturers required that the British Government pay the cost of equipping their facilities for the production of the tanks, and in some instances, this required extensive and costly rehabilitation. All of this was prior to Lend-Lease,

meaning cash payment was required, often in bullion. Ultimately, the British spent $16,570,000 expanding and improving the manufacturing facilities of the US railway equipment manufacturers who would build their tanks.

On 18 September 1940 the British signed their first contract for production of the M3, ordering 500 examples from Pullman Standard Car Company. Successive orders were placed with Baldwin, American Locomotive, Pressed Steel Car Company and Lima, although the latter ultimately would never produce the M3, rather entering production after the M4 was introduced.

The British very much wanted the radio mounted in the turret, operated by the commander, while the

**Above:** *By the time this photo was taken on December 13, 1940, in a shop at Aberdeen Proving Ground, a second pilot turret, of steel construction, had been installed on the Medium Tank M2A1. The original label of the photo refers to this as a "Radio Turret." It varied in numerous respects from the mockup photographed on this tank the preceding month, one prominent new feature (but one that would not carry over to the production turrets) being a square hatch on the sloping right side of the roof, in addition to the round hatch on the left side of the roof. Machining marks are present all over the turret's surface. Patton Museum*

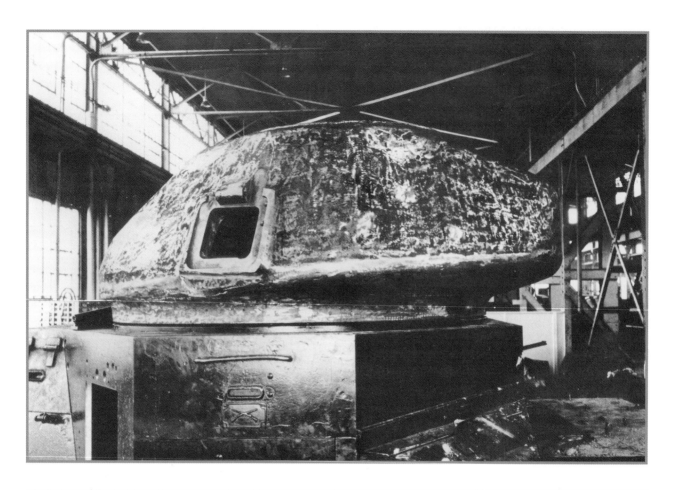

**Above:** *The steel mockup of the Grant turret of December 1940 lacked the perfectly flat rear panel on the center of the bustle, as seen on the mockup of November 1940. To the right is the pistol port on the right side of the turret. Patton Museum*

American design had the radio in the hull, with a task-specific radio operator in the crew. On 8 October 1940 a telegram was sent from the Dewar team to England, addressing the turret matter. It said, in part, "Ordnance Department have informed us unofficially but we are not able at this moment to say whether it would be confirmed by Defense Commission that we may have a different turret with a bulge in it for our own radio set if we wish.

"Unfortunately this would mean a complete re-designing of turret as owing to placing of guns the introduction of a bulge in present design of turret will introduce a considerable off centre load estimated to be about 400 lbs which can only be balanced by adding a similar weight at an appropriate place on opposite side of turret.

"We would most strongly advise turret without bulge should be accepted and we are sure that remote control switching from commander to radio set could be arranged…."

While retaining the standard 54-1/2" turret ring of the M3, Leslie Edward "Ted" Carr, noted British tank engineer, designed a new turret that could house the radio equipment.

The new turret also lacked a cupola, which it was felt added unnecessarily to the height of the vehicle. Not only was this a tactical issue, but also a logistics problem with the British Purchasing Commission being advised by cypher telegram "When transporting M3 Medium tanks on British railways it will be necessary to remove Cupola of U.S. design turret." The British dubbed their preferred version the General Grant, and its American counterpart the General Lee.

In October Douglas Pratt saw a mockup of the new M3 and immediately voiced his concern, chiefly that it was "as high as the tower of Babel." Even with that, he confessed he would "rather fight in it than any other tank."

# Chapter 3
# An overview of the M3 Medium Tank series

The agreement which led to the production of two types of turrets, one for US use, and another the preferred turret for Commonwealth use, gave rise to what many consider the two base types of tanks. It was the British who dubbed their preferred type the Cruiser Tank General Grant, and the US standard M3 medium the General Lee.

However, the variety of M3 Medium tanks was actually much more extensive than that, due in large part to the extreme shortage of radial air-cooled engines. As described earlier, the intent was to power the M3 Medium with the R-975 radial engine. However, demand for this engine for use in both armored vehicles and aircraft outstripped

**Above:** *With the Medium Tank M2A1 quickly rendered obsolete by rapid advances in technology and weaponry on the battlefields of Europe, the U.S. Army abandoned that program in favor of a new, more advanced one: the Medium Tank M3, which was standardized on June 11, 1940. The running gear of the M3 was similar to that of the M2A1, but the rest of the design was quite different, featuring a 75mm gun in the right sponson and a 37mm gun in a fully rotating, cast-armor turret, with a rotating cupola on top with a .30-caliber machine gun. After the British lost much of their armored force in the defeat in France in spring 1940, they submitted contracts for Medium Tanks M3, with the British version, designated the Cruiser Tank Grant I, having a larger, cast-armor turret with a bustle large enough to install wireless (radio) equipment. The U.S. version with the smaller turret was called the Lee. Some Lees found their way into British service, such as the example to the right, parked next to a Grant in North Africa. Imperial War Museum*

production capacity, leading the military to seek alternative powerplants. These included Diesel engines of the M3A3 and M3A5 as well as the unique Chrysler A57 Multibank engine used in the M3A4. With the exception, of a single experimental M3A1 test article, all the M3, M3A1 and M3A2 were powered by the R-975 radial engine, but differed in hull construction. That exception was the M3A1 pilot, which was repowered with Guiberson T-1400-2 radial Diesel engine for testing.

The initial M3, like most earlier US tanks, was of primarily riveted hull construction. This assembly technique inherently poses a significant hazard for the crew, and enemy shellfire can shear the rivets, allowing the rivets themselves to fly through the interior of the tank at high velocity, killing or wounding the tank crew, and potentially causing fires. Two alternate methods of upper hull construction were trialed to address this. The first was to cast the entire upper hull from armor. This resulted in the M3A1 variant.

The other alternative was to weld the superstructure plates together rather than riveting them. This was first used on the M3A2 and was subsequently adopted on the M3A5.

The British, rather than using the US military M-designations described above, preferred the Grant and Lee names, of course based on turret configuration. In fact, per a document located in the Dewar files, for the Grant, the only criteria that the British used when assigning designation was the engine configuration. All Grants were either Grant I or Grant II, depending up whether the powerplant was a R975 or a 6046. The naming of Lees was somewhat more convoluted, reflecting the US designations, and in some cases assigning names not only to variants that were not procured by the British as well as to variants that weren't actually manufactured at all.

**Right:** *Crewmen are taking a break on the engine deck of a Lee at a base in North Africa. To the front is a Grant I. The differences in the turret shapes and sizes may be compared readily. Patton Museum*

The designations given in the August 1942 Dewar document were:

| British Turret | US Turret | M-designation | Fuel | Engine |
|---|---|---|---|---|
| Grant I | Lee I | M3 | gasoline | R-975 |
| | Lee II | M3A1 | gasoline | R-975 |
| Grant I | Lee III | M3A2 | gasoline | R-975 |
| | Lee IV | M3 (Diesel) | Diesel | T-1400-2 |
| Grant II | Lee V | M3A3 (Diesel) | Diesel | 6046 |
| | Lee VI | M3A4 | gasoline | A57 |
| Grant II | | M3A5 | Diesel | 6046 |

No evidence has surfaced that M3A1 or M3A4 tanks were manufactured with Grant turrets. Similarly, the M3 and M3A2 Diesel models were not produced, and only one experimental M3A1 (Diesel) was produced by conversion.

**Above:** *As seen in a photo of a Medium Tank M3 with the nickname DESTROYER and registration number W-304326 painted on the sponson, the Medium Tank M3 in U.S. service featured a three-piece, bolted final-drive assembly; 13-tooth sprockets; plain rubber track shoes with no grousers; riveted armor; sponson doors; and vision ports covering all angles. Patton Museum*

**Above:** *The design of the rear of the Grant-type turret is seen on British War Department census number T-24241, in a photo taken at the Pullman-Standard Car Company plant in late 1941. A pistol port with a hinged flap with a Protectoscope viewing device on it is toward the rear of the right side of the turret. Another pistol port is on the right side of the rear of the upper hull. Sandshields are installed, and the two "pepper-pot" exhausts used on most of the Medium Tanks M3 are on the rear of the hull. Patton Museum*

**Above:** *The Medium Tank M3A1 substituted a cast-armor upper hull for the M3's riveted armor-plate upper hull. Cast armor had its advantages, including eliminating rivets, which could shear off and ricochet around the interior of the vehicle when a projectile struck a plate-armor joint. Cast armor also presented fewer flat surfaces to the trajectories of projectiles, providing greater protection. Registration number W-306032 is depicted here. Patton Museum*

**Above:** *Another means of eliminating the dangers posed by riveted-armor construction was welding the armor plates. The Medium Tank M3A2 featured an upper hull fabricated in that manner. Some rivets remained on the rear of the upper hull, and the final-drive assembly on the front of the hull continued to be of bolted construction, but for the most part, rivets were eliminated. This example is being tested at Aberdeen Proving Ground on January 1, 1942. National Archives*

Tanks equipped with Grant turrets were produced by Pullman Standard, Pressed Steel Car Company and Baldwin Locomotive Works exclusively. Pullman and Pressed Steel built only the Grant I (M3) model, beginning in August 1941. Baldwin, which began production of tanks for the British in October 1941, assembled a wide range of tanks, including M3, M3A2, M3A3 and M3A5 models.

Production of the Grant was discontinued at all three plants in July 1942.

In the following chapters we will look at the M3 medium tank series in greater detail. In order to present the material in a logical manner, we will be examining the tanks in groups based on powerplant.

**Above:** *The engine selected for the Medium Tank M3 was the Wright R-975-EC2, built under license by Continental Motors Corporation. This was a nine-cylinder, air-cooled, four-cycle radial engine with a displacement of 973 cubic inches. At Pullman-Standard's plant in Hammond, Indiana, on July 8, 1941, two of these engines are being prepared for installation in M3s. Military History Institute*

*Above:* A Medium Tank M3A5 is shown during testing. The tracks are an unusual (for an M3) type with three lateral grousers (two short ones over one long one), apparently the T49 model. *TACOM LCMC History Office*

**Above:** *An example of a General Motors 6046 Diesel engine is displayed. The engine was a twin in-line, two-cycle, 12-cylinder design with a displacement of 850 cubic inches. Owing to the fuel efficiency of the Diesel engine, the M3A3 and M3A5 were able to enjoy greater range than the radial-engine-equipped M3 medium tanks despite having a lower fuel capacity. General Motors LLC*

**Above:** *A Chrysler A57 multibank engine for a Medium Tank M3A4 is viewed from the output (front) end. This massive four-cycle, 30-cylinder gasoline power plant had a displacement of 1,253 cubic inches. Visible on the rear of the engine is part of the exhaust line. Vintage Power Wagons collection*

**Left:** *Shown here is a late-production Lee, registration number W-309733, which is listed in the Ordnance Department Armored, Tank and Combat Vehicles, 1940-45, issued in May 1945, as a Medium Tank M3 but was converted to a Medium Tank M3A4. Like the Medium Tanks M3A3 and M3A5, the M3A4 was conceived as a solution to a shortage of radial engines that was forecast in mid-1941. Chrysler quickly developed an engine powerful enough to propel the medium tank by joining together five six-cylinder L-head engines into a single unit with a common crankcase, designated the A57 multibank engine. The size of this engine dictated that the rear of the tank be extended, 15 inches for the upper hull and 11 for the lower hull. Bulges on the engine deck and engine-compartment floor gave clearance to, respectively, a radiator and fan. FCA North America Archives*

# Chapter 4
# The radial engine tanks M3, M3A1 and M3A2

One of the central elements in the design of the M3 Medium Tank family was the Wright R-975 Whirlwind engine. This engine had been developed by the Wright Aeronautical Company in the late 1920s as an aircraft engine. Assigned the model number J-6-9, the engine was used to power a number of aircraft, including the BT-9 and BT-15 military trainers.

The high horsepower to weight ratio of aircraft engines made them attractive to tank designers, and as noted previously, a R-975-EC2 was used in the M2. The same powerplant was also designated for use in the M3, M3A1 and M3A2, as well as a host of other US armored vehicles.

The tank powerplant installation differed from that used in aircraft. In an airplane, obviously the propeller forced air over the cylinder cooling fins, even when idling on the ground. In flight, the air flowing through the cowling would cool the engine. The enclosed engine compartment of an armored vehicle lacked that natural air flow, so an aluminum 14-blade axial-flow fan was installed on the flywheel.

Cooling air was drawn through a grill on the engine deck.

The engine, which burned 92-octane aviation fuel, developed 346 net horsepower at 2,400 RPM, and maximum torque of 812 lb-ft at 1,600 RPM. It differed from the aviation engine by having a 2 ¾-inch shorter crankshaft, different valve timing, and automatic rather than manual spark advance.

**Above:** *The Rock Island Arsenal in Illinois assembled four pilot vehicles for the M3 series of medium tanks: the first pilot Medium Tank M3, the first pilot M3A1, and the first and second pilots of the M3A2. Rock Island Arsenal completed and shipped to Aberdeen Proving Ground all four of these pilots by August 1941. The first pilot Medium Tank M3 was run for 35 miles to bring all of its oiling systems to proper temperature for observation, and then was shipped to Aberdeen Proving Ground on March 15, 1941. This tank, assigned registration number W-304191, is seen here during testing at Aberdeen on 28 March 1941. National Archives*

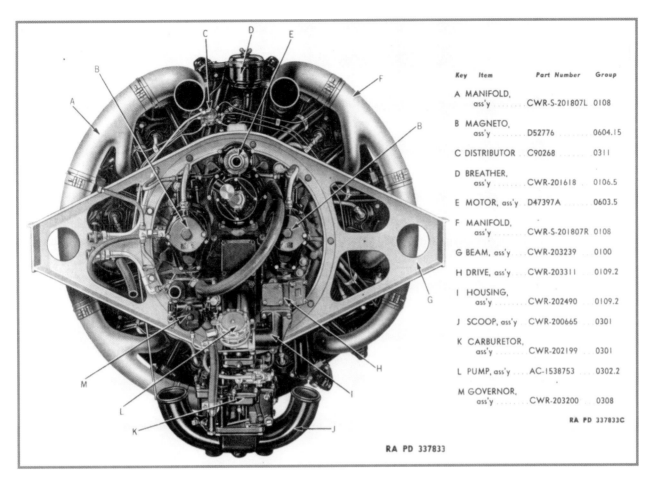

| Key | Item | Part Number | Group |
|-----|------|-------------|-------|
| A | MANIFOLD, ass'y | CWR-S-201807L | 0108 |
| B | MAGNETO, ass'y | D52776 | 0604.15 |
| C | DISTRIBUTOR | C90268 | 0311 |
| D | BREATHER, ass'y | CWR-201618 | 0106.5 |
| E | MOTOR, ass'y | D47397A | 0603.5 |
| F | MANIFOLD, ass'y | CWR-S-201807R | 0108 |
| G | BEAM, ass'y | CWR-203239 | 0100 |
| H | DRIVE, ass'y | CWR-203311 | 0109.2 |
| I | HOUSING, ass'y | CWR-202490 | 0109.2 |
| J | SCOOP, ass'y | CWR-200665 | 0301 |
| K | CARBURETOR, ass'y | CWR-202199 | 0301 |
| L | PUMP, ass'y | AC-1538753 | 0302.2 |
| M | GOVERNOR, ass'y | CWR-203200 | 0308 |

RA PD 337833C

RA PD 337833

**Above:** *The power plant for the Medium Tank M3 was the Wright R-975-EC2 Whirlwind nine-cylinder radial engine, which also was built under license by Continental Motors Corporation. The engine is seen from the rear, which includes the manifold assembly, the mounting beam, and engine accessories such as the breather assembly (top center), magnetos (left and right of the center of the engine), and the pump and the carburetor (bottom center). At the very bottom is the carburetor air supply. Patton Museum*

The initial production M3 tanks were used during the Carolina and Louisiana maneuvers, and trouble with the engine installation surfaced. Complaints came from the field bemoaning low power and short engine life – two problems intimately related.

Tests showed that some engines were developing fewer than 280 net horsepower, and often engines required an overhaul after less than 100 hours of operation.

Investigation of these problems showed that these problems could be traced to cooling problems as well as unsatisfactory intake and exhaust systems. Originally, the M3 was equipped with a pair of Vortox U7x18C air cleaners mounted inside the engine compartment at the rear. With this arrangement, air was expected to be drawn from the fighting compartment through the sponsons, then through the air cleaners and on to the carburetor through 3 ½-inch tubes. However, the engine compartment as well as the sponsons were heated by the engine, resulting in the air entering the carburetor to be as hot as 180 degrees. The result of the expanding intake air was that less fuel was introduced to the cylinders, resulting in lower power.

Further, the early tanks were equipped with external mufflers, most often referred to as pepper pot mufflers. This exhaust system resulted in considerable exhaust gas backpressure, reducing engine power.

Beginning on 21 August 1941 and continuing through 8 January 1942, Wright conducted a series of tests and experiments to rectify these problems. As a result of these tests, some changes were implemented in production tanks. Engine intake air was drawn from the fan shroud, routed through tubes insulated with asbestos to new air cleaners mounted on the outer rear wall of the engine compartment. This resulted in cooler intake air as well as easier servicing of the oil bath air cleaners.

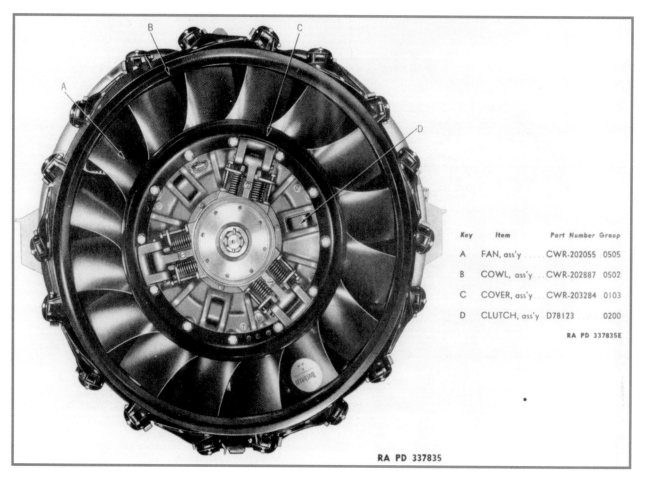

| Key | Item | Part Number | Group |
|-----|------|-------------|-------|
| A | FAN, ass'y | CWR-202055 | 0505 |
| B | COWL, ass'y | CWR-202887 | 0502 |
| C | COVER, ass'y | CWR-203284 | 0103 |
| D | CLUTCH, ass'y | D78123 | 0200 |

RA PD 337835E

RA PD 337835

**Above:** *A Wright/Continental R-975-EC2 Whirlwind engine assembly is seen from the front, with the cowl and the fan (with a De Bothezat logo sticker on one of the blades) hiding the engine cylinders. At the center is the clutch, which is built into the engine flywheel. Around the clutch are arranged its pressure springs. Patton Museum*

Also, the pepper-pot mufflers were replaced with straight through Maremont mufflers which exited through the rear of the tank, parallel to the stream of cooling air. In order to accommodate the new style mufflers, the engine exhaust collector ring had to be redesigned to discharge the gases at the top of the engine rather than at the bottom.

These changes had the added benefit of improving fuel economy as well as increasing power. During field testing increases of between 13 and 75 horsepower were reported. The correction of these deficiencies overcame many of the problems of the R-975 – power, fuel economy and service life – yet one problem remained, that of supply. Wright was straining to meet the requirements for aircraft engines. Therefore, in order to supply the needed engines for the M3 Medium Tanks as well as other armored vehicles, a licensing arrangement was worked out with Continental Motors, allowing the latter to produce the engines.

This was a fortuitous decision indeed, as Wright could only manage to produce 750 of the R-975 for tank use throughout their production, yet Continental was scheduled for 1,000 per month. The Continental engine was designated the R-975-EC2.

The production of the tanks themselves was even more convoluted. The design, as being advanced was for a tank with a hull made primarily of armor plates, which were precision cut then riveted together. It was anticipated that the vehicles would be assembled by railway equipment manufacturers, who not only had experience in assembling heavy stock and had the facilities to accommodate large components and assembly, but also had the excess manufacturing capacity due to the depression-driven downturn in railway equipment production.

On 23 November 1940 American Locomotive signed a contract with the government, which had been issued in September, to produce 685 medium tanks, and Baldwin Locomotive works signed a similar contract at a few days later. Chrysler's M2A1 production contract was amended to call instead for the production of 1,000 of the new M3. But, as illustrated in Chapter 2 the design of the M3 was far from complete. Thus, while these firms were the first to be contracted to build the tanks, the first M3 Medium tanks were not actually built by either.

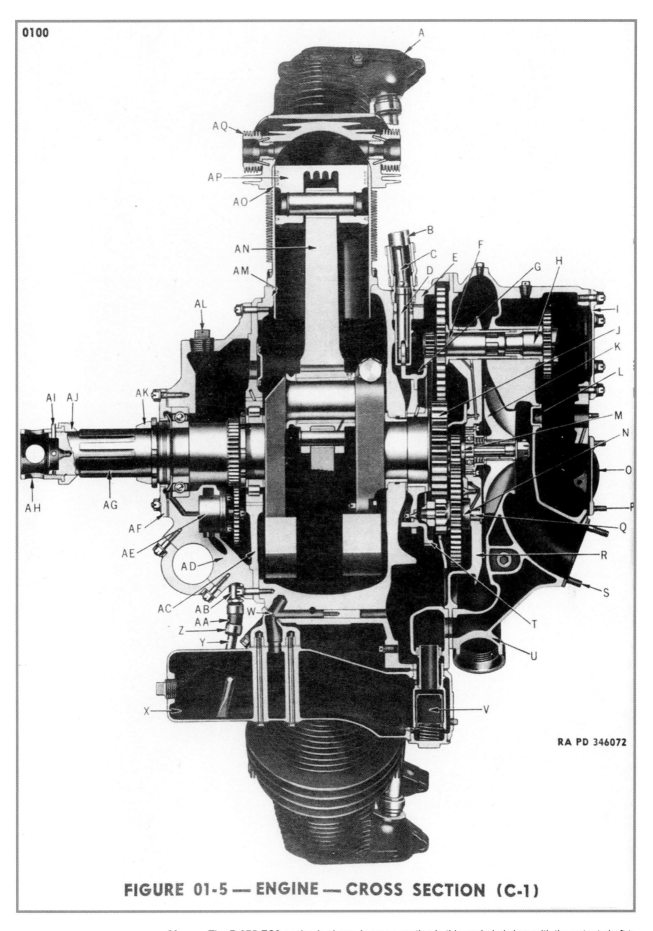

RA PD 346072

FIGURE 01-5 — ENGINE — CROSS SECTION (C-1)

**Above:** *The R-975-EC2 engine is shown in cross-section in this exploded view, with the output shaft to the left; the cylinders and crankcase at the center, showing the crankshaft, the balancer, a piston, and a rod; and, to the right, the accessory case, with gears and drives for the magnetos, generator, governor, fuel pump, tachometer, and so forth. Patton Museum*

**Above:** *A Wright/Continental R-975-EC2 Whirlwind engine is viewed from the left rear in a photo dated 16 March 1942. The fuel and oil lines are installed. The electric starter has not been installed between the two magnetos on the rear of the engine. National Archives*

**Right:** *A Wright/Continental R-975-EC2 Whirlwind engine equipped with the new mufflers and fishtail exhausts is viewed from the rear. Although this February 1942 photo shows an engine and exhaust system as installed in a Medium Tank M4, the arrangement was similar for the late Medium Tank M3. Patton Museum*

**Above:** *Late-production Medium Tanks M3 equipped with Wright/Continental R-975-EC2 radial engines eliminated the original "pepper pot" mufflers on the outside of the rear of the hull, substituting new mufflers inside the engine compartment with fishtail exhausts. Shown in this 1 August 1942 photo from Aberdeen Proving Ground is such an exhaust setup, featuring two Maremont mufflers with downward-pointing fishtail exhausts. Patton Museum*

**Above:** *A photo of the same engine and exhaust system shown in the preceding photo is viewed from the right side, showing the angle of the mufflers and the positioning of the fishtail exhausts. Patton Museum*

# Rock Island Arsenal

Despite what has been reported elsewhere, the log of activities at Rock Island Arsenal state clearly that the four pilot M3s were produced at Rock Island, and they included examples of each type of hull fabrication that would be used in the M3 medium tank program.

The February 1941 log provides the following insights: "Medium Tank, M3. The following is the status of the Pilot Medium Tank, M3, being manufactured at Rock Island Arsenal:

Hull – Completed except drilling for attaching parts.

Transmission – Being installed

Suspensions – Completed and installed

Tracks and Sprockets – Completed

One set Turret Rings – Completed and shipped to Aberdeen Proving Ground, February 10, 1941.

Controls – Drawings released to the shop, February 12, 1941. Patterns completed and castings scheduled for delivery the week of February 24, 1941.

Engine – Ready for installation but waiting the receipt of clutch throwout bracket casting which is part of the controls.

75 m/m Gun, T7 – Received at Rock Island Arsenal 2-21-41.

75 m/m Tank Mount – Completed with the exception of the Cone Worm and wormwheels, which are scheduled for delivery from Michigan Tool Company on March 10, 1941. Standard straight type worms and wormwheels have been manufactured and installed by the Arsenal in order that this mount may be completed and proof fired. Proof firing of this mount is scheduled for the week of February 24th.

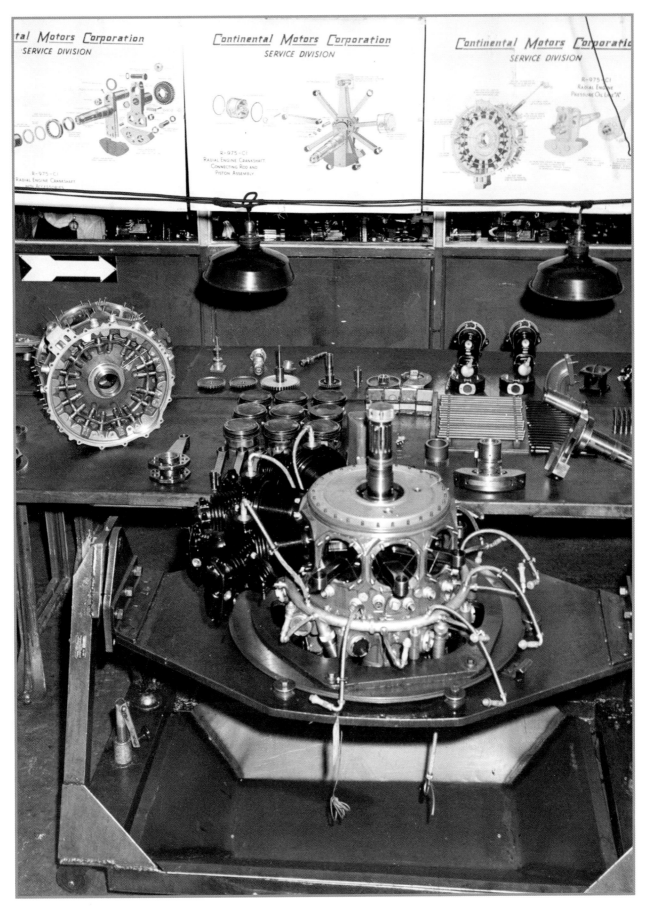

**Above:** *In a display promoting the Continental Motors Training School, the assembly of an R-975 engine is depicted. A partially assembled engine is on the stand in the foreground, while on the bench in the background are engine components, including a crankcase, cylinders, pistons, and more. The diagrams above the bench are for the R-975-C1 engine, an improved version of the R-975-EC2 used in some Sherman tanks. Jim Gilmore collection*

**Above:** *In a continuation of the display of Continental radial engines, a completed R-975 engine is on the stand. Components are on the table, and at the upper left is a poster showing cutaway diagrams of the four cycles of the engine: intake, compression, firing, and exhaust. Jim Gilmore collection*

**Above:** *The accessories section of an R-975 engine is on a stand, showing components that would be installed on the rear of the engine. Jim Gilmore collection*

**Above:** *The following series of photos was taken on 28 March 1941 to document the first pilot Medium Tank M3, registration number W-304191, assembled by the Rock Island Arsenal, shortly after its arrival at Aberdeen Proving Ground. Here, the pistol ports are open, a soldier is standing in the cupola, and the 37mm gun and its coaxial .30-caliber machine gun are elevated. National Archives*

**Above:** *The cupola ring on the roof of the first pilot, as well as early-production M3s, had a pronounced ledge where it jutted out on the left rear of the turret. Later, the design was revised so that the contour was bumped out such that the diameter at the bottom was carried straight up. National Archives*

**Above:** *The pistol ports are closed in this left-side view of the first pilot M3. The first pilot M3 lacked a left vision port on the cupola, but this feature would appear on production M3s. Strapped to the upper hull above the fender is a machine-gun tripod. A grab handle is above the crew door on the sponson. The crew door has three hinges on the forward side and a padlock hasp on the other side. National Archives*

**Above:** *The first pilot M3 had an angled antenna bracket on the left rear of the fighting compartment; a similar bracket would be used on very early production tanks but later would be supplanted by a bowl-shaped antenna bracket. To the right of the bracket are two handles for the fire-extinguisher system; the handles are horizontally oriented, with protective hoods over them. National Archives*

**Above:** *A rear view of the first pilot Medium Tank M3 shows the pepper-pot exhausts flanking the two engine-compartment access doors. Also in view are the rear tow eyes and clevises and the idler brackets. The tracks were the T41 model, a double-pin design with smooth rubber blocks. National Archives*

**Above:** *The first pilot M3 is seen from the right rear with the pistol ports and cupola vision ports open. Pioneer tools and a coiled tow cable are stored on the engine deck. National Archives*

**Above:** *Pistol ports are open on the turret and hull of the first pilot M3, registration number W-304191, at Aberdeen Proving Ground on 28 March 1941. The road wheels were part number D38501, a five-spoked design. The idler wheels were part number D37916, a six-spoked design. National Archives*

**Above:** *The pistol ports are open and the 37mm gun is elevated in this right-front view of the first pilot Medium Tank M3. The 13-tooth sprocket assemblies were part number D47366; there were several variations on this assembly, and the ones used on the M3s were the early type. A good view is available of the 75mm gun barrel, the rotor shield the barrel is seated in, and the horizontal rotor shield, through which the rotor shield protrudes. National Archives*

**Above:** *Prominent on the bow of the first pilot Medium Tank M3 is the final-drive assembly, an armored housing for the differential, steering-brake drums, and the final drives. This overall assembly was designated part E1233; the three individual castings were, from right to left from the driver's perspective, parts number E1230, E1232, and E1231. This vehicle has blackout marker lamps next to the service headlights, which would be standard on production M3s. National Archives*

**Right Above:** *An overhead photo of the first pilot M3 shows structural features such as the four armored fuel-filler covers, two each side of the engine-air intake grille on the engine deck; the T-shaped stiffener on the roof of the fighting compartment; the hatch doors on the cupola and the fighting compartment; and the dust cover over the gunner's periscope on the round plate over the 75mm gun mount. The turret lacked the three built-in fittings for installing lifting rings on the edge of the roof, which would be a feature of production turrets. National Archives*

**Right:** *The first Medium Tank M3 completed by the American Locomotive Company plant in Schenectady, New York, was the subject of a christening ceremony upon the vehicle's rolling out on March 19, 1941. Next to the M3 is the sponsor of the vehicle, Miss Beverly Lentz, daughter of W. L. Lentz, manager of the plant. Scott Taylor collection*

**Above:** *Members of the press, military and civilian VIPs, and others are gathered around the first M3 to roll out of the American Locomotive plant at Schenectady, on 19 March 1941. Among the guests was Undersecretary of War Robert P. Patterson. In the background is a DL-109 locomotive. Scott Taylor collection*

**Above:** *This photograph and the following one almost certainly document the rollout of the first Medium Tank M3 completed by the Baldwin Locomotive Works, in Eddystone, Pennsylvania. Baldwin built a total of 295 Medium Tanks M3 between June 1941 and March 1942. Baldwin Locomotive Works*

**Above:** *An army officer is addressing those assembled for the rollout of the first M3 completed by Baldwin Locomotive Works. The barrels of the .30-caliber machine guns are an early type, with long slots in the cooling jackets. Baldwin Locomotive Works*

**Above:** *This photo and the following series of images were taken to document an early Medium Tank M3 assembled by Baldwin Locomotive Works at Eddystone, Pennsylvania. The shot trap formed by the junction between the ring for the cupola and the left side of the turret, present on the first pilot M3, was eliminated on production M3s by building up the armor in that area. Baldwin Locomotive Works*

**Above:** *The two .30-caliber machine guns at the lower left of the glacis was a separate casting with two ports for the gun barrels. The casting was secured with rivets in a cutout in the glacis. On each fender is a service headlight with a so-called "blue-louver" (or "cat's eye") blackout lamp on its outboard side. A brush guard is bolted to each fender to protect the lights. Baldwin Locomotive Works*

It is estimated that this tank will be completed, ready for road test, March 8, 1941."

**The March log reported:**
Medium Tank, M3, Pilot. The manufacture of the Medium Tank, M3, Pilot, less Turret, has been completed at Rock Island Arsenal. This vehicle was operated approximately 35 miles, which was sufficient to bring all oiling systems up to proper temperature for observation. No undue troubles were encountered during this test run. The vehicle was shipped to Aberdeen Proving Ground on March 15, 1941, for further test."

**The April log reported:**

"Medium Tank, Pilot, M3, No. 2. The status of the Pilot Medium Tank, M3, with cast hull (General Steel Casting Corporation) is as follows:

Casting for upper hull and plate for lower hull have been received and are being assembled. Assembly of the hull 85% complete.

All armor plate castings for gun mounts have been received and are in process of machining. 50% completed.

**Above:** *The early Baldwin M3 is viewed outside of the plant. At this time, the registration number has not been painted on the sponsons. Baldwin Locomotive Works*

**Above:** *Two gentlemen in suits and ties and prewar-style tanker's helmets are standing in the hatches of the cupola and the fighting compartment. Whereas the hinges of the engine-compartment doors on the rear of the lower hull of some M3s were installed with slotted screws, the ones on this vehicle were welded. The right rear armored plate of the fighting compartment, directly below the man to the right, was fastened in place with slotted screws instead of rivets. This was so the plate could be removed in order to extract the 75mm gun from the tank or reinstall it. Baldwin Locomotive Works*

**Above:** *Whereas the first pilot Medium Tank M3, assembled by Rock Island Arsenal, had one grab handle for the engine-compartment doors, this early-production Baldwin M3 had two grab handles, side by side. The small hole on the center of the rear plate of the upper-hull overhang is the aperture for the manual starting crank. Baldwin Locomotive Works*

**Right:** *Civilians are gathered around a Medium Tank M3 at the Baldwin Locomotive factory, possibly during manufacturer's tests. The tracks of the vehicle have churned up the soft ground to the rear. The man standing in the cupola is wearing an army uniform. The barrel of the coaxial .30-caliber machine gun next to the 37mm gun has the early-style cooling jacket with elongated slots, while the 30-caliber machine gun in the cupola has the later-style cooling jacket with round perforations. Baldwin Locomotive Works*

**Above:** *A Baldwin Medium Tank M3 is undergoing manufacturer's performance tests on an earthen slope. The M3 was capable of negotiating a grade of 60 percent, which equates to about 30 degrees.*
*Baldwin Locomotive Works*

**Above:** *A Medium Tank M3 is being driven through a water course to evaluate the vehicle's ability to operate in deep water. To the right, a cameraman is filming the test. Patton Museum*

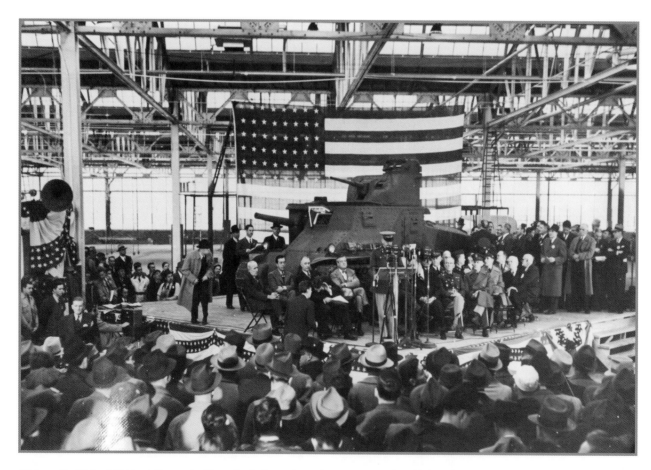

**Above:** *On 24 April 1941, civilian and military dignitaries and guests are convened at the Detroit Tank Arsenal on the occasion of the delivery of the first Chrysler production pilot Medium Tank M3 to the U.S. Army. Chrysler automobile dealers, salesmen, and distributors funded the construction of this vehicle and presented it to the U.S. government. Receiving the tank on behalf of the army was Maj. Gen. Charles M. Wesson, Chief of Ordnance, U.S. Army. Military History Institute*

**Above:** *The first Chrysler production pilot M3 is parked in a doorway of the Detroit Tank Arsenal in April 1941 after it has been operated; note the grease and lubricant stains and dirt on the tracks, suspension, and hull. This was the first M3 Lee to be equipped with regulation armor and weapons.*
*Military History Institute*

**Above:** *On the occasion of its 24 April 1941, official rollout, the first Chrysler production pilot M3 demonstrates its ability to crash through a telephone pole in front of a group of army officers and executives.  Library of Congress*

**Above:** *On the same rollout ceremony shown in the preceding photo, the first Chrysler production pilot Medium Tank M3 has part of a tree lying on top of it, apparently after exhibiting its power to force its way through woodlands. Military History Institute*

Gun Mount parts in process of machining, 50% completed.

Suspension 90% completed.

Gas Tanks 75% completed.

Interior parts of hull (racks, controls, subfloor, etc) in process of manufacture. 30% completed.

The Turret Casting received was rejected. 10 items of armor plate castings received from Chrysler were also rejected.

Every effort is being made to have replacements made as soon as possible.

Medium Tank, Pilot, M3, No. 3. The status of the Pilot Medium Tank, M3, with welded hull (Disston) is as follows:

Total of 10 hull plates have been received.

Preliminary set ups are being made for welded assemblies.

All armor plate castings have been received an it has been found that a number of these castings are rejected"

By May, substantial progress was being made on pilots 2 and 3, with the following notations:

"Pilot, Medium Tank, M3, No. 2

The status of this tank with cast hull (General Steel Casting Corp.) is as follows:

Turret casting received and rejected. Replacement has been received and is approximately 65% complete.

It is estimated that the preliminary test of this Tank will begin on May 27.

Pilot, Medium Tank, M3, No. 3

The status of this Tank with welded hull (Disston) is as follows:

Welding of all sub-assemblies has been completed

**Above:** *A wooden structure was not immune to the power of the M3 to punch its way through it, as shown in another photo from the 24 April 1941 rollout ceremony at the Detroit Tank Arsenal. Military History Institute*

**Above:** *The first production pilot M3 completed by Chrysler splashes through a pond during a demonstration of its fording capabilities during the rollout on 24 April 1941. The Medium Tank M3 had a maximum fording depth of 40 inches. Military History Institute*

**Above:** *In a final photo from the 24 April 1941 rollout of the first Chrysler M3, Major General Charles Wesson (left) chats with K.T. Keller (right) in front of the first and second pilot M3s built by Chrysler. The second tank was completed early and unveiled as a 'surprise' to visiting dignitaries. That company would complete over 3,240 M3 medium tanks: far more than any of the other firms that built the tank. Military History Institute*

and final welding will be completed on May 28, 1941.

Completion of the Tank is expected about June 16."

The June report makes no mention of Pilot No. 2, leading to the assumption that the tank had been completed. However, in addition to Pilot 3, the log also reports on Pilot 4. The status of these two pilots was:

"Medium Tank, Pilot, M3, No. 30 (sic), with Welded Hull (Disston)

Assembling and welding of the hull has been completed and the suspensions, gas tanks and transmission installed.

Turret, interior parts, engine, etc., now in process of assembly.

Preliminary road test scheduled to start June 30, 1941."

"Medium Tank, Pilot, M3, No. 4, with Welded Hull – (Carnegie Illinois Steel Company)

Hull received, completely welded. Suspensions and a majority of parts for this hull have been completed."

In July, the log provides:
"Medium Tanks, M3

The status of the two Pilot Medium Tanks, M3, now under manufacture at this Arsenal is as follows:

The Pilot Medium Tank, M3, with Welded Hull Plates, furnished by Disston, has been completed, road tested and shipped to Aberdeen Proving Ground on July 2, 1941.

Medium Tank, M3, with Welded Hull Plates, furnished by the Carnegie-Illinois Steel Company, assembly and welding of Hull completed."

August was the last mention of these vehicles in the monthly summary, stating that:
"The Pilot Medium Tank, M3, with welded hull (Carnegie-Illinois Steel Company) has been completed. This vehicle, less engine, transmission, turret, gun mounts, was shipped to Aberdeen Proving Ground August 9, 1941."

**Above:** *A weak point of the Medium Tank M3 was the crew doors on the sides of the upper hull. Thus, Aberdeen Proving Ground advocated for the deletion of the doors, installing instead an escape hatch in the floor of the fighting compartment. This Chrysler-built Medium Tank M3, registration number W-3058309, had the doors deleted but retained a pistol port on the right side. The vehicle was photographed on 30 September 1942, during testing by the Ordnance Operation, General Motors Proving Ground; chalked on the hull is "Received 9/7/42." Patton Museum*

**Above:** *Another Medium Tank M3 with the side doors deleted was registration number W-3028529. No pistol port was retained where the door had been on this side of the vehicle. The main gun on this tank and the one in the preceding photo was the long-barreled 75mm Gun T8, standardized as the 75mm Gun M3. Below the barrel of the 37mm gun is a tube-shaped counterweight, installed to make the operation of the elevation gyrostabilizer more effective. By this time, a ventilator with an armored splash guard around was standard equipment on the left front part of the fighting-compartment roof. Patton Museum*

**Above:** *After a regimen of testing and evaluation, the first Chrysler pilot Medium Tank M3, registration number W-301000, was returned by railroad to the Chrysler Tank Arsenal on May 17, 1945. Two men are holding up a sign with the details of this delivery, while workmen with crowbars prepare to remove the blocking. Patton Museum*

## British orders

The British placed orders with Pressed Steel Car Company, Pullman Standard and Baldwin Locomotive Works for a total of 1,685 tanks. Baldwin received an order for 685 tanks, with Pullman Standard getting an order for 500 tanks, and Pressed Steel getting an order to "build a pilot tank out of mild steel to be used for instructional purposes" plus 500 combat tanks. Michael Dewar telegrammed regarding this on 31 January 1942 that "Ultimately armour plate was supplied a standard M3 medium tank produced with result that 501 tanks will be manufactured on above contract…". An order was also placed with Lima Locomotive Works for 400 tanks, but production had switched to the Sherman before Lima completed any tanks.

The Ordnance Department awarded Baldwin a contract for medium tanks on 24 October, and the British Purchasing Commission placed their order on 4 November. A handwritten ledger titled "Register of Engines made by the Baldwin Works

1940," in the collections of the Smithsonian Institution, lists the orders sequentially. Construction numbers 62541 to 63225, referencing (serial) numbers 1002 to 1686, are shown with purchaser "United States Government War Department (Ordnance Dept) Military Medium Tanks M3." Construction numbers 63226 to 63910 are listed with purchaser "His Majesty's Government in the United Kingdom represented by the British Purchasing Commission."

In addition to the tanks themselves being placed on order, many of the key components were purchased separately and furnished by the British government to the assembly plants (the US government followed the same procedure). Those components were engines from Continental Motors, transmissions from Mack Manufacturing, armor plate from Republic Steel, 2,500 75mm guns and mounts from Empire Ordnance, 1,500 37mm guns and mounts from American Type Founders Corp. on order A-1964 and 1,000 37mm guns only from National Pneumatic Company on order A-2311.

**Above:** *The following series of photos of a Cruiser Tank Grant I completed by the Pressed Steel Car Company, of Hegewisch, a community area in Chicago, Illinois, appears to represent an official rollout, likely of the first Grant completed by PSCC, given the U.S. and British flags attached to the vehicle and the photo coverage given to the event. The number 501 is stenciled on the sponson. The 75mm main gun is installed, but the British-type turret lacks the 37mm gun and .30-caliber coaxial machine gun.*
*Pressed Steel produced 501 Grant Is,*

## Armament

When production of the M3 was being planned, the intention was that the primary armament would be the 75mm Gun, T6, an experimental low velocity anti-aircraft gun. However, it was learned that the gun would require several modifications in order to make it suitable for use in a tank. This include equipping the gun with a trigger type firing mechanism with provision for firing solenoid in lieu of the constant pull type mechanism, moving the cam opening mechanism from the left side of the breech to the right, rotating the recoil mechanism 90-degrees and equipping the breech with an operating handle. The T6 incorporating these modifications was initially designated the T7. However, following the Ordnance Committees approval of the Subcommittee on Mobile Artillery's 24 April 1941 recommendation, the T7 was adopted as Standard with the nomenclature "75-mm Gun, M2."

Testing of the installation of the M2 gun with gyrostabilizer in the M3 Medium Tank mounting at Aberdeen Proving Ground revealed that the gun was 3,618 inch-pounds out of balance. Aberdeen recommended that the length of the 84-inch tube be increased by at least ten inches to compensate for this.

By June of 1941 work was well underway on the T6 Medium Tank, which would evolve into the Sherman. As part of the trials, the length of the M2 gun tube was revisited. It was learned that a gun with a tube of 100.7 inches could be fitted without the barrel extending beyond the hull, or 112.9 inches before extending beyond the tracks.

It was also learned that the gun would need to be rotated 90-degrees to provide clearance at maximum depression. This rotation would require modifications to the breech mechanism to insure proper operation. The resultant gun, with a tube length of 118 3/8-inches, was designated the T8 during development.

**Above:** *Pressed Steel Car Grant I number 501 lacked the right pistol port on the turret and the driver's vision port. The fairly rough texture of the cast armor on the front of the right sponson, which houses the 75mm gun and rotor shields, is evident. Note too that the center part of the hinge for the pistol port on the sponson door has not been installed yet; two holes for attaching the lug are visible. Joe DeMarco collecton*

**Above:** *Three civilians, likely Pressed Steel Car employees, are aboard Grant I number 501 on the same occasion as the preceding photo. These photos were stamped with the date of printing, "Jul 13 1941," yet, despite the fact that at least this one Grant I was virtually complete and in running condition by that date, the official production dates of the Pressed Steel Grant Is were August 1941 to July 1942. Joe DeMarco collecton*

**Above:** *Several men, including one about to snap a photo with a camera, are watching Grant I number 501 as it rolls along a dusty road, presumably at the Pressed Steel Car plant at Hegewisch. A detail worth noticing is the well-defined, straight line between the upper part of the turret and the lower, shaded part. Joe DeMarco collecton*

**Above:** *The Pressed Steel Grant I is observed from the front, showing the driver's detachable windshield, which is equipped with a wiper. With the 37mm gun and the gunner's sight not installed in the turret, the left trunnion brackets for the 37mm gun mount and the gunner's sight rotor are visible just inside the turret. The tracks are the model WD-212, which is the part number for an assembly of four links. Current sources often refer to these tracks as the double-I. Two manufacturers produced the WE-212 tracks: Burgess-Norton, and Inland Steel. Joe DeMarco collecton*

**Above:** *Pullman-Standard completed 500 Cruiser Tanks Grant I at its plant in Hammond, Indiana, between late July 1941 and July 1942. This Grant I was photographed before being completed at Pullman-Standard on 15 April 1941. The shield for the 37mm gun is simply resting on the front of the turret, not having been seated flush in its opening. The left pistol port hasn't been installed on the turret. To the front, the final-drive assembly hasn't been installed, and a pipe has been rigged across the front of the hull to hold the sprockets temporarily. Two pipes have been installed in the openings for the bow machine guns, for effect, and the 75mm "gun" is a section of pipe. National Archives*

As a longer tube would also result in higher velocity, and hence greater armor penetration, the Subcommittee on Tank Armament urged that the new gun be installed in the M3 medium tanks as early as possible given the state of M2 gun procurement

On 28 June 1941 the Ordnance Committee approved the Standardization of the T8 as the "75-mm Gun, M3." At the same time the new gun was approved for procurement, and the M2 guns were reclassified as "Substitute Standard." The new guns were to be incorporated into production as soon as practicable. The Adjutant General approved all of this on 15 July 1941.

Ordnance issued a production order to Watervliet Arsenal for 1,308 T7 (M2) guns on 17 July 1940. The cost of the guns was $1,972.00 each. The first of these were shipped in April 1941. Ultimately, 1,897 M2 guns were produced. In February 1942 production began to shift to the M3, and both types

were produced concurrently until June 1942. The M3 had first been ordered on 4 June 1941. The first 385 M3 guns were shipped in March 1942, along with 65 M2 guns.

As mentioned earlier, the 2,500 guns ordered by the British were produced by Empire Ordnance of Philadelphia. The order included 2,100 M2 guns at $2,700 each, and 400 M3 guns (presumably the 400 M3s were intended for the 400 Lima-built Sherman tanks).

Empire began shipping the M2 guns in August 1941, and the last a year later. The firm began shipping M3 guns in July 1942.

By way of comparison, in 1941 only Watervliet and Empire were producing M2 guns, with the combined production through December 1,216 guns. On the other hand, production of the M3 for US delivery only (excluding Great Britain) was 1,342 tanks. This is the reason so many period

**Above:** *The same uncompleted Grant I shown in the preceding photo is viewed from the right front at the Pullman-Standard factory in Hammond, Indiana, on 14 April 1941. The sprocket rings were tacked with three bolts and nuts apiece to metal drums, not actual sprocket-assembly drums. National Archives*

photos show the tanks absent their main gun. This deficiency was evident to planners early on, and in an effort to combat, in October 1940 a third manufacturer was added to support the M3 program. C.H. Cowdrey Machine Works, a precision tool manufacturer in Fitchburg, Massachusetts, was issued contract 953-ORD-1140 to produce the weapon. Before production began, the firm was purchased by American Type Founders, Inc., of Elizabeth, New Jersey.

It would be April 1942 before the gun deliveries began to outstrip the tank deliveries. However, it would be M3 production by Oldsmobile, which began in May 1942, that truly put the gun into mass production. While May deliveries by Oldsmobile were only 144 guns, in June 1,076 were delivered, and soon the GM Division was delivering almost twice as many as all the other manufacturers combined.

The turret armament of the M3 was a 37mm antitank gun. In order to meet the requirement that the Medium Tank T5 (see Chapter 1) be armed

with a 37mm gun, work began in 1937 on adapting and improving the 37mm field gun. It was decided that two types of breech mechanisms would be developed for the improved gun, one manually operated, and the other a semi-automatic breech. The decision was made to develop the manual breech first, to allow subsequent development of various ammunition components, with development of the semi-automatic breech to follow. The 37mm antitank gun with manually operated breech was standardized as the "37mm Gun, M3."

The newly developed light tank M2A4 was to be armed with this weapon, however there were concerns that because the muzzle of the gun extended beyond the bow of the tank, that the weapon would be subjected to damage when operating in close quarters. Thus, on 3 August 1939 the decision was made to produce the same gun, although with a barrel six inches shorter for this application. This gun was first designated M3A1, and on 13 October 1939 was redesignated as M5.

**Above:** *The first Cruiser Tank General Grant I to be completed at Pullman-Standard's plant in Hammond, Indiana, is being backed onto a railroad flatcar for shipment on 25 July 1941. The 37mm gun and coaxial machine gun and the 75mm gun were not installed on this tank and others shipped from Pullman on that date. As completed, the Grant tanks were painted in a dark color, presumably Olive Drab. National Archives*

**Above:** *Pullman-Standard workers are blocking and securing the first two Grant tanks to be shipped from the Hammond plant, on 25 July 1941. Note the tall storage box atop the sponson of the front vehicle and the short box on the tank to the rear. The WD-212 tracks are installed on both Grants. National Archives*

**Above:** *This is the first Cruiser Tank General Grant I built by Pullman-Standard at Hammond, Indiana, for the British Purchasing Commission; this work came under contract number A-1381. The photo was taken on 25 July 1941. No census number had been painted on the sponson at this point, but presumably this vehicle was number T-24189. The forward parts of the sand skirts are installed.*
National Archives

**Above:** *It is not clear if this was the first Grant completed by Pullman-Standard; if not, it is a very early example, as the photo is dated 3 August 1941, a week after the preceding photo of the first Pullman-Standard Grant was taken. The partial sand shield is already slightly crumpled at the front corner, being fabricated from sheet metal. This vehicle lacked storage boxes on the sponsons. National Archives*

**Above:** *In an elevated view of the Pullman-Standard Grant on 3 August 1941, the part numbers cast into the three sections of the final-drive assembly are visible: from the viewer's perspective they are, left to right, E1230, E1232, and E1231. To the rear of the cutout on the top of section E1230 is a siren. The part number is also visible on the front of the 37mm gun shield below the gunner's sight port: D47321. Note the guard for the 75mm gunner's sighting periscope on top of the sponson. The periscope and holder traversed in an arc in unison with the traverse of the gun. On the front right corner of the turret is the aperture for the 2-inch Mortar Mk. I; note the ribbed or stepped surface inside the aperture. The turret hatch ring and hatch doors have not been installed. National Archives*

**Above:** *The Pullman-Standard Grant is observed from the upper rear in a photo dated 2 August 1941. On the right rear of the turret roof is a base for mounting an antenna. Production Grants typically had another antenna mount to the rear of the turret hatch, but this is not installed. However, there is a small hole on the turret roof a foot or so to the rear of the hatch, which was the lead-in for the electrical wiring for an antenna in that position. On the left vertical plate of the rear of the fighting compartment, a small, square piece of steel has been attached to the place where the antenna mount was installed on the Medium Tank M3 for U.S. Army service, as British Grant tanks didn't have an antenna in that location.*
*National Archives*

**Above:** *Taken on the same date as the preceding photo is this left-rear view of the first, or a very-early, Pullman-Standard Cruiser Tank General Grant I. Mounted on each side of the overhang at the rear of the upper hull was a combination taillight assembly. The left and the right assemblies were not identical. The left one, seen here, contained a blackout light over a service and stop light. The right taillight assembly, seen in the next photo, had a blackout stop light over a blackout light. National Archives*

Work to develop a semi-automatic breech continued under the authority of an Ordnance Committee action of 17 August 1939. This resulted in the 37mm Gun, M5E1, which featured a counter recoil opened, spring closed breech. The new weapon was presented at a conference at Aberdeen Proving Ground on 5 September 1940, and on 24 October 1940 the semi-automatic gun was Standardized as the "37mm Gun, M6," and at the same time the M5 was reclassified as Substitute Standard.

As Standardized, the 76 ½-inch long M6 fired a 1.92-pound armor piercing round at 2,900 feet per second at a range of up to 12,850 yards. When firing 1.61-pound high explosive rounds these numbers dropped to 2,600 feet per second and 9,500 yards. Eight ounces of powder were used.

Proof testing of the M6 at Aberdeen showed that the weapon as installed was breech heavy, and it was recommended that the tube be lengthened to counterbalance the gun. This would have a couple of added benefits. First, the muzzle velocity would increase about 55 feet per second. Secondly, this would make the tube the same length as that of the M3, which would serve to expedite production of the M6 by two months.

On 24 April 1941 this change was approved by the Ordnance Committee, with the further stipulation that the longer barrels not be used as replacements for the M5 gun which was used in the M3 light tank, and that the barrels be so marked.

Watervliet Arsenal completed its first 18 series-produced M5 guns in February 1940, ultimately producing 506 of the weapons during that year. Production of the weapons continued through July 1941, by which time a further 944 had been produced. The final five Watervliet-produced guns were shipped in August and November, bringing the total production to 1,455.

**Above:** *The same tank is seen from the right rear on 2 August 1941. The WD-212 tracks provided better traction on sand and soft earth than the smooth treads used on the U.S. Army's M3 medium tanks. Indiana Historical Society*

The first production order for the M6 was issued to Watervliet Arsenal in January 1941, with the first 70 of the guns being completed in March 1942, with 27 more in April, then no further guns until July.

Clearly, the requirements of the US Medium Tank program alone exceeded Watervliet's production, not to mention the British Medium Tank program nor the light tank program's use of the M5 (M3 light tank) or M6 (M3A1, M5 light tanks).

Thus, in July 1940 the Boston Ordnance District issued an order for 800 M5 37mm guns to United Shoe Machinery Corp of Beverly, Massachusetts. United Shoe began shipping guns in April 1941, with 85 weapons. The New York Ordnance District ordered 1,380 M6 guns from United Shoe on 20 October 1941, with the first of these being completed in January 1943, too late for the Medium Tank program.

The second commercial contractor enlisted in the 37mm tank gun program was National Pneumatic Company of Rahway, New Jersey. This firm's peacetime business was the production of pneumatic door openers of the type used on streetcars and buses.

The New York Ordnance District issued an order on 12 September 1940 to the company for 3,667 M5 guns. This order was later reduced by 1,667 guns when the M6 became standardized.

The company began shipping the M5 in April 1941, and the M6 in November of that year. When production of the M5 gun began at the company the unit cost was $1,612.00; by the time production of the M6 ceased in July 1944 the unit cost had dropped to $592.00.

The final commercial firm engaged in the production of the 37mm tank gun was American Type Founders of Elizabeth, New Jersey. The company's initial order was placed by the New York Ordnance District in order to fill the British Purchasing Commissions order A-1964 for 1,500 M6 guns. American Type Founders did not produce the M5. The company made its first shipment of the M6 in August 1941, ultimately producing 905 guns in that year. Production of the M6 by American Type Founders was discontinued in January 1942, at which time 6,626 of the weapons had been completed.

**Above:** *Cruiser Tank General Grant I census number T-24241 is shown fully fitted out at the Pullman-Standard plant in Hammond, Indiana. This vehicle was part of the plant's October 1941 production. The sand shield on this example had a flat front end, as opposed to the curved front seen in the preceding photos. National Archives*

It is helpful to note the following production statistics:

|  | 1940 | 1941 | 1942 |
|---|---|---|---|
| M2A4 (M5 gun*) | 325 | 40 | 10 |
| M3 light (M5 gun*) | 0 | 2551 | 3256 |
| M3A1 light (M6 gun*) | 0 | 0 | 4581 |
| M3A3 light (M6 gun*) | 0 | 0 | 2 |
| M5 light (M6 gun*) | 0 | 0 | 2074 |
| M5A1 light (M6 gun*) | 0 | 0 | 784 |
| M3-series Medium (M6 gun*) | 0 | 1342 | 6058 |
| Total requirement M5 | 325 | 2591 | 3266 |
| Total requirement M6 | 0 | 1342 | 16755 |
| *specified weapon |  |  |  |
| 37mm gun production |  |  |  |
| M5 | 506 | 3766 | 0 |
| M6 | 0 | 1317 | 23839 |

While it can be seen from the table above, the annual supply of guns exceeded the annual requirements from 1940-1942, that was not the case on a monthly basis. With regard to the M3 medium tank program alone (negating the 2620 M6 guns needed for Cadillac light tank program), 1,342 M6 guns were needed in 1941, while the total production was only 1,320 units.

This situation continued into 1942, when M6 gun production lagged behind tank production by 400 units monthly for the first two months of the year. It is not at all surprising that as an expedient measure, the M5 guns were installed in numerous M3 medium tanks.

**Above:** *Grant I T-24241 had the tall storage box on the left sponson and the short box on the right side. Four L-shaped brackets on the outboard side of the left box served to secure it in place. The lid of the box was hinged on the inboard side: on the outboard side of the lid were two padlock hasps, with a spring-loaded snap hook on a retainer chain provided for securing each hasp. National Archives*

## Cast hull tanks

As noted in the previous chapter, the riveted-hull M3 was not the only variant of the R-975-powered tank to be produced. In 1939 the General Steel Castings Corporation of Eddystone, Pa, began experimenting with single-piece hull castings.

Formed in 1928, General Steel Castings was principally involved in the production of major components such as locomotive beds and cylinders, as well as other heavy cast components for locomotives and railcars. That the firm was located in Eddystone, as was Baldwin, should come as no surprise as Baldwin owned 32.37% of the business. American Locomotive owned 13.14% and Pullman 8.54%. The other major stockholder was American Steel Foundries, with a 38.33% share. On 30 July 1929, General Steel Castings acquired competitor Commonwealth Steel Company, including that firm's relatively new facilities in Granite City, Il.

On 27 July 1940 approval was granted for manufacture of an experimental cast armor upper hull for the M3 Medium Tanks, as well as five turret castings. In September of 1940 the Ferrous Metallurgical Advisory Board formed a subcommittee to draft specifications for cast armor as well as to advise on production techniques.

In late 1940 and early 1941 three cast armor upper tank hulls for the M3 were tested at Aberdeen Proving Ground, all three having been made by the General Steel Castings Corporation at their Eddystone, Pennsylvania plant. The first two were for the US M3, and the third for the Canadian M3, also known as the Ram. The first hull for the US tank underwent a firing test at Aberdeen Proving Ground on 19 September 1940. Lt. Colonel John Christmas issued a brief report, with the summary that the hull "...is too brittle and lacks ductility and toughness characteristics desired. This is evidenced by the type of fractures and the back spalls..."

**Above:** *The design of the rears of the sand shields are displayed in this right-rear view of Grant I census number T-24241. The right storage box is similarly appointed to the left box, with four L-brackets on the outboard side and two lock hasps with snap hooks on retainer chains. In addition, the lid of the right box has footman loops around the edges. Note the bracket for a radio antenna on the left rear of the turret. These photos of T-24241 were dated on the negative 12 November 1941. National Archives*

A second General Steel hull casting, fittingly referred to in documentation as "Cast Armor Hull #2," of an improved design and metallurgy arrived on 17 March 1941, and was subjected to firing tests on 19-20 March. These tests included being fired on with 37mm and .50-caliber armor piercing rounds, as well as 75mm proof rounds. Lt. Colonel Christmas also wrote a summary of this test on 2 April 1941 saying, "It is concluded from the above tests that this cast top hull has withstood a remarkable ballistic test and that it has very satisfactorily met all ballistic requirements of Spec. AX3-492. It has definitely proved that a casting of this size and varied dimensions can be made with satisfactory ballistic qualities. Since this top hull has been only slightly damaged in this extensive ballistic test, it is recommended that be returned to the manufacturer for repair and machining preparatory to incorporating it in the construction of a Medium Tank M3."

Colonel Christmas's sentiments were echoed a couple weeks later by Lt. Col. Frank Williams, Liaison Officer at APG to Chief of the Armored Force, who on 15 April 1941 wrote:

"1. Two cast steel hulls were made up by the General Steel Casting Company, Eddystone, Pennsylvania. One hull was sent here for ballistic test, the other was machined and sent to Rock Island Arsenal where will be made up into a Medium Tank, M3.

2. The cast steel hull that was sent here passed every specification for cast armor with something to spare. In addition, this cast hull resists other types of fire (particularly as regards shock) very well. As a result of these tests it was recommended from here to the Chief of Ordnance that –

a. A cast upper hull far the Medium Tank, M3 be standardized as a alternate construction at an early date.

b. One of the firms now making the Medium Tank, M3 be directed to employ this form of manufacture for the tanks it is making, and change to be made as soon as the tank manufacturer can accomplish this without delaying his production schedule.

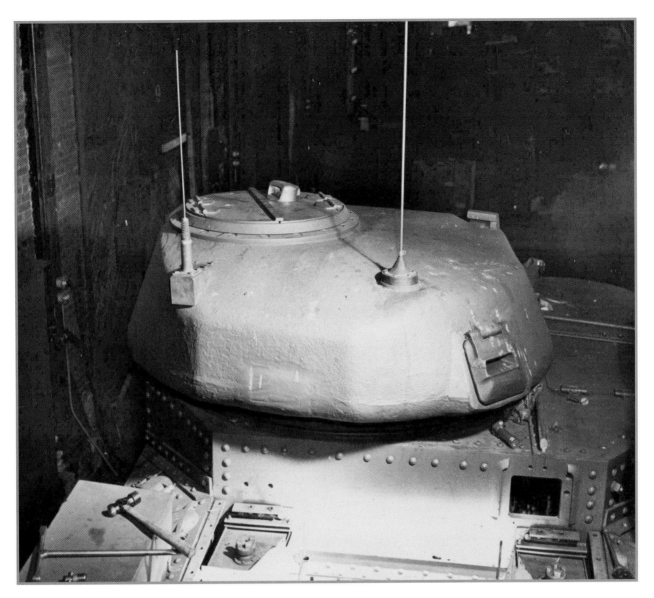

**Above:** *A Grant I is under assembly in the Pullman-Standard plant in late November 1941, displaying the two antennas for the No. 19 wireless set installed in the turret bustle. The hatch ring and two hatch doors are installed on the turret. The vision port is not yet installed on the right rear of the fighting compartment. Two holes on the left side of the vertical center plate of the rear of the fighting compartment are associated with the still-to-be-installed fire-extinguisher handles. The deck plates and engine-air intake grille are not installed, and overspray from the white paint in the engine compartment is on the darker-colored paint above it. National Archives*

3. The advantages of the cast steel hull over the homogeneous armor plate are as follows:

a. Eliminates bolts and rivets

b. The cast hull can be rounded to some extent, thereby denying direct impact from projectiles

c. A great reduction in the amount of work involved in manufacturing the hull

d. The machined hull will cost about fifty cents per pound to manufacture, thus creating a saving of approximately three thousand dollars per tank.

e. General Steel Casting Company state that they will be able to manufacture four fully machined cast armor hulls per day without expanding their present facilities.

f. The weight of the cast steel hull exceeds that of the hull made up of homogeneous armor plate by only two hundred pounds.

4. Colonel Christmas informed that an Ordnance Committee Meeting will be held in Washington at an early date in order to initiate a program of construction of the Medium Tank, M3 with cast steel hulls by the American Locomotive Works (sic)."

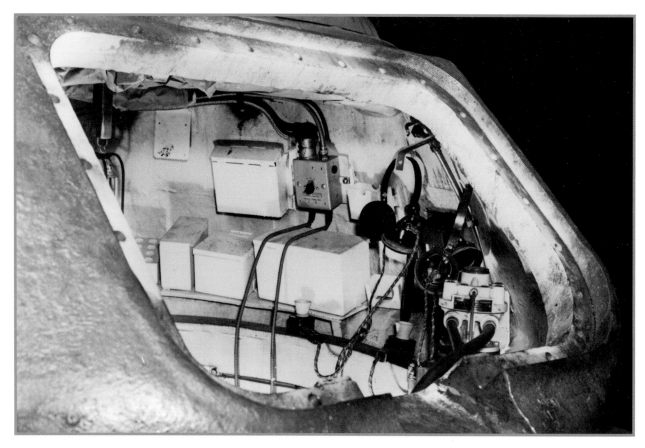

**Above:** *A Pullman-Standard photo dated November 21, 1941, shows the left side of the interior of a Grant turret through the opening for the 37mm gun mount. On the sidewall of the turret, among storage boxes, is an intercom control box. Two headphones are stored on hooks in the front of the turret; below them are two hand-held microphones. National Archives*

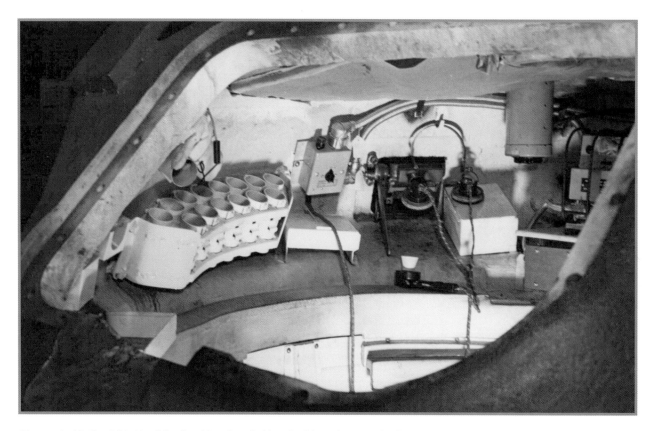

**Above:** *Inside the right side of the Grant turret are holders for 14 smoke grenades for the 2-inch Mortar Mk. I, along with an intercom control box, headphones, microphone, and other equipment. Behind the headphones is the right pistol port, to the rear of which is a storage box for vacuum tubes (or valves, in British parlance) for the wireless set. National Archives*

**Above:** *As seen through the opening for the 37mm gun mount in the front of a Grant turret at the Pullman-Standard plant on November 21, 1941, in the turret bustle is a No. 19 wireless set, with a guard in the form of curved bars in front of it. The cylinder to the left is an aerial variometer, mounted below the right antenna on the turret. National Archives*

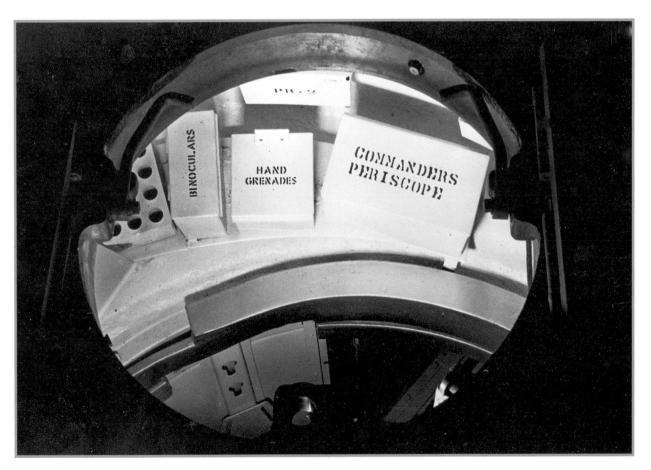

**Above:** *Looking down through the turret hatch to the left interior of the turret, directly inside is a storage box for two spare Protectoscope prisms. Farther down are, left to right, a storage rack for 12 signal cartridges, and storage cases for binoculars, hand grenades, and the commander's periscope. Patton Museum*

**Above:** *This view through the hatch of a Grant turret at Pullman-Standard on October 16, 1941, shows the forward right part of the turret basket, including the diamond-tread floor, storage racks for 37mm ammunition, boxes for 700 rounds of .30-caliber ammunition and spare periscope heads, and a fire extinguisher. Patton Museum*

Contract W-670-ORD-20 for the cast M3A1 hulls was issued by the Philadelphia Ordnance District to General Steel's Granite City facility on July 1941. The contract was completed in April 1942.

The Canadians, who ultimately produced their own M3 derivative, the M3 Ram with a cast upper hull, were very interested in the previously mentioned tests. Colonel F. F. Worthington (Canadian) on 24 March 1941 reported the results of the firing trials of the cast M3 hull held at Aberdeen. His assessment was that cast and plate armor had equal protection at thicknesses over 1 ½-inches.

The British commissioned a one-piece upper hull casting of their own design from General Steel Castings as well, and that casting was shipped to Aberdeen as well, where it was subjected to ballistic tests on 27-28 May 1941.

Of those tests, Colonel Christmas reported, "The resistance to penetration of this hull is comparable to the cast armor Top Hull #2 cast by the General Steel Castings Corp. and tested here recently. However, although the two hulls have approximately the same weight, the Canadian hull is thicker and has much more high obliquity

surface and hence is considered to offer more protection than Top Hull #2."

As mentioned earlier in this chapter, Rock Island completed the second pilot of M3 Medium tank in May 1941. That tank, Ordnance serial number 2372, Army registration number 304192, featured a General Steel Castings cast armor upper hull. It was shipped to Aberdeen Proving Ground without a turret on 4 June 1941. On 27 June it was being used for tests of American Steel Foundry track.

In July the tank was used as a test bed for Guiberson Diesel T-1400 number 1. Installation of the engine was completed at midnight on 10 July, and at 2:15 AM on July 11 tank 2372, in the company of five medium tanks powered by R-975 engines embarked on a trip to Carlisle, Fort Littleton, McConnellsburg, and Gettyburg PA, returning to Aberdeen at 12:45 PM the next day.

On August 9 1943 2372 was used as a target for firing tests of a PaK 40.

On 19 June 1941 OCM 16860 approved the construction of M3s with cast armor upper hulls, and on 9 October 1941 OCM 17301 designated such tanks as M3A1.

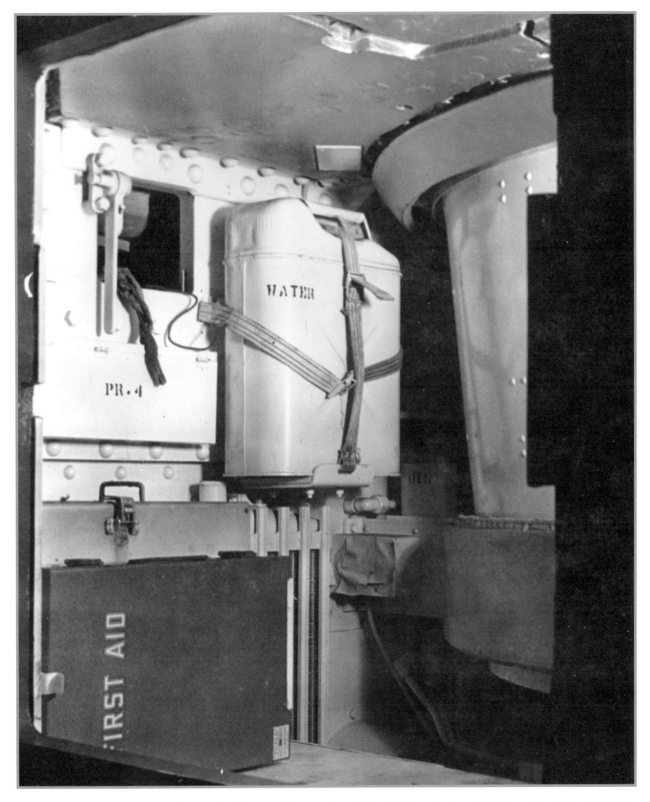

**Above:** *Looking toward the rear through the right door of a Grant at Pullman-Standard on September 11, 1941, toward the top are the rear pistol port with Protectoscope and a container for drinking water. To the left side of the pistol port is its operating lever. Below the pistol port is a box for spare Protectoscope prisms; farther down is a first-aid kit, to the right of which is the oil cooler. To the right is the turret basket. At the top right is the hatch in the roof of the fighting compartment. Patton Museum*

The American Locomotive contract was amended, and in February 1942 the M3A1 began to be produced alongside the M3 in Schenectady, and by the next month the firm was turning out more cast hull M3A1 Lees than riveted M3s.

Strangely, despite the many apparent advantages offered by the M3A1, none would see combat. Rather, all were used in the US as training vehicles.

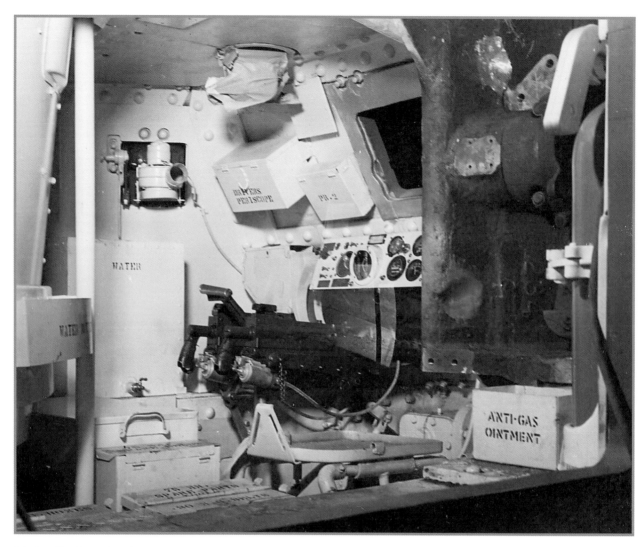

**Above:** *The front of the fighting compartment of the Pullman-Standard Grant is viewed through the right door, with the 75mm gun not installed. To the right is the interior of the horizontal rotor of the gun mount. In the background are the driver's vision port and instrument panel, as well as storage boxes for a periscope and Protectoscope prisms, and the two .30-caliber machine guns, with firing solenoids next to the grips. What appears to be a small ventilator blower fitted with an electrical cord is mounted on the side pistol port; below it is a drinking-water chest with a spigot near the bottom. National Archives*

## M3A2
## Welded Hull Radial Engine

As mentioned previously, Rock Island Arsenal-produced pilots 3 and 4 featured hulls assembled by welding. Pilot number 3, with hull plates made by Disston steel and welded together by Rock Island Arsenal personnel, was completed with turret, road tested and shipped to Aberdeen Proving Ground on 2 July 1941. This tank was Ordnance serial number 2373, Army registration number 304193.

At Aberdeen this tank was subjected to one of the most unusual test programs that this author has uncovered documentation of to date. On 1 July 1942 it was planned that the tank was going to be subjected to a 1,000-mile automotive test. This

test was specifically directed to be done "largely cross country and enough of it over difficult terrain to determine whether sufficient wear or distortion develops to adversely affect operation." On 7 July this plan was amended so that immediately after the 1,000-mile test the tank would be subject to a firing test "to determine its resistance to shock and to develop any weaknesses that may be present in the welds." Prior to the firing test, Aberdeen was to remove or "other wise protect components such as armament, engine, transmission system, etc., likely to be injured by firing as this firing test is of the hull only."

Harry J. Rouse, Associate Engineer at Aberdeen wrote on 26 July that "at the rate mileage is being put on, it will be at least ten days before it completes the 1000 miles required."

**Above:** *The driver's seat of the Grant, also seen in the preceding photo, straddled the rear of the transmission. It was mounted on tubular supports and lacks the seat back and cushion. To the rear of the seat are storage boxes for spare parts and tools for the 75mm gun, .30-caliber ammunition, and books. To the right of the seat is the transmission gear-shift lever. Farther forward, on each side of the transmission, are the steering levers. To the left front of the seat is the left steering-brake housing; the hex plug near the top would be removed to adjust the brake with a deep-socket wrench. National Archives*

On 2 August Chief of Ordnance General Charles Wesson sent a teletype to Aberdeen directing that the 1,000 mile test be reduced to 500 mile test, after which the proof firing was to be conducted, at "the earliest practicable date." Wesson's message continued, "Teletype report is requested. This information needed in connection with Ordnance Committee action authorizing the use of welded construction in production Medium Tank M3."

On August 7, after the tank had completed its automotive test at odometer reading 565, the 37mm gun was proof fired, then the power train assembly and engine were removed. The tank was then towed to the firing range, where 37mm and 75mm proof slugs were fired at it. In an after-firing summary, Major J.E. McInerney reported that "The forward end of the hull bottom is warped slightly upward at the center. It is believed that this bending of the bottom occurred while the vehicle was being towed to the range for the ballistic test of the hull. During this period the power train was removed from the front end of the vehicle and the vehicle was towed on its bogie wheels With the front end removed the rigidity of the forward portion of the hull is decreased considerably and great strains are set up within the hull structure during towing, especially on turns." McInerney concluded "The welds of this vehicle have given very satisfactory performance during the road test and also the ballistic test. This type of fabrication is highly recommended."

**Above:** *The creation of a M3 with a cast armor hull was a part of the medium tank plan from early on. Shown here is the first of the proposed armored upper hull, photographed prior to ballistic testing at Aberdeen Proving Ground in September 1940. National Archives*

**Above:** *The first armored, shown here, produced by General Steel Castings Corporation, did not pass the ballistic tests. This led to a redesign and production of an additional test hull. National Archives*

**Above:** *The second prototype upper cast armored hull for the M3 produced by General Steel Castings is shown in one of the Aberdeen Proving Ground shops. Markings on the hull indicate the armor thickness at various points. National Archives*

**Above:** *In addition to the hull itself, the armored side doors were redesigned as well. The sponson mount for the 75mm main gun was integral with the hull itself. National Archives*

**Above:** *While creating and heat treating such a large armored casting as this is time consuming, there is considerably less labor expense in manufacturing a tank hull by casting as opposed to the riveted construction method used on the first M3 pilot. This results in a lower cost. National Archives*

**Above:** *Even more important that cost, the crew of a cast hull tank does not face the hazard of sheared rivet heads in the event that the tank comes under enemy fire. National Archives*

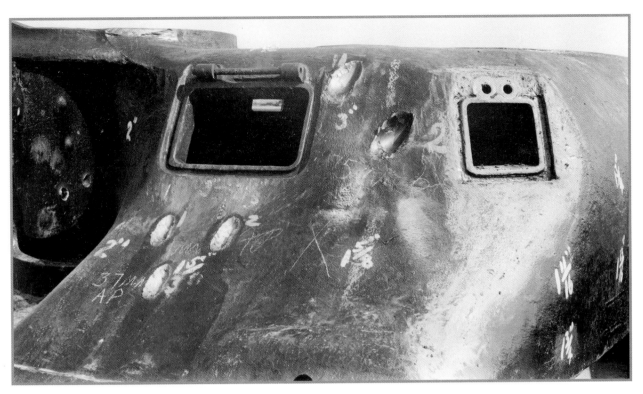

**Above:** *The second experimental cast hull passed the ballistic test with flying colors, with minimal damage from 37 and 75 mm rounds, as shown here. This hull was subsequently repaired and incorporated in the first pilot cast hull M3 assembled at Rock Island. National Archives*

**Above:** *Rock Island Arsenal built the pilot cast hull M3, incorporating the previously-tested cast upper hull manufactured by General Steel Casting Corporation; this vehicle was shipped to Aberdeen Proving Ground on 4 June 1941, without a turret. It was later used for automotive testing, including testing the Guiberson T-1400 radial Diesel. Joe Demarco collection*

Armament: 1-75 m/m; 1-37 m/m M6; 3 cal. .30 machine guns; 1 cal. .45 machine gun
Armor: 3/8" - 2"
Clutch: Rockford Multiple dry disc
Crew: 6
Engine: Guiberson T1400 9 cyl. air cooled Diesel, 350 HP at 2400 RPM
Fuel capacity: 175 gallons
Fording depth: 40"
Ground clearance: 14"

Ground pressure: 13.55# per sq. in.
Height: 123"
HP to weight ratio: 10.95 HP per ton
Length: 222"
Speed: 25 MPH
Steering: controlled differential
Suspension: vertical volute springs, front sprocket drive
Track: Ordnance rubber bushed outside guided
Transmission: Caterpillar 5 speed synchromesh
Weight: 63,880#

**Above:** *The Medium Tank M3A1 was in most respects identical to the Medium Tank M3 except that it had a cast-armor upper hull. The shape of this hull dictated certain adjustments to the layout of the vehicle, such as installing a new fighting-compartment hatch and redesigning the side doors. Shown here is M3A1 registration number W-306032 and Ordnance number 1962, while undergoing tests at Aberdeen Proving Ground on 6 December 1941. Patton Museum*

**Above:** *The same M3A1 shown in the preceding photo is seen from the right, showing the redesigned side door with its rounded shape. As the upper hull was cast, the sponson for the 75mm gun mount was part of the casting, and thus lacked the visible joint the Medium Tank M3 had where the cast sponson joined the plate armor to the rear of it. National Archives*

**Above:** *The new hatch door for the M3A1 was moved to the rear, and was positioned on the angle where the fighting-compartment roof transitioned to the engine deck and rear sponsons. Initially the door was hinged on the front, but this made it difficult to lift, so later it was changed so the hinge was on the rear of the door. The part number of the door was in raised letters on it: D38464. National Archives*

**Above:** *Two bowl-shaped antenna brackets were on the rear of the fighting compartment of the Medium Tank M3A1, as opposed to one on the left rear of the fighting compartment of the Medium Tank M3. The taillight assemblies were recessed in the overhang at the rear of the upper hull, with the lenses flush with the armor. National Archives*

**Above:** *A Medium Tank M3A1 is splashing through water during testing. Attached to the muzzle of the 75mm gun is a counterweight, which compensated for the short length of the barrel with reference to the proper functioning of the elevation gyrostabilizer, which kept the gun at the correct elevation on a target as the tank moved over terrain. With the counterweight installed, there was less friction when the gun was elevated, thus aiding the proper functioning of the gyrostabilizer. Allen County Historical Society*

**Left Above:** *The left front of the upper hull of the M3A1 had a pronounced step, with the pistol port located on the upper part. The apertures for the two .30-caliber machine guns were on a small bulge that was integral to the lower left corner of the glacis. Note the bulge in the frontal armor above the driver's vision port. An aperture for a 2-inch smoke-bomb mortar is visible on the right front of the turret roof. National Archives*

**Left:** *Welded to the hull between the left side door and the forward-side vision port of Medium Tank M3A1 W-306032 was a bracket for a radio antenna; this was in addition to the two antenna brackets on the rear of the fighting compartment. On this vehicle, the part numbers of the two outboard sections of the final-drive assembly were cast on the sides of the housings for the final-drive gears. National Archives*

**Above:** *Rock Island Arsenal constructed two pilot tanks with welded hulls. The first one, serial number 2373, shown here, was ordered on 31 January 1941, and was shipped complete with turret to Aberdeen Proving Ground on 12 July 1941. This tank was manufactured with hull armor plates made by Disston and welded together at Rock Island Arsenal. National Archives*

**Above:** *As with the cast hull, the welded hull was an effort to both reduce the combat hazard inherent with riveted construction, with the further benefit of reduced manufacturing costs. National Archives*

**Rght:** *Unlike production tanks, 2373 had fabricated sheet metal rear fenders. The tank was equipped with a pre-production turret casting, as evidenced by the lip beneath the commander's cupola. Subsequently, the welded hull, radial powered M3 was authorized for production and designated M3A2 in September 1941. National Archives*

**Above:** *The markings on this tank on 21 July 1941 indicate the angles between adjacent armor. At the time of this photo the tank was undergoing automotive testing at Aberdeen. National Archives*

**Above:** *The second welded hull pilot, serial number 2374, was shipped to Aberdeen Proving Ground incomplete (without the engine, power train, and turret) on 9 August 1941. The hull for this tank had been shipped to Rock Island Arsenal completely assembled, with Rock Island installing the suspension and interior components. At Aberdeen it was subjected to firing tests. In this, the only photo yet to surface of 2374, shows that at the time of the firing test, no main armament was installed. The partially completed vehicle was subsequently shipped to Baldwin for repair and completion. This is evidenced by the large opening at the right in this photo (just behind the builder's plate), which should house the 75mm gun. National Archives*

**Above:** *In the end, only 12 production M3A2s were completed, all by Baldwin Locomotive Works, between January and March 1942. Shown here is a Baldwin-built M3A2, numbered 1040 on the front and sponson, during tests at Aberdeen on 1 January 1942. National Archives*

**Above:** *Baldwin Medium Tank M3A2 number 1040, undergoing tests at Aberdeen Proving Ground on 1 January 1942, displays its right side. The vertical panel on the right side of the rear of the fighting compartment retained its screwed-on construction, as it was necessary to remove this panel when changing the 75mm gun. National Archives*

**Above:** *The same M3A2 is viewed from the upper front during a pause in tests at Aberdeen on 1 January 1942. The hinges of the side doors were fastened with large, slotted screws and were not welded. National Archives*

**Above:** *With the exception of the lack of rivets, the Baldwin-built M3A2 was similar in appearance to a standard Medium Tank M3. The hinges of the engine-compartment doors on the rear of the lower hull were welded, not screwed. This turret is a good example of a type that had a smooth, built-up transition between the left side of the cupola ring and the turret. National Archives*

**Above:** *Baldwin-constructed Medium Tank M3A2 number 1040 is observed from the left rear during testing at Aberdeen on 1 January 1942. On the top of the sponson near its front end are two armored covers for fuel fillers. The one on the left is for the 2 1/2-gallon fuel tank for the auxiliary generator, and the one to its right is for the fuel tank in the left sponson. National Archives*

**Above:** *Medium Tank M3A2 number 1040 is viewed from the right at Aberdeen Proving Ground on 1 January 1942. Aberdeen Proving Grounds' evaluations of this tank disclosed that the welded hull offered more protection than the riveted hull and also weighed slightly less. The welded hull was also less time-consuming to construct. National Archives*

**Above:** *As seen in a frontal view of Baldwin M3A2 number 1040 at Aberdeen, the armored fairing for the two .30-caliber machine guns remained a separate part that was riveted to the glacis. Hex bolts with lock nuts were used to join together the flanges separating the three sections of the final-drive assembly. The joints between the armor plates of the hull were extremely neat. Note the extreme wear to the rubber shoes of the tracks. National Archives*

**Above:** *Baldwin M3A2 1082, believed to be the second and only other M3A2 Lee, is shown at Aberdeen Proving Ground on 30 January 1942, displays what appears to be an atypical rivet pattern in the area of the 75mm gun sponson and right side crew door. If the rivet pattern of M3A3s is considered the norm for Baldwin-built, riveted hull tanks, then this tank has 'too many' rivets, while 1040 has too few. The possibility exists that this tank, 1082, is in fact Rock Island pilot 4, which was shipped incomplete to Baldwin for completion, but no documentation of the origin of 1082 has yet surfaced.*

**Above:** *The following sequence of photos documents a welded Medium Tank M3A2 hull produced by Baldwin Locomotive. There is evidence that this may have been the first welded hull completed by Baldwin, as other photos exist of office and factory workers posing in and with this hull. A close examination of the photo shows, through the side door, details of the interior, including the welded joints between the armor panels. The armor panel on the right rear of the fighting compartment remains a screwed-on component, to allow for removing the 75mm cannon for repair or replacement. Baldwin Locomotive Works*

**Above:** *In a left-side view of the Baldwin M3A2 welded hull, note the splash guard around the sides and bottom of the pistol port, and the two holes on top of the sponson for the fuel fillers, which have slightly raised rims around them. Baldwin Locomotive Works*

**Above:** *In a rear view of the same M3A2 welded hull, holes are cut in the rear of the lower hull for the pepper-pot exhausts and the engine-compartment doors. Tow eyes are installed on the lower part of that panel. Note the splash guard on the sides of the pistol port on the right rear of the fighting compartment, and the two holes for fuel fillers to the sides of the opening for the engine-air intake at the front of the engine deck. Baldwin Locomotive Works*

**Above:** In a frontal view of the Baldwin M3A2 hull, a rectangular opening has been left on the lower left of the glacis for the fairing for the two machine guns. The ribbed bulkhead on the front of the lower hull appears to have been installed for support only and was not a permanent part of the hull structure. Baldwin Locomotive Works

On 30 August Lt. Colonel Christmas ordered the tank reassembled and driven an additional 500 miles. Of this, he wrote, "The object of this additional road test is to more definitely prove the success of welding for tank fabrication. Complete inspection of all welded joints should be made of this hull in its present disassembled condition. Cracks adjoining any of the three 75mm A.P. penetrations should be punch marked so as to note any possible extension that may occur during the 500 mile run. At the conclusion of the test, a second inspection for cracks and misalignment or change in plate angles at the welded joints is desired."

M3 pilot number 4 was assigned Ordnance serial number 2374 and Army registration number 304194. The hull plates of this tank were made by Carnegie Illinois Steel Company, who also welded them together and shipped the completely welded hull to Rock Island Arsenal. Personnel there proceeded to assemble this vehicle, including suspension assemblies, etc. However, the tank was not complete when it was shipped to Aberdeen on 9 August 1941. When it left Rock Island it did not have engine, transmission, guns or turret. The only photo located thus far of this tank at Aberdeen was taken on 28 August 1941,

and is of the interior. At that time it had been subjected to a firing test and still lacked the 75mm gun.

The firing test on tank 2374 was conducted on 30 August 1941. Four rounds of 75mm A.P. M61 were fired at the hull. The first round struck just in rear of the left door, at a junction of three welds, causing a partial penetration. The middle weld cracked near the point of impact, for an exterior distance of 9-inches and an interior distance of 6-inches. The other three rounds did not cause any welds to fail.

Major McInerney wrote at the conclusion of the test, "This test has been shown that the Carnegie-Illinois welded hull is comparable to the Rock Island welded hull recently tested at the Proving Ground, in that the welds hold up extremely well. Of course, impacts at certain points on a welded hull will cause the weld to crack but this does not compare to the danger resulting from rivet heads knocked off by impacts on hulls of riveted fabrication. The welded structure also compares very favorably with cast hulls. We again emphasize our recommendation that welded fabrication be used in place of riveted or bolted fabrication wherever possible."

*12128-4*

**Above:** *The welded hull has been hoisted to permit photographing its top, providing details of the top of the 75mm gun sponson, the T-shaped brace and the hatch on the fighting-compartment roof, and the openings for the fuel fillers and the engine air intake on the engine deck. Baldwin Locomotive Works*

**Above:** *A Medium Tank M3A2 at the Engineer Replacement Training Center area at Fort Belvior, Virginia, has been painted in a four-color disruptive camouflage scheme. The lightest color is on the bottoms of the 37mm and 75mm gun barrels, for countershadowing purposes. Communications and Electronics Command History Office.*

**Above:** *The same M3A2 in four-color disruptive camouflage paint is seen from the left side. The .30-caliber machine guns had been removed from the bow and the cupola. This turret had the more smooth and built-up transition between the left side of the cupola ring and the turret than the pronounced ledge seen on many M3 turrets. Communications and Electronics Command History Office.*

**Above:** *The disruptive camouflage scheme applied to the M3A2 at Fort Belvoir was not in widespread use in the U.S. Army, and the application of it to this tank have been part of a training exercise for Engineer replacement troops. Communications and Electronics Command History Office.*

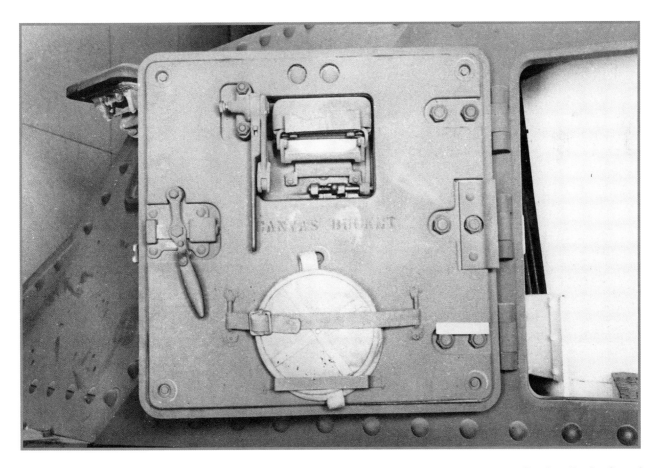

**Above:** *The following series of photos dated 20 June 1942, were taken at Aberdeen Proving Ground to document interior storage provisions in the Medium Tank M3 as part of Project No. 3-19-1. The vehicle used was Ordnance number 1026. Depicted here is the interior of the left side door. At the top is the inside of the pistol port, showing the Protectoscope holder and the operating lever of the port door. On the left is the latch handle for the door, and at the bottom is stored a collapsible canvas bucket, with "CANVAS BUCKET" stenciled above it on the door. Patton Museum*

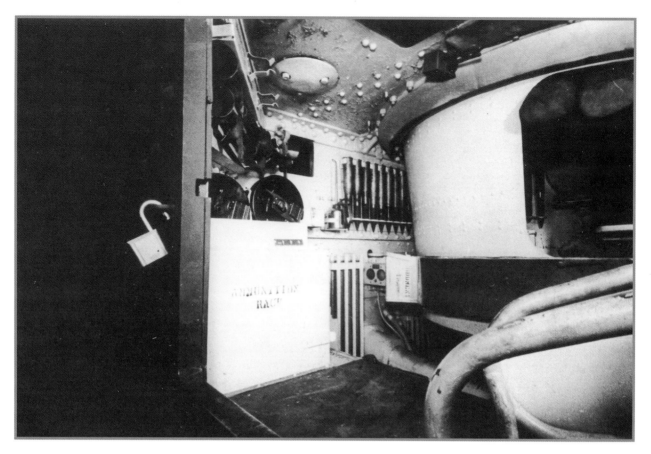

**Above:** *The rear of the fighting compartment, the turret basket, and, to the lower right, the recoil guard of the 75mm gun, are seen through the right side door. On the rear bulkhead are, left to right, clips for storing a Thompson submachine gun, below which are a tripod and Thompson ammunition magazines; an oilcan, and a 37mm ammunition rack. To the rear of the turret basket is an oddments tray. Below the turret basket is the drive-shaft housing. Patton Museum*

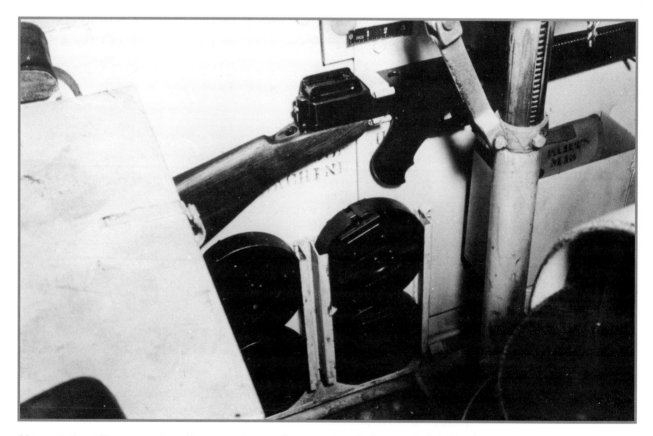

**Above:** *A stored Thompson submachine gun and ammunition magazines for it are on the left side of the lower hull to the left of the driver's station. Patton Museum*

**Above:** *The storage arrangements on the right rear of the fighting compartment are viewed from the perspective of the driver when he turned his head to the right rear. In the corner of the compartment are a stored Thompson submachine gun, tripod, .45-caliber magazines, and a storage box for 37mm ammunition. In the foreground is the elevating hand wheel for the 75mm gun. Patton Museum*

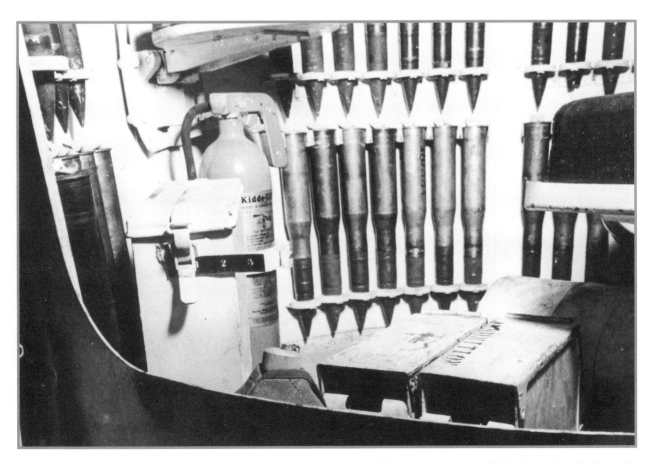

**Above:** *The interior of the turret basket of M3 Ordnance number 1026 is viewed from the front, with the loader's seat to the left, the gunner's seat to the right, ammunition boxes on the floor, 37mm ammunition stored on the basket, and a fire extinguisher below the loader's seat. Patton Museum*

**Above:** *The turret basket interior is seen from the left rear, with the gunner's seat to the left, the combination pump and motor for the Logansport hydraulic traverse below the seat, and the loader's seat, fire extinguisher, and 37mm ammunition storage on the opposite side. Patton Museum*

**Above:** *The Logansport hydraulic-traverse motor and pump unit is viewed close-up from the rear. This unit combined a hydraulic pump, right, and an electric motor, right, to draw hydraulic oil from the reservoir and pump it to a control valve, which then apportioned pressurized oil to the traverse motor to drive it in the desired direction. General Motors LLC*

**Above:** *A view from the front of the turret basket shows, the gunner's seat, right, with the hydraulic-traverse motor and pump below and to the rear of it. To the far right, part of the hydraulic-oil reservoir is in view, next to which are the suction hose (lower) and the pressure hose (upper). General Motors LLC*

Remarkably, such was the state of US tank production and availability that after the firing tests of both 2373 and 2374, and the 1,000-mile road testing of 2373, on 24 September 1941 Aberdeen was advised that "The Office of Chief of Ordnance, has directed the Philadelphia Ordnance District to make a complete tank of the Carnegie welded hull and repair penetrations and cracks in the Rock Island welded tank. Shipping Order No. 123676 dated September 9, 1941, covers the Carnegie hull, and Shipping Order No. 123777 dated September 23, 1941 covers the Rock Island tank. The Proving Ground is authorized to ship these two units to the plant of Baldwin Locomotive Works at Eddystone, Pennsylvania…"

Based on the favorable test results, OCM item 17201 of 11 September 1941 recommended that "welding of approved types be authorized as an alternative method of fabricating tank hulls and turrets" and "That the Medium Tank, M3, when equipped with welded hull be designated: Medium Tank, M3A2."

The justification for this was the positive report of the road and firing tests, which listed several advantages to welded assembly, including:

"(1) Reduction in weight for a given ballistic resistance or increased protection within a given weight limit;

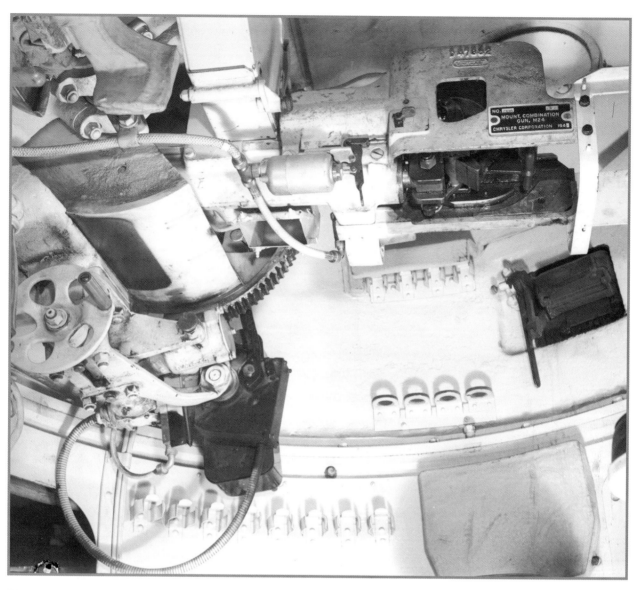

**Above:** *The perspective of this view of the interior of the turret is from the lower left looking upward at the 37mm gun and its mount. The data plate on the side of the recoil guard identifies the unit as "MOUNT, COMBINATION GUN, M24" manufactured by Chrysler Corporation. Also in view are the elevating hand wheel (lower left), the crash pad for the gunner's sight (upper left), and, below the gun, the elevating sector and the lower part of the rotor shield. The dark-colored box on the lower part of the far side of the gun mount is the gyrostabilizer control unit. Note the pistol port on the turret toward the right. General Motors LLC*

(2) Elimination of rivet heads and angles on the interior surfaces;

(3) Reduction in machine work;

(4) Elimination of flying rivets and entrance of splash through joints;

(5) Reduction in cost and time required in fabrication."

On 11 September 1941, Ordnance Committee minutes 17302 approved welding as an alternative means of fabricating the M3 Medium tank, and provided the designation of M3A2 for such tanks. Baldwin began delivering M3A2 tanks in January 1942, but production came to an end in March, after only 12 had been completed, the result of the shift to Diesel power for the welded-hull tanks. Two of the twelve were destined for US forces, while the remaining ten were built as Grants for the British.

**Above:** *The stabilizer control unit is the dark-colored box to the lower right. This was part of the gyrostabilizer system for the 37mm gun, which acted to keep the gun trained, in elevation, at a target even as the tank moved, including over rough ground. To the upper left is the elevation sector, underneath he 37mm gun. General Motors LLC*

**Above:** *Some of the 37mm ammunition stowage on the right-rear quarter of the turret and turret basket is viewed from behind the gunner's seat back. Also in view is the recoil guard of the 37mm gun. Patton Museum*

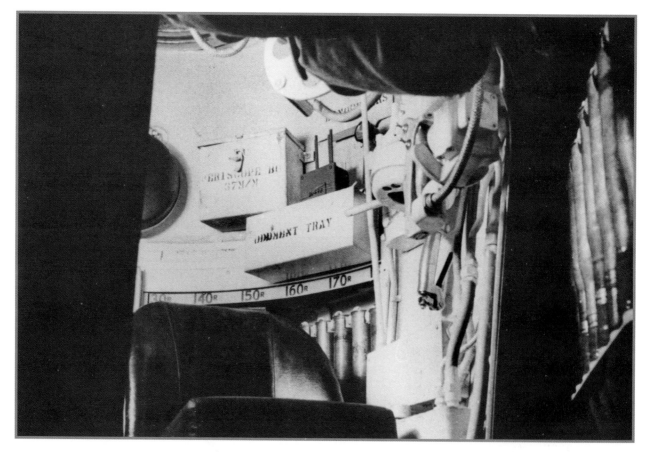

**Above:** *In a view of the left rear of the turret of Medium Tank M3 Ordnance number 1026, which was taken through the crew-access opening in the front of the turret basket, a periscope storage box and an oddment tray are at the center of the photo. Also present is stored 37mm ammunition. Around the turret ring are azimuth marks, from 130 degrees right to 170 degrees right. At the bottom is the gunner's seat. Patton Museum*

**Above:** *To the rear of the driver's seat (lower left) and to the front of the turret basket is the driver's detachable windshield and windshield-wiper assembly. To the right are mockups of radio equipment.*
*Patton Museum*

**Above:** *This photo shows an installation of an SCR-508 short-range radio set in the rear of the left sponson of a Medium Tank M3. The photo was taken by or for the Signal Corps Laboratories, Fort Monmouth, New Jersey, on June 23, 1942. National Archives*

# Chapter 5
# The Diesel Tanks
# M3A3 and M3A5

Diesel engines offer a number of advantages over gasoline engines for use in tanks and combat vehicles. Among these are the much higher flash point of the fuel, making fire a significantly lower risk, greater fuel economy, which results in a greater range for a given fuel capacity, and increased low speed torque.

On 28 May 1937 the Commander of the First Cavalry recommended that all future procurement of combat cars be with Diesel engines. On 4 June 1937 the Infantry Board recommended that up to a total of 50% of the M2 tanks being procured be powered by Diesel.

On 2 February 1939 authorization was given to modify the pilot light tank M2A2E2 to use the General Motors Detroit Diesel Division 6-71 6-cylinder Diesel engine along with an automatic

transmission. In this configuration the engine developed 165 horsepower and 575 lb-ft of torque.

The GM 6-71 engine was part of a family of engines which was designed in 1937. The engines were offered in two, three, four and six-cylinder configurations, each with using the same 71 cubic inch displacement cylinder design arranged in the various combinations. Thus, the 6-71 was a 6-cylinder, 2-cycle inline engine. Because it is a two-cycle engine, it is relatively easy to make the engine run in either direction, requiring only the reversal of the cylinder head, blower and camshaft. The significance of this will be seen later.

As a result of generally favorably initial tests of this and other Diesel engines, increasing numbers of Diesel powered combat vehicles were ordered in the Fiscal Year 1940 and 1941 appropriations.

**Above:** *In August 1941, as a hedge against predicted shortages of Wright/Continental R-975-EC2 radial engines, the U.S. Army ordered an experimental power plant consisting of two General Motors Diesel engines, designated the Model 6046, for use in the Medium Tank M3. The resulting vehicle would come to be designated the Medium Tank M3A3 in vehicles with welded hulls, and the Medium Tank M3A5 for riveted hulls. To test the concept, a Model 6046 engine was installed in a pilot vehicle, Medium Tank M3 registration number W-301026, photographed at Aberdeen Proving Ground on November 26, 1941. Patton Museum*

**Below:** *The Medium Tank M3A5 pilot, registration number W-301026, displays the large, new overhang on the rear of the upper hull, which enclosed the radiator. An air deflector below the overhang directed engine exhaust and engine-cooling-air exhaust to the rear instead of downward, to reduce the amount of dust stirred up by the vehicle. Patton Museum*

**Below:** *From the side, the pilot Medium Tank M3A5 looked like any other early-production M3, except for the enlarged overhang at the rear of the upper hull. Patton Museum*

**Above:** *A Model 6046 twin-Diesel engine shipped in April 1945 is displayed. The power plant consisted of two GM 6-71 Diesel engines that fed power into a common transfer gear case. Even if one of the engine banks was damaged or disabled, the power plant could still operate at enough horsepower to keep the tank under motion. Shown here is the front end of the engine. General Motors LLC*

At about the same time General Motors Limited, the British arm of GM, approached the British Admiralty with an eye toward selling them a marine version of the three-cylinder 71 series engine. The Admiralty trials of this engine came to the attention of the War Office, who was seeking additional sources of engines for their Valentine infantry tank. Collaborative work between the War Office and General Motors produced a version of the 6-71 suitable for this application, the 6-71S. After five months of negotiation, the British Purchasing Commission on 27 September 1940 placed an initial order for 250 of the engines for installation in Valentines being produced in Canada.

Through time, the 6-71, known in this application as the model 6004, became well liked by the British for use in tanks.

As noted previously, the introduction of the M3 series of tanks coincided with the United States overall coming to a war footing. The M3 was designed around the Wright R-975 aircraft engine; an engine that was not only increasingly in demand for the expanding tank program, but also in demand for use in aircraft. Despite Continental being contracted for license production of the engine, in 1941 there was still far greater demand for tank engines than there was R-975 production capacity.

By virtue of the block design of the 6-71, it was possible to marry two of the engines together, creating a relatively compact yet powerful engine.

The fan end is at the rear of the engine and rear of the tank. Both engines are right hand rotation. The blocks and cylinder heads are symmetrical at both ends and relative to each other. Each engine has its own clutch.

In the twin unit power pack, the two blocks are

placed parallel to each other and are joined by the engine transfer case gear housing, in which the drive gear of each engine turns a single driven gear for the pair of engines. The driven gear then turns the drive shaft.

In order to make the powerplant as compact as possible, the blocks and heads are oriented such that all the engine driven accessories are located on the outboard sides of the blocks, with only the exhaust manifolds and water outlet manifolds between them.

Each engine had its own clutch, which in normal circumstances were operated together by the driver. However, in the event of a failure of one engine, that could be disengaged, allowing the tank to be operated on one engine, without the further load of turning the inoperative engine.

On 4 August 1941 the Under Secretary of War approved awarding a contract to General Motors to install a dual 6-71 Diesel engine in a M3 Medium Tank.

The 28th Chrysler-built M3, registration W-301026, was shipped to the General Motors Diesel plant in Redford Township, Michigan, about 25 miles from the Chrysler-operated Detroit Tank Arsenal.

The GM twin Diesel was substantially larger than the R-975, requiring some changes to the engine compartment and rear hull. The engine compartment doors of the M3 were replaced with a single plate. The hull rear side plates had to be extended rearward, as well as down to the level of the track. The rear plate had to be extended downward a similar distance, and was arranged such that it sloped out from the rear of the vehicle.

**Above:** *The 6046 twin-Diesel engine is viewed straight-on from the front; crewmen and mechanics were taught to call this the "flywheel end" of the engine and the opposite end the "fan end," to avoid any confusion. The oblong assembly in the lower foreground is the transfer gear case, at the center of which is the output shaft, which connected to the drive shaft. General Motors LLC*

**Above:** *In a right-front view of the engine, the starter for the right engine bank is the black object on the side of the crankcase. There is one starter for each engine bank; they are 24-volt units and are mounted on the flywheel housing. The bullet-shaped object alongside the crankcase to the rear of the starter is the right-hand oil strainer. Above the strainer is the air-inlet housing; three air cleaners were attached to the top of the housing but are not installed here. A total of six air cleaners were required. General Motors LLC*

These changes were made to accommodate the radiators.

A deflector shield was installed to prevent the cooling air and engine exhaust gases from stirring up dust, thereby disclosing the tank's location to the enemy.

The top plate of the engine deck was replaced with one including two hinged armored air intake louvered doors.

Also, the lower portion of the bulkhead between the engine and fighting compartment was moved forward about one foot to accommodate the bellhousings of the engines as well as the clutch and transfer case.

Thus modified, the vehicle underwent testing at the General Motors Proving Ground in Milford, MI from 9 October through 19 November 1941. After the conclusion of those tests, the tank was then driven

547 miles from Milford to Aberdeen, MD, leaving 21 November and arriving in Aberdeen on 24 November.

As was often the case during the war, decisions were made prior to testing being finalized, and even before certain formalities were completed. Such was the case with the GM twin Diesel. On 11 November 1941 a directive was issued to Baldwin "that all M3s are to be diesel driven, starting with the 87th U.S. Tank and the 221st British."

A cypher telegram from the British Purchasing Commission to England of 28 November 1941 advised, "U.S. Ordnance intend change medium tanks from Baldwin's production from Whirlwind engines to twin G.M. 6/71 Diesel engines these give tank much improved performance and pending confirmation from you have informed U.S. Ordnance that these tanks will be acceptable to us if approved for use in their army."

Testing at Aberdeen continued until 28 April 1942. However, based on the initial success of the tests at the GM Proving Ground, OCM 17440, dated 21 November 1941, recommended the adoption of the twin 6-71 engine as an alternative power plant for Medium Tanks and provided the designation of M3A3 for medium tanks equipped with this power plant.

On 29 October 1941 an expansion of the GM Detroit Diesel Division plant to permit the production of 1,000 twin Diesel units per month was approved by the Undersecretary of War.

On 13 January 1942, a conference was held to discuss the various engine options available for tanks. Those attending were General Devers, General Somervell, Colonel Cheves, Colonel Christmas, Colonel Cummings and Colonel McAuliffe. At that time, Diesel was still the stated favorite fuel for US tanks. The Armored Corps wanted to eliminate many of the engines then being used in tanks and armored vehicles. In particular, they wanted to eliminate the radial

engine, whether gas or Diesel-fueled. General Devers stated specifically that he did not want any further orders placed for the Guiberson engine.

Colonel Christmas advised those attending that "the output of General Motors Diesel engines would permit the issue of medium tanks with these engines for eight American Armored Divisions by the end of June. This was subject to the qualification that defense aid requirements could be met by the supply of other tanks and tanks then in the hands of troops which might be replaced by the Diesel engine tank."

On 23 January 1942 the Undersecretary of War approved a second expansion of the Detroit Diesel facilities. This expansion would increase capacity of the plant to 2,000 units per month.

All these plans were reversed on 7 March 1942 when Major General James Ulio, 7 days after becoming the Adjutant General, decreed that:
"All wheeled vehicles (including half-tracks) will be gasoline powered.

**Above:** *The 6046 engine is seen from the right side. At the upper left, to the immediate rear of the right valve cover, is the right fan drive; the five-blade cooling fan is not installed. To the immediate front of the fan drive and above the valve cover are the right thermostat housing and air-bleeder valve. The mechanism with the pipe elbow on the bottom rear of the engine, to the immediate rear of the oil strainer, is the right oil cooler. General Motors LLC*

**Above:** *The fan end, or rear, of a 6046 twin-Diesel engine, as shipped on 4 April 1945, is displayed. The bright-toned discs at the top of the engine are the fan drives. The two discs toward the bottoms of the engine blocks are vibration dampers. General Motors LLC*

**Above Right:** *A final view of the 6046 twin-Diesel engine as shipped on 4 April 1945, is from the right rear. The two inverted elbows at the upper center of the rear of the engine are exhaust-manifold elbows. General Motors LLC*

**Right:** *A view of the left side of the 6046 engine reveals that the features on that side were virtually identical to those on the right side. A starter was provided for this side of the engine as well as one for the right side. General Motors LLC*

6046-E
(AS SHIPPED)
4-4-45
8

6046-E
(AS SHIPPED)
4-4-45
3

**Above:** *Baldwin Locomotive assembled this Grant tank with a welded hull. Note the use of some rivets where the side plate armor met the 75mm gun sponson. The design of the forward, curved part of the sand shield is of interest; tabs on the top of the shield were bent 90 degrees and screwed to the vertical part of the shield. Counterweights are on the 75mm gun barrel and the 37mm gun mount. As 2-inch Mortars Mk. III (Smoke) were often in short supply when the Grant tanks were being assembled, many vehicles that lacked the mortars had a piece of armor welded over the aperture on the right front of the turret roof, as seen here. Baldwin Locomotive Works*

**Above:** *A Baldwin-built, riveted-hull Grant tank, census number T-24051, has been loaded on a civilian tractor-semitrailer for transport. This was a late Grant tank, part of Baldwin Locomotive's June 1942 production. The wheels were the C85163 stamped, solid-spoke type, with solid rubber tires. Baldwin Locomotive Works*

**Above:** *The same Grant, T-24051, is seen from the right side on the flatbed semitrailer. Pieces of tape are over the opening for the Protectoscope on the side door and the opening for the 2-inch smoke mortar on the upper-right front of the turret. Baldwin Locomotive Works*

**Left** *In a photo of the same Baldwin Locomotive Grant tank from the right front, WD-212 tracks are installed. Below the driver's port is a small bracket for attaching the hold-open brace for the port. The British designation for Grants with welded hulls and gasoline engines was Grant III, while the term for vehicles with welded hulls and Diesel engines was Grant IX. Baldwin Locomotive Works*

**Above:** *Two Baldwin Locomotive Grant tanks have been loaded, front-to-front, on a railroad flatcar. The one on the left is a riveted-hull, Diesel-engined (note the tall overhang on the rear of the hull) vehicle, census number T-23736, and the tank on the right is T-23735. A reference to "O. O. Melbourne" is stenciled on both vehicles, apparently a reference to tanks destined for Australian service. For the long voyage, sealant material has been applied over the pistol and vision ports, side doors, gun mounts, and removable panels on the right rear of the fighting compartments. Baldwin Locomotive Works*

"Present program of gasoline powered tanks will be continued and developed to the fullest...

"Production of the Diesel-powered tanks will be continued to utilize the production capacity for Diesel engines to the fullest, until sufficient capacity for gasoline-powered tanks is developed. (emphasis added)

"Diesel-powered tanks will not, as far as practicable, be sent overseas with our troops but will be held for service in the United States and for training use."

It would be decades before the US Army would again standardize on Diesel-powered tanks. However, Diesel-powered Lees and Grants would definitely be built for our Allies. Production of these tanks was going full-steam when the Office of Chief of Ordnance sent Army Service Forces the following information on 13 June 1942:"From a production standpoint, for the calendar year 1942, 53% of medium tank engines will be the Wright 975 and 31% will be the twin General Motors engines... "...since the General Motors Diesel engines are acceptable to, and in some instances preferred by the British and the Russians, who are obtaining approximately two-thirds of the medium tanks in

our program, no reason is seen to stop the manufacture of General Motors Diesel engines for medium tanks, even if our production objectives would allow us to do so."

As described in Chapter 4, as a result of testing of welded hull assembly, it was "...the final recommendation that welded fabrication be used in place of riveted or bolted fabrication for armored vehicles whenever possible."

While it was initially hoped to manufacture all the Diesel-powered tanks with welded hulls, the production facilities with which to weld the hulls were inadequate for the demand. This led to the realization that a number of the tanks would have to be built with riveted hulls. Accordingly, on 22 January 1942 OCM 17677 was approved, which assigned the designation M3A5 to riveted M3 with 6046 engines, and retained the M3A3 designation for welded hull tanks with the Diesel engines.

General Henry Aurand, Director of Defense Aid/Chief of the International Division, Army Service Forces had tentatively assigned the entire production of Baldwin Locomotive Works to the British. The British responded to this information by asking that the British-style turret be installed

DO NOT
HUMP
THIS CAR

**Above:** *A Diesel-engined, riveted-hull Grant is loaded on a flatcar at the Baldwin Locomotive plant. Sealant has been applied to areas and details on the vehicle where moisture might infiltrate. Baldwin Locomotive Works*

**Above:** *A welded-hull Grant, T-23914, is ready for transport on a flatcar at Baldwin Locomotive. This vehicle was part of the plant's May 1942 production. A very close inspection of the photo reveals that the overhang on the rear of the upper hull is the tall type, indicating that this is a twin-diesel-powered vehicle. Stenciling door-sealing material references the "LINK NO. T-23914," same as the census number, as well as the "MSU" number A-1960, same as the production order number. Baldwin Locomotive Works*

on all of the vehicles, a position that Brigadier General John Christmas supported. Christmas, however, looked deeper into the practicality of this on 17 July 1942.

Responding to his inquiry, both Major White and Major W. S. Toothacker advised Brig. General Christmas that this was a bad idea, citing the delays this would cause in deliveries, which at that point were projected to be completed in November. Further, it was stated, "When a crisis for a sudden shipment arises, we won't be able to use this type which will be different than others."

## The other Diesel

On 17 September 1941, as a result of testing of the M2A1 Medium Tank equipped with the T-1400 Guiberson Diesel engine, it was recommended that this engine be used in future medium tanks, rather than the Wright R-975. Specifically, the Armored Force Board report stated "The Guiberson T-1400 Engine be considered a more suitable engine for use in medium tanks than the Wright R-975 Engine. As many medium tanks as possible should be equipped with the Guiberson T-1400 Engines…"

In July 1940 the government and Guiberson Diesel Engine Company had entered into contract W-741-ORD-5917 calling for the production of 170 T-1400 and 323 T-1020 radial Diesel engines.

In June 1941 an additional contract, DA-W-271-ORD-34 was issued for 500 T-1400 and 50 sets of spares.

On 21 September 1941 the Defense Plant Corporation entered into an agreement with the Guiberson Diesel Engine Company to build and equip a facility in Garland, Texas, to permit the monthly production of 500 of the T-1400 Diesel engines.

The T-1400-2 that had been successfully installed in the M2A1 was removed from that vehicle and installed in cast-hull M3 number 2372 as described in Chapter 4.

The tests were favorable in many ways, with the tank having greater torque at low RPMs and almost double the fuel range. However, the engine was unreliable, necessitating frequent repairs. The Guiberson T-1020, developed for use in light tanks, suffered the same issue. A meeting was held in the Office of the Chief of Ordnance in Washington on 17 December 1942 to discuss this.

**Above:** *The same Grant shown in the preceding photo, census number T-23914, is viewed from the right front on the flatcar at Baldwin Locomotive. Shipping stencils are on the 75mm gun barrel and the sealant material on the gun sponson. Baldwin Locomotive Works*

**Above:** *A welded-hull Grant tank with no census number painted on the hull is ready for transport on a flatcar at Baldwin Locomotive. The bogie wheels on this vehicle are the open-spoke model, part number D38501. Baldwin Locomotive Works*

**Above:** *As the side doors of the Medium Tank M3 series was an Achilles heel of the protection of these vehicles, sometimes the doors of later-production tanks were shed of their hinges and were welded in place. Such was the case with this Baldwin Locomotive Medium Tank M3A3, registration number W-305249. With the side doors immobilized, the grab handles above them were removed. Welded to the glacis was a box for storing grousers: metal fixtures that were attached, at intervals, to the tracks to give them better traction on snow, mud, and soft ground. Notably, all the Grants were built with hinged, opening doors. Baldwin Locomotive Works*

While most of the meeting concerned the T-1020, the meeting discussed Guiberson radial Diesels in general. While by this time, production of the GM Diesel was well underway, a transcript of that December meeting does provide some valuable insights.

Lt. Col. V.W.B. Wales, with the Army Ground Forces, stated "We like the Diesel engines because the fuel is not inflammable, and eliminates the fire hazard. We like them because they give a larger radius of operation with the same amount of fuel, and we like them because they give better operation at lower engine speeds. They also eliminate engine interference with radio."

Lt. Colonel Joseph M. Colby, of the Tank-Automotive Center, offered, "…we are getting reports from Russia, that are very hot, condemning the gasoline engines and stating that they want Diesel engines."

General John Christmas's remarks not only echoed Colby's, but expanded on them. He stated, "..the Russians insist on Diesel engines, and the

British prefer them, and when we get a good one, no one will disagree with them. The second thing, about the Guiberson engine – we have invested a lot of money in that since 1935, and have the license on it. The 7 or 8 years we have been working with it have certainly shown an improvement on it.

"The Guiberson Company didn't show an interest in the engineering side of the their engine. I think the cancellation of their projects by the Services of Supply have given them religion."

On 23 May 1942 the contracts for the T-1400 engines were cancelled, as was a lease agreement between Guiberson and the Defense Plant Corporation covering the lease of the Garland, Texas plant. That plant was subsequently leased to Continental Motors for the production of R-975 gasoline engines on 27 August. Continental planned to produce 750 engines per month.

The dealings with the Guiberson Diesel Engine Company were looked into by the House Procurement and Buildings Subcommittee of the

**Above:** *Medium Tank M3A5, Ordnance number 1465, is viewed from above during acceptance tests at Aberdeen Proving Ground, Maryland, on December 31, 1942. The left door, stripped of the hinges, pistol port, and lock hasp, is welded to the upper hull; the U-shaped splash guard for the pistol port, however, remains in place. The two grille/doors on the engine deck, a feature of the M3A3 and M3A5, are partially visible under the layer of dirt that has accumulated on the vehicle. Baldwin Locomotive Works*

**Above:** *As seen in a right-front view of M3A5 Ordnance number 1465 at Aberdeen on December 31, 1942, the pistol port remained a feature on the welded-on right side door. Baldwin Locomotive Works*

**Above:** *Samuel Allen Guiberson, III (right) along with Fred Thaheld pose with one of the ill-fated T-1400 radial Diesel engines at an exhibition in 1941. National Air and Space Museum*

**Above:** *The armored housing for the radiator, jutting from the rear of the hull, and the exhaust deflector below the housing are displayed in this left-rear view of M3A5 Ordnance number 1465. A metal strap supports each side of the exhaust deflector. A shovel and a tow cable are stored on the engine deck.*
*Patton Museum*

**Above:** *As a result of testing of the Medium Tank M3 at Aberdeen Proving Ground, the Ordnance Department recommended that automatic transmissions be evaluated in these vehicles. Thus, the twin-Diesel-powered vehicle in this photograph, registration number W-304468, was equipped with two Hydramatic transmissions and was designated the Medium Tank M3A5E1. Patton Museum*

**Above:** *The experimental pilot Medium Tank M3A5E1 is viewed from the front in January 1942. The weapons had been removed from the vehicle. Patton Museum*

**Above:** *As seen in this right-side view of the Medium Tank M3A5E1, the rear of the upper hull had the characteristic high extension found on Lee tanks equipped with twin-diesel engines. Patton Museum*

Committee on Expenditures in the Executive Departments.

In the report of the investigation of overpayments, it was noted that, "…not withstanding such delinquency in delivery – apparently warranting termination of both contracts for default – the payment to Guiderson for termination of contract No. W-741-ORD-5917 exceeded by $144,862.16 the entire sum payable for the completed contract, while the payment for conract No. DA-W-271-ORD-34 – under which the government received no engines – equaled 90 percent of the contract price. "It appears, also, that the settlement agreement was made as set forth above, although vigorous and categorical objections thereto were voiced by a legal representative of the St. Louis Ordnance District – the contracting agency concerned – and by the disbursing officer to whom the voucher covering payment pursuant thereto was presented. Those objections, in pertinent part, were as follows:

(a) That the No. 1400 engine was unsatisfactory and much money, critical materials, and labor were wasted in experimenting with it. That the contract was entered into as a production, not an experimental contract. That the contractor grossly misrepresented that the No. 1400 was a perfected engine."

It is worthwhile to state here that the proposed Guiberson-powered M3 tanks were to be designated M3A1 (Diesel), rather than M3A3 or M3A5 as were designated the GM 6046-powered vehicles.

Although there have been multiple reports that 28 M3A1 (Diesel) built, thus far the author has been unable to locate any primary source documents confirming this. Rather, concerning the Guiberson T-1400 Ordnance Committee item 22178 of 25 November 1943, referring to a memorandum dated 10 July 1943, states, "…there has been only one vehicle built to date using this engine, and there are 111 such engines now in storage in the Ordnance warehouse at Omaha, Nebraska." Item 22178 goes on to recommend, "That the Ordnance Department be authorized to dispose of the Guiberson T-1400 Diesel Engines on hand in accordance with regulations pertaining to obsolete material."

**Above:** *Part of the test equipment for Medium Tank M3A5E1 registration number W-30446 was a bicycle-wheel rig mounted on the rear of the vehicle. Patton Museum*

# Baldwin
# Diesel-powered tanks

Records suggest that Baldwin completed their first Diesel-powered medium tank, M3A5 serial number 1087, for the US Army in January 1942.

The next 5 M3A5s, delivered to Great Britain, were completed in February, followed by a dozen more in March. In April 97 were completed, with the British getting 88 of them. Production of the M3A5 peaked in May at 106, with all but one going to Great Britain. These were followed by 97 the following month, with all assigned to the British, with that country getting their final group of M3A5s the next month, when they received 74 of the 115 produced. The M3A5 remained in production exclusively at Baldwin until December 1942, with all of the August-December production being delivered to the US Army.

Baldwin built their first welded-hull Diesel-powered M3A3 in March 1942, the same month that the last gasoline-powered M3 was completed. The M3A3, serial number 1084, the first Baldwin-built M3A3, was driven from Baldwin's Eddystone, PA plant to Aberdeen Proving Ground on 15 March 1942. The GM 6046 powerplant had been subjected to a run-in period of 5 to 6 hours prior to being shipped to

Baldwin, and once the tank was completed, it was driven 27 miles on a cross-country course by the manufacturer, prior to leaving for Aberdeen. During the road march RPMs were limited to 1,700-1,900 up until odometer reading of 75, and after that RPMs were raised to 2,000, up until odometer reading of 103. At that point the left engine developed a loud knock, began smoking and lost power. That engine was shut down and the tank proceeded using the right engine only.

Examination of the engine at Aberdeen revealed that the engine failure was caused by improper machining of a fuel injector, allowing the spray tip to break off into the cylinder, punching a hole in the piston.

A new piston, cylinder liner, injector, connecting rod and wrist pin were installed in the engine, and after a three-hour no-load break-in period for the engine, testing of the M3A3 began.

This problem brought attention to a manufacturing issue regarding the injectors, which was quickly corrected, and production of the M3A3 (and M3A5) continued unimpeded.

A report prepared by the Records and Reports Section of the Tank and Combat Vehicle Division dated 22 May 1942 stated that 23 M3A3 welded

**Above:** *A rear view of the M3A5E1 provides a clear depiction of the large plate on the rear of the upper hull. The bicycle-wheel instrumentation has been removed for this photo. The turret is traversed to about the 2:00 position, and the cupola is traversed to the rear. Patton Museum*

hull tanks and 441 M3A5 riveted Diesel were on order for the British, with 590 and 10 respectively on order for the US. Ultimately, while the total remained the same, the breakdown changed to 83 M3A3 and 381 M3A5 going to the British with both types on Production Orders A-1960 and T-4155. The Production Order for the 464 GM Diesel US tanks was T-693, the same document that called for the production of the M3 and M3A2 models for the US.

The ten M3A3 and single M3A5 produced by Baldwin in December 1942 were the final M3 mediums of any type produced.

So far no documents have surfaced that differentiate the M3, M3A3 and M3A5 by British army census (T-) number. Thus, the best that can be offered in this regard is that some of the tanks in the T-23652 to T-23741 range were Diesel-powered, and that those in the T-23742 to T-24188 range were certainly Diesel-powered.

# Chapter 6
# The Multi-Bank tanks M3A4

The Chrysler A-57 Multi-Bank is unquestionably one of the most interesting powerplants ever installed into a tank. Various histories of this amalgamated powerplant have stated that the individual engines making up the A-57 were bus engines or truck engines.

However, a Chrysler document dated 7/19/43 states that the engines comprising the Multi-Bank were the model C-34 Chrysler. This is consistent with the information recorded in the "Record of Army Ordnance Research and Development in World War II, Ordnance Development of the Chrysler A-57 (Multi-Bank) Tank Engine," which says that the engine is a "…multiple installation of

the of the Chrysler 'Royal' six….", as the 115 brake horsepower C-34 was the powerplant used in the Royal sedans. The Royal was Chrysler's entry-level 6-cylinder car of the era.

As recalled by Harry T. Woolson, Chrysler Engineering Division Executive Engineer, during an early July 1941 Engineering conference "…a message was given to the effect that high authority in Washington has advised Chrysler management that capacity for producing the current tank engines is limited, and Chrysler's suggestions are urgently needed for producing tank engines in a hurry.

**Above:** *The Medium Tank M3A4, like the M3A3 and M3A5, reflected an effort to supply a power plant to supplement the original radial engine of the Medium Tank M3. The M3A4 featured a Chrysler A-57 multibank engine, which combined five six-cylinder L-heads around a common crankcase, resulting in an engine with a star-like shape when viewed from the front or rear. The A-57 was a large engine, requiring the extension to the rear of the upper hull and the lower hull, resulting in the main identifying feature of this tank. Depicted here is the pilot M3A4, W-304741, during testing at Aberdeen Proving Ground on 13 February 1942. National Archives*

**Below:** *The photo, taken 12 November 1941, shows what is likely the first A-57 Multi-Bank engine nearing completion. The next day the multi-bank would run for the first time, and only a few days later it would be powering a tank. Here, three of the C-34 blocks have been installed, and the starter and Bendix is visible at upper right. Vintage Power Wagons collection*

"Also, the 9-cylinder (Wright R-975) engine which now is being used is somewhat underpowered for 30-ton tanks.

"While the logical step, under ordinary circumstances, would be to design a suitable engine, speed being the all-important consideration, something quicker is needed.

"A possible solution suggested is to use an automobile or truck engine in multiple which has had a background of years of successful operation and which is completely tooled, to produce a unit have the desired power for tank propulsion. Such a unit is not to be considered as an ultimate tank engine, but simply as a stop-gap until a more suitable design could be developed. The design of such a unit was immediately started."

Initially, four engines 90-degrees apart were considered. However, Ordnance wanted more power, so five were used instead. The top engine was vertical, bottom pair 7.5-degrees from horizontal and other pair at 27-degrees. The basic Chrysler C-34 was a 250.6 cubic-inch displacement 6-cylinder engine developing120 horsepower at 3800 rpm and 200 lb-ft of torque at 1600 rpm. It had a 6.6:1 compression ratio, 3 7/16-inch bore and 4 ½-inch stroke.

On 15 July 1941 Ordnance issued a Letter Contract to Chrysler for the production and experimental installation of three of the engines. The estimated cost of the work was $25,000, plus a fee of $1,250. On 20 October 1941 the formal contract was issued covering this work, which raised the cost from $25,000 to $120,000, but the

**Above:** *Workers prepare to place block number one on top of the crankcase of an A-57 engine in the Chrysler plant. While complex appearing when fully assembled, each of the five engines would individually look very familiar to mechanics of the era, as they were standard 6-cylinder L-head engines. Vintage Power Wagons collection.*

fee remained the same. This would again be raised on 10 December to $171,000, and again on 9 March 1942, to $755,000.

On 22 August 1941 Chrysler president K.T. Keller wrote to Big Bill Knudsen that "Our boys have found a way to put five engines together so none has a tendency to gather oil. You will find that we have developed a very ingenious arrangement of firing so that when the five engines are mothered to one shaft, we get smooth firing order."

Dynamometer testing of the first Multi-Bank started at 3:06 AM on 13 November 1941. On 15 November the engine was installed in a tank, and two days later the pilot M3A4 with Multi-Bank began undergoing tests at the Dodge Truck Proving Ground (as the Tank Arsenal test track was not complete).

On 17 December 1942 Harry Woolson and Chrysler Chief Engineer of Engine Design Melbourne "Mel" L. Carpentier applied for a US patent for the "multiple engine power plant," with Chrysler as the assignee. The patent was granted on 22 April 1947.

The Ordnance Committee, per Item 17578, on 23 December 1941 designated riveted hull tank powered by the Multi-Bank engine the M3A4. Final approval of the use of the A-57 in the M3A4 was given by the Ordnance Committee on 26 December 1941.

The Multi-Bank engine, given the Chrysler model number A-57, was substantially larger and heavier than the R-975. This required a number of changes in the tank so to accommodate it. For the pilot tank, the engine compartment was lengthened 18-inches, although in the production vehicle this was reduced to 11-inches. The combined effect of the relocation of the engine, as well as its greater weight, shifted the center of gravity of the M3. To provide better weight distribution, the suspension spacing was increased, moving the rear bogie as well as the idler to the rear. This change also lengthened the track run, the tank now requiring 83 shoes per side, rather than the 79 of the other M3-series tanks. As a result of the longer track, the 34-ton M3A4 actually had slightly lower ground pressure than did the M3.

Again, due to the larger size, the two vertical fuel tanks usually found in the M3 engine compartment were eliminated, with the sponson tanks being enlarged to offset the fuel loss. A 4 ¼-inch blister in the floor of the tank, and a similar one on the revised engine deck, provided clearance for the engine cooling fan.

Also related to the stuffing of the oversized engine into a small engine compartment, accessibility for service, especially to engine-mounted equipment, was challenging. The R-975 was 45-inches wide, while the A-57 was a full ten inches wider.

Because of the increased load on the suspension, Chrysler developed a new bogie, the D47527. On the D47527 the upper return roller was offset on a support arm rather than being centered on main bracket casting. Instead, centered at the top of the casting was a symmetrical skid. The M3A4 was the only version of the M3 to leave the factory with this suspension assembly, although it was also used on early M4A4 Shermans.

The individual engines are designated by number with the top engine being number one, then numbered consecutively in a clockwise direction when the engine is viewed from the distributor end. Each cylinder of each engine is numbered in order also starting at the distributor end. The firing order for each engine is 1-4-2-6-3-5, with an interval of 120-degrees between cylinders. The number one cylinder of each engine fires approximately 24 degrees later than the number one cylinder of the engine preceding it in numeric order. The starter, which was mounted between the number one and

**Above:** *A Chrysler A-57 Multi-Bank engine is seen from the left rear, showing the intricate networks of exhaust lines, water lines, and carburetor-air ducts. Five distributors are on the rear of the engine. In fact, the technical manual for the A57 engine referred to this end of the engine as the "distributor end." To the front of the engine is the radiator. FCA North America Archives*

number two engines could bring the engine to life at speeds as low as 30 RPM, easing starting when cold or with low batteries.

The engines are mounted on a central casting, and are synchronized through herringbone gears mounted on the end of each engine crankshaft, which turn a central gear.

On 2 December 1941 Chrysler submitted a quote for furnishing 100 multibank engines and adapting the M3 hull to accommodate the new powerplant. On 13 December Chrysler got a telephone call from the Army advising that a contract was being issued for 109 of the tanks, rather than the quoted 100. The Letter of Intent, Supplement Number 12, which covered that work arrived on 6 February 1942. It authorized expenses up to $1,635,000.00

for the project. This contract was formalized on 26 February 1942.

Production pilot of M3A4 was completed at the Chrysler Engineering Laboratory and sent to the Utica Tank Proving Ground for tests on 15 May 1942.

Series production of the Multi-Bank engine began on 7 April 1942. Through its production run, two major variants were produced, as well as a third, slightly lesser variant. We will refer to the first major variant the early engine. This engine was used in all the M3A4 tanks as well as M4A4s through serial number 2304. The later engine was not originally installed in the M3A4, but was used on M4A4s serial number 2305 and up.

**Above:** *In a 19 January 1943, photo, an A-57 Multi-Bank engine is viewed from the left side with the radiator removed. The ring gear can be seen just inside of the fan, and three of the engine's five Carter carburetors are visible stacked along the centerline of the engine. FCA North American Archives*

**Above:** *The front of the A-57 engine is shown without the fan, shroud, and the radiator to encumber the view. The A-57 technical manual called this the "radiator end" of the engine. The front engine mounts are jutting from each side of the lower part of the engine. FCA North American Archives*

The early A57 had a water pump on each of the five blocks. The water pump was similar to what was found on the engines in their civilian application. On the late engines this was replaced by a single large water pump, which greatly reduced maintenance. The 24-volt generator on the early engines was mounted on the number 2 engine and was driven by that engine's water pump belt.

The early engines had the fuel pump mounted on the distributor end of the crankcase and driven by an accessory shaft, whereas on the late engines the fuel pump was mounted on the distributor end of engine four.

Perhaps most noticeable, the carburetors of the early engines were staggered around the individual blocks, while on the late engines, the carburetors were all in one plane near the top of the engine.

The first production M3A4 was built on 3 June 1942. Being introduced late in the M3 series production, the series-built M3A4 did not have side doors. Ultimately, 33 M3A4s were built in June. That same month, production of the M4A4 Sherman with the Multi-Bank engine began. Chrysler would be 73 more M3A4s in July, with production of the type wrapping up with three final tanks in August. In fact, on 3 August 1942 Chrysler ceased production of any M3 variant.

Chrysler records indicate that all the production M3A4 tanks were shipped to Camp Chaffee, Arkansas where they were assigned to the 6th Armored Division. After initial familiarization and training, they then took part in the Louisiana Maneuvers, and then were shipped to the Desert Training Center. While numerous Multi-Bank powered M4A4 Shermans saw combat, it appears that the M3A4 was only used in a training role.

**Above:** *Another view of the radiator end of the engine, with the various engine accessories such as the carburetors, starter, and oil filters in place. At bottom center is the flywheel. Vintage Power Wagons collection*

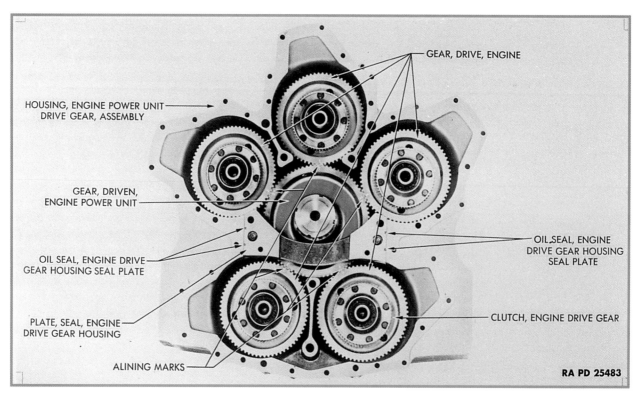

GEAR, DRIVE, ENGINE

HOUSING, ENGINE POWER UNIT
DRIVE GEAR, ASSEMBLY

GEAR, DRIVEN,
ENGINE POWER UNIT

OIL SEAL, ENGINE
DRIVE GEAR HOUSING
SEAL PLATE

OIL SEAL, ENGINE DRIVE
GEAR HOUSING SEAL PLATE

CLUTCH, ENGINE DRIVE GEAR

PLATE, SEAL, ENGINE
DRIVE GEAR HOUSING

ALINING MARKS

RA PD 25483

**Above:** An M3A4, registration number W-304741 is climbing a 50 percent grade (27 degrees) at Aberdeen Proving Ground on 25 February 1942. Along with the lengthening of the hull of the M3A4, the center and rear bogie assemblies were relocated to the rear, resulting in an additional spacing of six inches between the bogies. Note the mismatched bogie brackets: the front and center ones have two horizontal ribs, while the rear bracket lacks this feature. National Archives

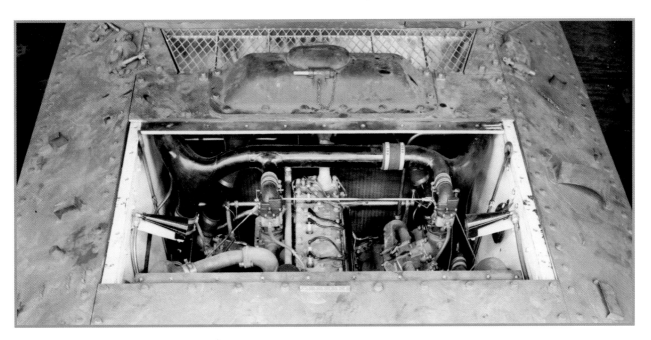

**Above:** The A57 engine installation in a Medium Tank M3A4 is viewed from the rear with one of the access plates removed at Aberdeen on 14 February 1942. To the front of the opening is a new feature: the cover for the radiator, with an oblong access door on it. The engine-air grille was redesigned, tapered so the front edge was wider than the rear edge. The vertical fuel tanks in the engine compartment had been deleted and the sponson fuel tanks enlarged; thus, there were only two fuel fillers for the main tanks, with an additional filler on the left side for the fuel tank for the auxiliary generator. National Archives

**Left:** On the radiator end of the A-57 engine, the engine drive-gear housing has been removed, exposing the five engine drive gears around the central, driven gear for the engine power unit. The driven gear operated the output shaft, visible on the center of that gear. Vintage Power Wagons collection

**Above:** *Two fishtail exhausts were on the rear plate of the upper hull of the pilot Medium Tank M3A4, as seen in a photo of an example under testing at Aberdeen Proving Ground on 13 February 1942. This plate replaced the stepped overhang on the rear of the upper hull found on preceding models of the M3. A taillight assembly is below each of the exhausts, under the overhang of the rear of the hull. The fairing over the radiator is visible on the engine deck. Patton Museum*

**Above:** *A right-side view of the pilot M3A4, registration number W-304741, at Aberdeen Proving Ground on 13 February 1942, illustrates several features of this model of Lee medium tank: the fairing for the top of the radiator on the engine deck; the extended rear of the upper hull along with rearranged rivets; and the slightly greater distances between the bogie assemblies. Patton Museum*

**Above:** *From the front, the pilot M3A4 looked identical to a typical Medium Tank M3. Patton Museum*

**Above:** *For scale, a soldier is standing to the front of the pilot Medium Tank M3A4, registration number W-304741 at Aberdeen Proving Ground on 13 February 1942. Because of the greater length of the upper hull, there were more rivets on the sides of the sponsons. Patton Museum*

# Chapter 7
# Production & modification

While the US and Great Britain placed their tank orders almost concurrently, it was recognized that Britain was at war, while the US was preparing for war. Thus the conscious decision was made to give manufacturing priority to the British tanks, as far as practical. That the first M3s produced were US Lees as largely attributable to its turret design having been finalized far earlier than had been the Grants.

As noted earlier in this book, certain key components were in short supply, notably guns, transmissions and engines.

The shortage of guns is discussed at some length in Chapter 4, and the engines in various other chapters. The transmission was another key assembly which was in terribly short supply.

Production of the transmission, designed by Spicer, was originally contracted to Mack by the government. The government then furnished the transmissions, like the engines, to the tank manufacturers.

The M3 transmission and final drive assembly included three large castings, which were then bolted together to form the nose of the vehicle. This assembly is often referred to by its drawing number, E1233. The externally visible portions of the final drive assembly includes casting E1230, housing, steering brake drum, right; E1232 carrier, differential; and E1231 housing, steering brake drum, left. The right (from inside the tank) casting, E1230, was notched to provide clearance for the 75mm sponson-mounted gun.

**Above:** In a photo dated 30 January 1941, patterns of parts for the Medium Tank M3 are under inspection at the Chrysler pattern shop. The man at the upper left has his hand on a pattern for a final-drive, while the one to the upper right is checking over a pattern for a transmission housing. To the bottom left is the pattern for a 37mm gun shield, and a turret pattern is to the lower right, with a bogie-bracket pattern next to it. National Archives

**Above:** *In the Chrysler pattern shop on 30 January 1941, the technician in the foreground is inspecting a pattern for a bogie bracket. Marked on the upper surface of the bracket is the part number of this model of bogie: D37893. On the bench in the right background is the pattern for an idler bracket. Military History Institute*

Mack Manufacturing, builders of the famed Mack trucks, was contracted to produce 2,408 transmissions to be used in Alco and Baldwin M3 production. Of these, 900 were for the British Purchasing Commission and 1,508 for the US military. In September 1941 this was augmented by a contract issued to Iowa Transmission Company, a subsidiary of agricultural equipment giant John Deere, while Chrysler was contracted to build their own transmissions. Mack, unable to completely tool up for production by the scheduled date, owing to a shortage of vertical boring mills, produced the first two transmissions largely by hand.

The first Mack transmission was shipped to Alco, and following the successful demonstration of their first pilot tank, it was removed and hastily shipped to Baldwin, where it was installed in that firm's pilot, allowing the tank to be presented to the government.

In February 1941 a Joint Production Committee was established to facilitate the leveling of distribution of such common parts so that the production rate was optimized. The Dewar files note that, "free interchange of components could be made between British contractors and U.S. contractors, exemplified in the supply of armour plate and 37 mm guns by us to the U.S. and the supply of Transmissions and 75 mm guns from the U.S. to our contractors. This interchangeability ultimately gave way to a 'pooling' of all free issues, and allocation fo such components that were in short supply by the U.S. Ordnance to the contractors so as to obtain maximum possible overall production."

The United States launched into such an ambitious expansion of tank manufacturing that on 5 March 1942, Colonel John Christmas wrote to General Wesson stating "That tank production in this country is now so well established and is planned for such large facilities and quantities of tanks that shortly the over-all requirements of the United Nations can be furnished by the United States."

**Above:** *The Chrysler Defense Arsenal, also called the Detroit Tank Arsenal, in Warren Township, Michigan, was one of the four manufacturers of the Medium Tank M3. In this photo, two M3s, Ordnance numbers 2 and 3, are under assembly. These two tanks were built under contract W-ORD-461 and were assigned registration numbers W-301000 and W-301001. In the rear of the fighting compartment of the tank to the left are visible the oil cooler and its guard and 37mm ammunition racks. To the rear of that vehicle, a workman is operating a grinder on a fender assembly, complete with the headlight brush guard installed.*

# The tank factories

## American Locomotive Company

The British Purchasing Commission had approached American Locomotive in July 1940 to produce 300 examples of the Cruiser Tank Mk VI Crusader, a design of the Nuffield Mechanisations and Aero LTD. As mentioned in the previous chapter, the US government objected to American firms producing tanks not used by the US military. No doubt referencing this, the Alco-produced wartime publication "American Locomotive Went to War" states that "Company officials and technicians went to the Rock Island arsenal. They made studies. And they agreed to build 300 M-3 medium tanks."

Fortune magazine reported that, "on a hot day in July, 1940 William S. Knudsen, who was born in Denmark, and (Alco) President (Duncan W.) Fraser, who was born in Nova Scotia, sat down in Mr. Knudsen's office in the Federal Reserve Building in Washington and agreed on terms. The conversation between these two seasoned production men, one speaking with a Danish accent and the other with a Scottish burr, is said to have set a record for saving words – but it has resulted to date in more than $60 million in tank orders…"

This discussion is reflected by this passage in the Alco publication, "Told to go ahead the Company proceeded without formal orders. Actually, Alco undertook the job in July 1940, and when formal orders came through in November of that year, the number had been raised from 300 to 685."

**Above:** *In the early stages of M3 production, easily the component in shortest supply was the transmission and final drive assembly. Although developed by Spicer to Ordnance specifications, the initial contractor to produce these was Mack. Mack Historical Museum*

**Above:** *The transmission protruded from the rear of the assembly and extended into the fighting compartment of the tank, where it was coupled to a driveshaft extending to the rear of the tank, where the engine and clutch are located. Mack Historical Museum*

That formal order was the 20 November 1940 War Department contract. This contract estimated the cost of the project at $1,155,000 for equipping the plant and $34,250,000 for actually producing the tanks. The production contract was cost plus a fee of 7% agreement, with the 'cost' not the actual cost, but rather what the cost should be; an effort by the government to force Alco to control costs, rather than to increase costs in order to maximize their commission. Similarly, the plant portion of the contract was further broken down such that Alco would be paid a fixed fee of $1, plus cost, for equipping the plant. Equipping the plant required over 100 new machine tools, which could only be used for defense work, as well as rearranging the plant to make room for tank production.

**Above:** *Shown here, from left to right, are the center section casting, which will house the differential, next to it is the steering brake housing (left hand, in this instance) and at fire right is the left final drive housing. Mack Historical Museum*

Thus, it would be 20 November before the first tank contract was issued to American Locomotive (Alco), and that would be for production of M3 Lee tanks for the US government. American Locomotive completed the company's first M3 in April 1941, and although the British may have been the first to approach Alco, all the M3s built by the firm were built for the US government. Later, however, the firm would build Sherman tanks destined for the British.

In order to build the tanks, rather than an assembly line, Alco set up a seven-station assembly process in the vast erecting hall in Schenectady, alongside the area where steam locomotives were essentially handcrafted. This somewhat unusual arrangement allowed workmen to shift between tank and locomotive production as the supply of materials dictated on a daily basis. The lower hull was fabricated in Alco's boiler shop, then transported to station one in the erecting hall. At that station the fuel tanks were installed, along with the casting for the 75mm gun mount, and the driver's door installed. At station two, the transmission was installed, followed by station three and the installation of the radial engine, along with the drive shaft. At station seven the track, turret, 75mm gun, fenders, lights and siren were installed. The turret castings used by Alco were poured by General Steel Castings Company.

In addition to rearranging the plant in order to produce the tanks, Alco also had to acquire over 100 new machine tools to enter tank production. Fortune magazine reported that, "On April 19th almost five months to the day after the contract was signed – American delivered to Robert P. Patterson, Undersecretary of War, the first medium tank (thirty tons) to be completed by an industrial company in this country."

As mentioned in Chapter Four, in addition to the riveted hull M3, Alco also produced the cast hull M3A1, utilizing upper hull castings manufactured by General Steel Casting Company. Compared to the laborious cutting, drilling and riveting of the hull plates of the M3, the casting of the M3A1 hull was vastly labor-saving. A 17 March 1943 report by General Steel Castings states, "The tank top hull cast in one piece of armor steel replaces approximately 130 separate plates, shapes, castings, etc., and, in the older designs, many rivets, bolts and nuts required in the assembly of the riveted counterpart. While the welded counterpart does not of course, include the rivets and bolts, there still remains the balance of many plates, shapes and castings that must be fabricated and assembled. A substantial saving in man hours is brought about by our innovation through elimination of all assembly works on the floors of the tank builder with respect to the hulls themselves, which are furnished as a completely finished product." That said, production of a single cast hull took about two weeks – homogenizing hull, heated to 1,850 to 2,000 degrees, soaked at that temperature for 6 to 10 hours and allowed to

**Above:** *A Mack employee inspects a left-hand brake housing, identical to the unit in the foreground. Behind the employee are parallel lines of left and right brake housings with the final drive housings mated to them. The telltale notches of the M3's right brake housings are evident on the row at right.*
*Mack Historical Museum*

air cool slowly. This was followed by annealing, heating the hull to 1,100 to 1,250 degrees for 4-6 hours, then air cooling. Hardening – heating to 1,500-1,700 degrees for 2-6 hours then quenching in water bath; tempering, requiring heating to 1,000-1,250 degrees for 4-10 hours, followed by air cooling.

Time Magazine reported that it took 1,100 man-hours to assemble the riveted hull, but only 100 man-hours to complete the cast hull.

**Above:** *The complete transmission, differential, brake and final drive assembly weighed several tons –
Mack advertising of the period boasted that it weighed "more than 300 times the weight of a passenger
car transmission." Not surprisingly, even the bare castings required material handling equipment to
safely move. Mack Historical Museum*

# Baldwin
# Locomotive Works

Among the builders of the M3, Baldwin Locomotive
Works of Eddystone, Pennsylvania was unique in
it was the only firm contracted to build both the Lee
and the Grant. Evidence suggests that Baldwin
was the first firm actually contracted to produce the
M3 medium tank. On 24 October 1940 the
company was awarded contract W-ORD-483, in
the estimated amount of $35,277,500.

On 4 November 1940 the firm also signed contract
A-1960 with the British Purchasing Commission
calling for the production of 685 M3 Grant medium
tanks.

In both cases, the contracts were for cost plus a
fixed fee, and specified that "the sum of $2,300.00
should be paid on delivery of each tank as partial
payment representing payment of rental charge
payable by the contractor to Defense Plant
Corporation on the cost of machinery, equipment
and facilities to be leased by the contractor from
Defense Plant Corporation plus the sum of $5.00
each for carrying charges, and that upon payment
of each such partial payment title to an undivided
1/1370ths of said machinery, equipment and
facilities should vest in the Government."

The first M3 Lee produced by Baldwin rolled out of
the works on 24 April 1941. Installed on the tank
was the same transmission that had been
previously installed on the first Alco tank when it
was rolled out five days prior.

*Right: Workers at the American Locomotive plant in Schenectady, New York, are assembling the lower
hull of a Medium Tank M3 on 6 November 1941. The sides were 1 1/2 inches thick, while the floor
varied in thickness from 1 inch at the front to 1/2 inch to the rear. Scott Taylor collection*

**Above:** *The differential has been joined to the brake housings and await installation of the final drives and transmission. The steering brake bands (shoes) are visible through the inspection ports, whose cover plates have not yet been installed. The prominent nut at the top of each brake band is the adjustment nut. Mack Historical Museum*

**Above:** *Upper-hull construction is underway on an M3 at American Locomotive on 6 November 1941. The man to the left is securing a hex bolt; nuts, bolts, and washers are installed in approximately every other rivet hole to hold the plates in place temporarily until rivets are driven in. The worker to the right is machining the edge of a vertical plate with a grinder. Scott Taylor collection*

**Above:** *An American Locomotive welder is fabricating a bogie wheel in a jig for a Medium Tank M3 using a General Electric Type W-25 welding electrode. Each bogie wheel required over 30 feet of 1/4-inch fillet weld. In addition to arc welders, GE AC welders also were used in assembling these wheels.*
*Scott Taylor collection*

The Baldwin roll out was attended by Under Secretary of War Robert P. Patterson, who addressed a crowd of 500 saying, "This is more than just a tank. It is a tank the design of which embodies the fruit of lessons learned in the Battle of France. One can almost say that this tank has been through fire. The Battle of France was fought and lost less than a year ago. The drawings for this tank were completed less than six months ago. Yet here it is ready to be manned by a crew from the new Army, which itself was not in existence a year ago."

Despite the propaganda-pleasing words of Patterson, things at Baldwin went far from smoothly. As mentioned, the Baldwin contract was on a cost-plus basis, specifying that the company would receive a $2,397,500 fixed fee which "shall constitute complete compensation for the Contractor's services, under this Title, including profit." The remaining almost 33 million dollars in

the contract were the estimated cost of the tanks. This contracting procedure would resurface in a 9 April 1942 when C.B. Smith, who was in charge of procurement for the tank division of the War Production Board, received a letter from engineer C. F. Schneff, reporting on the conditions at Baldwin. Schneff wrote:

"This outfit today again shipped 4 tanks and they are staggering along out of one component today and another tomorrow just their lack of skill in planning, their requirements and then following up their plans. At this long last they seem awakened to their deficiency and are taking steps in the right direction to remedy the trouble. I am putting in a word here and there when I can secure a listener and tomorrow I go out to hustle some supplies for them in Philadelphia, Newark, N.J., and Cincinnati, Ohio. I expect to be in Philadelphia, Friday, Newark, Saturday and Ohio on Monday."

**Left:** *Sprockets for M3 medium tanks are being fabricated by four cutting torches mounted on a master-pattern wheel, thus automating the process. The sprockets were first cut from steel stock and then further refined. The site was the American Locomotive plant in Schenectady, on 6 November 1941.*
*Scott Taylor collection*

**Above:** *A 37mm Gun M5 or M7 in a Mount M24 is being lowered by means of a chain hoist onto the turret of a Medium Tank M3 at the American Locomotive plant in Schenectady on 6 November 1941. The Browning .30-caliber M1919A4 coaxial machine gun is already installed in the gun mount; its barrel is visible on the near side of the 37mm gun barrel. In the absence of lifting eyes on the gun shield, special lifting fixtures were installed in screw holes on the shield for attaching the hoist. One of these is visible below the big hook on the hoist chain to the right. Scott Taylor collection*

"Baldwin is an old, supremely self-satisfied, secretive outfit, that regard myself and the Government Ordnance men here as outsiders to be tolerated with passive resistance, told nothing and spoken too (sic) only when necessary. They are on a cost plus basis, so they more they spend the merrier – hence their impatience with a chap like myself, who might be tactless enough to point our (sic) inefficiencies in their operations, however politely, and besides might report things to Washington. They are a devious crowd (as mentioned in a previous report) and might, if I do get in their hard (sic) which I am leaning backwards not to do) concoct some complaint concerning me

in order to discredit me in Washington. If I followed my personal inclination, I would turn my back on this plant and keep going indefinitely. But, I'm staying right here with them to see if we can keep them producing in spite of themselves. I return here again next Tuesday or Wednesday from the West and will probably be here next week until Friday.

"As an example of how they work, I'll cite an instance of today. They build the riveted hull British tank, with a cast housing containing the rotor of the 75 M.M. gun. The machining of this housing is done on planers and their capacity is very limited.

**Above:** *Like most vehicle manufacturers, the American Locomotive Company had its own test ground, where it evaluated the serviceability and performance of its tanks before delivering them to the government. This Medium Tank M3 has become well mired during a test run through a mudhole at the ALCO test ground on 6 November 1941. No registration number is on the tank, but the code "L-3-10" is painted on the sponson, and "46" is marked on the rear of the fighting compartment. Scott Taylor collection*

**Above:** *Registration number W-305757 was the first M3 built by American Locomotive (ALCO), and indeed the first M3 completed by any commercial firm. Like many other early production tanks, it wound up on a firing range. Here it is on the range at Aberdeen when it was just two months old, being subjected to .30-caliber fire. Joe Demarco collection*

**Above:** *A pair of M3A1s prepare to leave the American Locomotive plant by rail. In the foreground is W-306058, with its serial number, 1988, scrawled on the side. Interestingly, this tank can also be seen in Chapter 9. This tank, the 31st M3A1, was built in March 1942. Steve Zaloga collection*

**Right:** *Workmen in Alco's Schenectady works put the finishing touches on an M3A1. Adjacent to this tank an M3 is just beginning its assembly, while an overhead crane swings another M3, this one nearly complete, into place. Robert Yarnell Richie collection, Southern Methodist University*

**Above:** *Visible beneath the boiler of this steam locomotive being assembled by Alco are a pair of partially complete M3 tanks, while at left can be seen the turret and 37mm gun of a M3, as well as the tracks. Alco M3s were not built on a moving assembly line, but rather on a series of seven assembly stations. Coincidentally, Germany's Tiger tanks were built in much the same way. When Alco began producing M4 (and later tanks), assembly line methods were used. Robert Yarnell Richie collection, Southern Methodist University*

**Above:** *This July 1942 scene shows a later production M3A1 hull at the Granite City, Illinois facility of General Steel Castings Corporation. While the experimental casting used on the Rock Island built prototype was poured at the firm's Eddystone, Pennsylvania facility, the production castings were created in Illinois. Joe Demarco collection*

**Above:** *This casting does not include the side doors found on the early production M3A1s. Alco reported receiving their first hull casting without side doors at the end of March 1942. The turret splash rail, which appears to have been added to the casting in May/June, is clearly visible. Joe Demarco collection*

**Above:** *From this unusual angle the inside of the casting can be seen, including the firewall separating the fighting compartment from the engine bay. Joe Demarco collection*

**Above:** *This hull appears to have been cast such that the roof hatch hinges upward. Later production M3A1s had upper hatches that swung down. Joe Demarco collection*

**Above:** *The bullet splash guard clearly shown here wrapped around the front and side of the turret race. When an incoming round, especially small arms, impacts the armor, the bullet sprays small, high velocity particles that can enter a tank through very small openings, with lethal consequences. The splash guard around the turret ring was to prevent the "splash" from entering the tank between the turret and hull, and to protect the turret rotation. Joe Demarco collection*

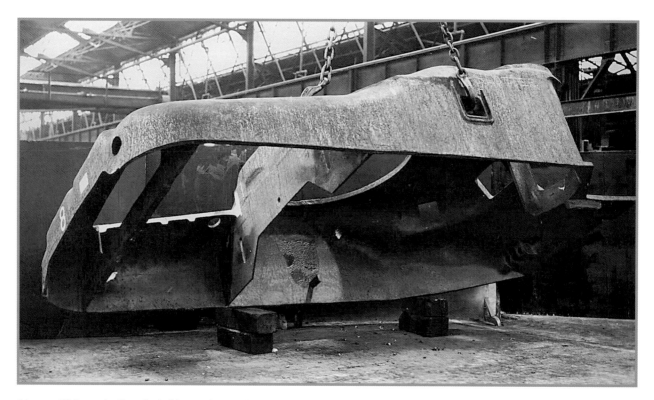

**Above:** *While production of a hull by casting requires much less labor than assembly by riveting or welding, the casting and quenching process is time consuming. The heat treatment process for the M3A1 hull took 22 hours, and involved several steps. Joe Demarco collection*

**Above:** *The very first Baldwin-built M3 poses outside one of the buildings of the company's famed Eddystone (Pennsylvania) works on 5 June 1941. The Army registration number, W-305072 has been painted in white in an elegant Railroad Roman font, typical of the company's normal products. This soon enough will give way to military Blue Drab stenciling. Notably, the 75mm gun, which was present at its April 1941 rollout, has been removed, no doubt because these weapons were in short supply. Southern Methodist University*

**Above:** *Chassis with riveted hulls are under assembly at Baldwin Locomotive Works. They are on trolleys mounted on tracks, for moving them from station to station on the assembly line. The vehicles in the foreground are in an early stage of construction, still lacking the turrets, the final-drive assemblies, the armaments, and most of the interior appointments. The bogie assemblies have been installed, and at least 13 more bogie assemblies are on the factory floor in the left foreground, awaiting installation.*
*Baldwin Locomotive Works*

**Above:** *Riveted-hull Medium Tank M3 chassis are moving along the assembly lines at Baldwin Locomotive. This photograph is a continuation to the left of the scene in the preceding photo, taken on the same occasion. Chalked here and there on the chassis are inspection marks, such as "OK" and arrows pointing to areas needing more attention, mathematical notations, and the occasional graffiti, such as "STINKEY" scrawled on the hull to the far left. Baldwin Locomotive Works*

I have been urging them to recruit some milling machines in their rod shops to relieve these planers and boost the output. I made another appeal today and then under promise of secrecy they said that they had acquired considerable additional outside capacity on planers that would solve their problem! But nobody must be told! And I wouldn't have been told except that I nailed them down and told them just how the mills could do the job despite their opinions otherwise. How is that for cooperation? I have developed a friendship with one of their executives who privately advised me that the word was passed to their General Foremen on the tank line to "tell me nothing."

"Of course, I play dumb about their attitude and keep offering to help them in any way within our ability and possibly we shall ultimately get under their skins. Their management to my mind is incapable and while the plant is enormous (7,000) and impressive, they are doing a poor job."

Despite this, Baldwin was able to complete the 685 Lees and 685 Grants ordered by the US and British governments respectively. The first of the Baldwin-built Grants was accepted in October 1941. Both the Grants and the Lees had turrets cast by General Steel Castings Corporation. The Grant turret bore WF2 markings indicating their British designation. The "Chronology of Ordnance Vehicles" published by Baldwin Locomotive Works Engineering Department in October 1945 lists the following milestones in the firm's production of the M3 series medium tanks for the British:

**Above:** Chassis for twin-Diesel-powered vehicles without the turrets or engine decks installed are viewed from behind in the Baldwin Locomotive factory. Note the white paint on the forward bulkhead of the engine compartment in the vehicle in the left foreground. A censor with an airbrush touched up this photo by spraying black tint over the turret openings, side doors, and engine compartments, to hide any details in the interiors of the hulls. Baldwin Locomotive Works

11-4-40   Order received for 685 for M3 Medium Tanks, gas engines, riveted hull.

4-29-41   First M3 completed and shipped to US Army.

10-6-41   Production of M3A2 began – gas engine, welded hull.

11-20-41  Ordnance Department directs that all M3s are to be Diesel driven, starting with the 87th US tank and the 221st British.

3-17-42   First British M3A5 completed, Diesel engine, riveted hull.

9-1-42    British order of 685 completed.

Breakdown of Models of M3 for the British

| | |
|---|---|
| M3 gas riveted | 211 |
| M3A2 gas welded | 10 |
| M3A5 Diesel riveted | 381 |
| M3A3 Diesel welded | 83 |
| Total | 685 |

However, interestingly the US Government took one of the British Grants (and notably, NOT the one that was until recently in possession of the US Ordnance Museum, that tank is actually a Lee which has had a Grant turret mounted on it). To replace the tank "appropriated" by the US, a M3A5 Lee from order T-693 was supplied to the British, with census number T-29141.

**Above:** *In June 1942, Grant cruiser tanks were under assembly at Baldwin Locomotive. Interestingly, the tanks on the line to the right have welded hulls, while those to the left have riveted hulls. Significantly, it can be seen that both bow machine gun ports on all of these tanks have been welded closed. The 75mm guns have been installed in the riveted-hull Grants. Both lines of tanks have the WD-212 tracks, while rolled up in the foreground are T41 track assemblies. Stenciled on the hulls are what are evidently manufacturer's numbers: the letter B over a number in the 560 to 580 range. Baldwin Locomotive Works*

12295-6
6-42

**Above:** *In early December 1941, welders at Baldwin Locomotive, in Eddystone, Pennsylvania, are fabricating bogie wheels. The positioning stands were "home made" at the plant from pipes and scrap steel. Scott Taylor collection*

**Above:** *Workmen pose for their photo next to a fully armed riveted-hull Medium Tank M3 (or possibly M3A5) at the Baldwin Locomotive plant. On the flatcar in the right background are two ships' propellers. Baldwin Locomotive Works*

**Above:** *The majority of the M3 medium tanks were assembled at the Chrysler Defense Arsenal, also referred to as the Detroit Tank Arsenal, in Warren Township, Michigan. This plant was still under construction when M3 production began there in mid-1941. In this interior view of the factory during that period, a steam locomotive is being used to generate steam for building services at the plant until the factory's steam plant was completed. To the left is a concrete truck, with a pile of coal for the locomotive's boilers to its side. FCA North America archives*

Recognizing in July 1942 that all the M3A3 and M3A5 tanks that Baldwin was yet to produce had been tentatively assigned to the British, it was requested that in view of this, all the tanks be equipped with British-type turrets, regardless of whether they were on US or British contracts. Responding to this inquiry, on 4 August 1942 General Christmas wrote to Major General D.H. Pratt, stating that, "...very little can be accomplished in this respect before late October at the earliest because the change to the British type of turret involves also a considerable number of other changes, as you know. Further, such changes will slow production and mitigate against reaching our production objectives. Since the Baldwin Locomotive Works will complete their orders for Medium Tanks, M3A3 and M3A5 in November, we consider it impracticable to make this change.

"There is also the additional fact to consider that if we change to the British type of turret in these tanks in the case of emergency these tanks could not then be available for assignment to other troops should the Munitions Assignment Board find this desirable."

General Christmas advocated another responsibility for Baldwin on 4 August 1942, writing "...the jigs, fixtures and other tooling applying to the Medium Tanks, M3 at Chrysler and such other plants have been making Medium Tanks, M3 as necessary are saved in order that we may make additional Medium Tank, M3 parts as required after the manufacture of Medium Tanks, M3 have been discontinued." Christmas continued, "The matter of becoming a source of M3 parts in the future has been taken up with Chrysler...and it was decided that Chrysler was not the best place for this on

**Above:** *Five of the key men in the history of the Chrysler Detroit Tank Arsenal gather in the 85% complete building on Sunday 16 March, 1941. From left to right are Edward J. Hunt, Operating Manager of the Arsenal; Herman L. Weckler, Vice-President and General Manager of Chrysler Corporation; Lt. Colonel H.W. Rehm, Commanding Officer of the Arsenal; W. S. Knudsen, Chairman of the Office of Production Management; and B. E. Hutchinson, Chairman of the Chrysler Corporation. Military History Institute*

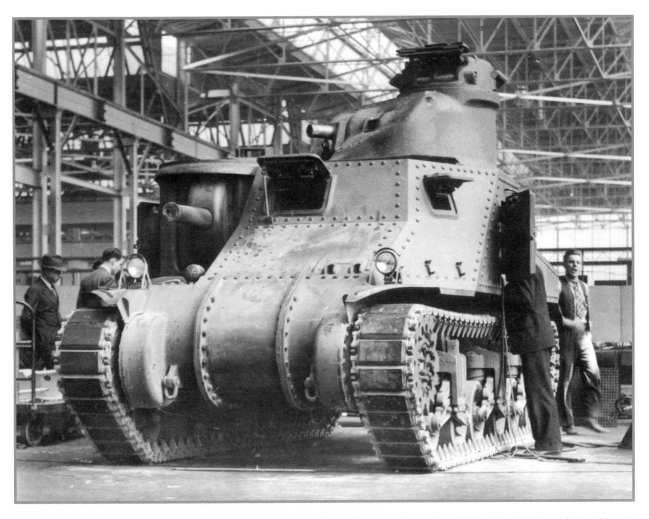

**Above:** *Based on a comparison of the negative number of this photo with those of other Chrysler Defense Arsenal photographs, this vehicle appears to be Chrysler's first production pilot Medium Tank M3, completed by Chrysler in April 1941. Although the Mount M24 for the 37mm gun has been installed on the turret, the gun itself has not yet been mounted. TACOM LCMC History Office*

account of the cost involved and the fact that Chrysler Tank Arsenal does not lend itself to job work." Christmas concluded, "It is very important that we set up at once a definite, sensible plan for the procurement of M3 parts for this tank after it has gone out of manufacture. In view of the fact that Baldwin has a job shop and will remain in the M3 manufacture longer than any other firm, it is likely that Baldwin would be a good continuing source of M3 parts."

## Pressed Steel Car Company

John MacEnulty, President of Pressed Steel Car Company, negotiated with the British Purchasing Commission, seeking a tank contract. This $28,455,000.00 contract was signed on October 25, 1940, and called for the production of 501 General Grant tanks. This production was to take place at the Pressed Steel's then-derelict Hegewisch Plant in the suburbs of Chicago.

Pressed Steel had closed and abandoned the Hegewisch plant in 1932, and in the following years it had suffered extreme decay, including the loss of the roof as well as the hardwood block flooring.

Pressed Steel was headquartered in Pittsburgh, and it was there that the company initially set up the offices of the "Pressed Steel Car Company, Inc., Armored Tank Division."

Frank Powelson, an engineer with Pressed Steel was tasked with the rehabilitation of the Hegewisch plant, which began on 20 February 1941 and was completed on 9 April 1941.

To oversee the engineering of the tanks, Pressed Steel hired Carl Hansen, originally from Copehagen, and Alex Blain, from Glasgow, Scotland. In Early October the tank engineers moved to Hegewisch.

Hansen, Blain and their 30-member engineering staff received 1,500 vellum copies of prints for the M3 on Christmas Day, 1940. The engineers

**Above:** *The first Chrysler production pilot M3 is parked in a doorway of the Detroit Tank Arsenal in April 1941 at the time of its official rollout. All weapons are installed, including the two machine guns in the bow, the muzzles of which are visible. TACOM LCMC History Office*

**Above:** *Driving at or near maximum speed, a Medium Tank M3, registration number W-305870 has just been launched off of a ramp during a test of its suspension's ability to withstand the shocks of extreme driving conditions. Note the sag in the tracks and the articulation of the rear bogie wheels as they cross over the timber on the edge of the ramp. National Archives*

**Above:** *The same M3 shown in the preceding photos, W-305870, is fully airborne after driving off the ramp to the left. The bogie-wheel arms are at or near the maximum lower limits of their travel. FCA North America archives*

**Above:** *An apparently freshly completed Medium Tank M3 is exiting the Chrysler Defense Arsenal. The left track is in need of tightening, with much slack visible below the sprocket. Note the evidence of uncompleted construction on the grounds around the plant. FCA North America archives*

**Above:** *A newly minted M3 is being driven along an access road outside of the Chrysler Defense Arsenal. The registration number of this vehicle will be stenciled on the sponsons at a later point. FCA North America archives*

**Above:** *The first pilot Chrysler Medium Tank M3 is observed from the front during a manufacturer's test drive shortly after its completion on 12 April 1941. A temporary cover is installed in the muzzle of the 75mm gun, to keep out foreign objects. FCA North America archives*

**Above:** *The first pilot Chrysler M3 is viewed from another perspective during manufacturer's testing in April 1941. Here, the driver has opened his vision port and is looking out of the port. Chrysler dealers and salesmen funded the construction of this tank and then presented it to the U.S. Army in a ceremony on 24 April 1941. Chrysler built this tank and another one, the second Chrysler M3 pilot, before it had finished installing all of its tooling for mass-producing the M3 medium tanks. TACOM LCMC History Office*

immediately set out to produce assembly drawings and determine what machinery was needed to equip the plant.

Representing the British Purchasing Commission at the Hegewisch facility as the engineering team was hard at work was Ernest Murphy. So impressed by Murphy's demeanor and knowledge was the management of Pressed Steel that in February 1941 the firm hired him, and on 1 April he was named Vice-President and placed in charge of the plant.

On 13 July 1941 Pressed Steel completed their first M3 Grant. The Lend-Lease Act of 11 March 1941 (H. R. 1776) caused the US Government to serve as a middleman between the various tank contractors and the British Government. As a result, the final 180 of the 501 tanks ordered by the British Purchasing Commission were actually completed under US government supervision. In a related matter, In January 1942 deliveries of tanks to the Britain were capped at 180 tanks per month.

The WF2 turrets used by Pressed Steel were cast by Union Steel Casting Company.

# Pullman Standard Car Company

The British Purchasing Commission contracted with Pullman Standard on 18 September 1940, agreeing to purchase 500 M3 medium tanks with the British-type (Grant) turret. This contract called for a target production rate of 45 tanks per month.

Pullman completed its first of the tanks for the British Purchasing Commission in July 1941, but production would not reach the target of 45 monthly until January 1942. While this was a month following Baldwin and American Locomotive, nevertheless Pullman was able to complete the last of the 500 British tanks in July 1942. All of Pullman-Standard's M3 production were Grants for the British, and featured WF2 turrets cast by General Steel Castings Corporation.

**Above:** *Chrysler executives have gathered around an M3 medium tank, likely the first pilot vehicle, outside of the plant. This factory employed a workforce of approximately 10,000 men and women in World War II. TACOM LCMC History Office*

Incidentally, on the 14th of July 1941, at the urging of General Charles Wesson, the US army began negotiating with the firm to build medium tanks, which would be for the M4A2 Sherman.

It should be noted that when Pullman began building Sherman tanks in April 1942, those tanks were built in a larger building, also on the Pullman grounds. The building which housed M3 production was too small to permit subassembly feeder lines, which the larger 313,000 square-foot building could accommodate.

The first Pullman-built Grant, T-24189, although completed in July, was not shipped until 27 October 1941, when it was dispatched to the Suez.

# Chrysler

The foundation of Chrysler's involvement in the M3 program was set forth in Chapter 2 of this book. In that chapter is discussed how the company came to be involved, and how the construction of the Chrysler Detroit Tank Arsenal was orchestrated.

It is worthwhile to consider that when Big Bill Knudsen approached K.T. Keller concerning what became the Tank Arsenal, Knudsen envisioned a "one-stop shop," with the Arsenal even rolling its own armor plate. That level of self-suffeciency was abandoned even before ground was broken, but when the facility opened in 1941 much of the manufacturing was done on site. However, as the war wore on the Arsenal became less of a manufacturing facility and more of an assembly plant.

Ground was broken for the Tank Arsenal on 9 September 1940, with Chrysler President K. T. Keller, Vice-President Frederick Zeder, and company General Manager Herman Weckler present, along with Colonel R. Z. Crane of the Ordnance Department present. On 7 November E. J. Hunt was appointed operating manager of the Tank Arsenal, and on the 18th the steel of that arsenal began to go up. That steel work would be completed on 28 January 1941. The structure consumed 6,500 tons of steel, assembled with 170,000 nuts and bolts, along with 90,000 rivets.

**Above:** *Chrysler workers are wrestling an industrial riveter into place while fastening an angle iron to the inside of the left upper hull panel. The angle iron, the front end of which is visible, will support the roof of the fighting compartment while also forming a structural joint between the roof and the side of the upper hull. FCA North America archives*

On 8 January 1941 the US flag was formally raised over the partial complete arsenal, with a number of Army and Chrysler dignitaries present.

On 20 January planning of a concrete figure-8 test track on the tank arsenal grounds began.

On 28 January, the completed 1/3 of the building was partitioned off, and because the arsenal powerhouse was not yet complete, a steam locomotive was moved in on the internal rail siding. The locomotive then provided steam to heat the building.

On 10 February parts for the first tank began to arrive, and three days later the completed portion of the building had risen to 700,000 square feet. On 17 February the plant powerhouse was completed and brought on line, releasing the steam locomotive previously used.

On 15 March 1941 the R975 was set in place in the first Chrysler-built M3. The chassis of this tank was completed on 12 April and it was driven 20 feet that day.

Exactly one month later the Tank Arsenal building was complete, and construction began on the test track. The Arsenal building, two blocks wide and five blocks long contained 51,000 tons of concrete, 200 miles of wire housed in 55 miles of conduit supplying, among other things, 7,000 lights. Twelve miles of pipe were used to distribute steam, water and compressed air. Glass, comprised of over 80,000 panes, covered 6 ½-acres of external surface of the building. Yet, despite the vast size of the building, it would soon be expanded.

In a ceremony on 24 April 1941, the first Chrysler-built M3 was delivered to the US Army. A campaign among Chrysler dealers raised enough money to pay for this tank, and it was presented to the Government as a gift. This event, which was extensively covered in news of the day, was attended by numerous Chrysler officials as well as Major General Wesson, Chief of Ordnance, Major General Adna Chaffee, head of the armored force, as well as Major General Bonesteel, Brigadier Generals Gladeon Barnes, D. H. Campbell, N. F. Ramsey and Lt. Colonels John Christmas and Rehm, the latter the Commanding Officer of the

**Above:** *An entire industrial riveter is visible in this scene of M3 hulls under construction at Chrysler Defense Arsenal. The riveter was shaped like an enormous horseshoe, with the rivet-driving mechanism on one side of the bottom and the rivet bucker on the other side. The whole unit was suspended from an overhead hoist. FCA North America archives*

Tank Arsenal. From the Office of Production Management in attendance were Bill Knudsen, John Biggers, A. R. Glancy, W.W. Knight and H.T. Bodman. Politicians, in the form of Congressman Louis Rabout, Governor Murray Van Wagoner and mayor Edward Jefferies, Jr. were also present.

As a surprise, on the same day a second M3 was rolled out of the Tank Arsenal, thereby setting a standard for early delivery. These two tanks were part of the initial 1,000 tanks on the initial Chrysler production order T-519.

In order to accept the donation of the first tank, the contract had to be modified. Therefore on 22 May

1941 Supplemental contract 1 was issued. The same document changed the specified vehicles under contract from M2A1 to M3, provided for installation of guns and sights by the contractor, and increased the unit cost of each tank from $33,500 to $37,779.

On 6 June 1941 Chrysler received a supplemental order of 152 M3s on production order T-1506. These tanks were originally scheduled to be completed after the initial order of 1,000 tanks was completed and before work began on the 1,600 tanks on production order T-1473. The government had considerable confidence in Chrysler when awarding these additional

**Above:** *With bogie assemblies awaiting installation in the foreground, Chrysler assembly-line workers are working on the rear of an M3 hull. The small plates for the side of the overhang of the rear of the upper hull have been installed. A rare view is available of the seldom-seen inner surface of a bogie bracket, to the left. Library of Congress*

contracts, because as of this date, only the two initial, hand assembled, tanks had been completed by the company. An Independence Day memo stated that on that day, four M3 tanks were on the assembly line in various stages of completion, and the first full-production M3 built by Chrysler was completed on 10 July. In fact, by the end of July Chrysler had completed only seven tanks.

As the month wound down, on 29 July Chrysler Comptroller L.A. Moehring and Dodge's Lester Lum "Tex" Colbert met with Army officers in Washington, who took the Chrysler men to task, stating that they were slow to produce tanks and transmissions. Among the Army officers complaining was Detroit Arsenal commander Colonel Rehm, who opined that some of the equipment in the Arsenal could be operating on Saturday and Sunday. Major D. J. Crawford stated that Chrysler was failing in its duty to the United States with regard to tank production. By this time, Chrysler attorney Nicholas Kelley had joined the meeting, and heard it reiterated that Chrysler should have agreed to build more in 1941.

Kelley, quickly tiring of the insults, responded telling the officers that early on Chrysler had offered the army the option of building a plant that could build ten tanks per shift, or five tanks per shift, and the Army had opted for the lesser capacity. Thus, in his estimation, it was the government at fault, not Chrysler, for creating a plant with inadequate capacity.

Major Crawford responded that before 1 January 1943 the government wanted tanks in addition to the 4,752 already on order, and that they wanted all of these tanks built as fast as humanly possible, that price was no factor, and if possible the work should be done 24-hours per day, 7-days per week.

By 1 August 1941 M3s were being built on three assembly lines at the Detroit Tank Arsenal, and on the next day the government sent Chrysler a letter of intent for a further 2,000 M3s. These were later contracted for on Supplement 8, signed 4 February 1942.

**Above:** *Medium Tank M3 hulls are moving on a conveyor along the Chrysler assembly line on June 20, 1941. Brackets for storing machine-gun tripods have been installed on these hulls, but hinged covers for the vision ports and pistol ports have not been mounted yet. TACOM LCMC History Office*

**Above:** *An assembly-line worker is carrying out his tasks on the front end of a Medium Tank M3 at the Chrysler Defense Arsenal on 20 June 1941. The vertical volute springs are visible on the bogie assemblies on the right side of the lower hull. Track-support rollers will be installed later. TACOM LCMC History Office*

**Above:** *A worker in bib overalls is making adjustments to the interior of the right side door of a Medium Tank M3 at the Chrysler Defense Plant on 20 June 1941. Other workers are installing components inside the hull and on the roof. TACOM LCMC History Office*

Many of the same men who were present for the 29 July meeting were present again for a meeting on 5 August 1941 to again address the matter of tank production. However, for this meeting the senior officer present was Brigadier General B. O. Lewis, Chief of Production Service Branch. General Lewis stated that he recognized that a 24-hour per day, 7-day per week operation was not feasible. Ultimately, a three-shift, six day per week schedule was agreed upon.

By the end of August, Chrysler, responding to a government request, had provided an estimate for a 150,000 square foot addition to the arsenal, which would be used for shipping service parts for the tanks, as well as providing a facility for the fabrication of experimental tanks. Tank production for the month of August was 50 vehicles, as compared to 7 for the previous month. By 12 September total production had risen to 100 vehicles. The initial contract required that 25 tanks be completed by 5 September. Just over a month later, company representatives were shown a sample of the M4 Sherman, foretelling the Arsenal's future.

October 11 saw considerable correspondence between Chrysler Vice-president B. E. Hutchinson and the Ordnance Department's Colonel John Christmas. The correspondence revolved the two-fold objective of switching to M4 Sherman production and expanding the tank arsenal to attain production of 750 tanks per month. The expansion would require a shift in operations of the arsenal and the relocating of considerable machinery. As initially planned and built, the Arsenal was almost a complete manufacturing facility, with virtually the entire tank built on site. The expansion however would require the transfer of various subassemblies, such as suspensions, sprockets, track, transmissions, idlers and other components to other Chrysler plants, and in some cases subcontractors.

Additionally, the Arsenal would need to be lengthened to 1,830 feet long, an extension of 450 feet, rather than the 300-foot extension previously proposed to accommodate the spare parts operation. Further, an additional 100-foot wide bay running the entire length of the building would need to be added. Beyond that, a 50 x 130-foot, four-

**Above:** *Three lines of M3 chassis are under production at Chrysler on 6 August 1941. The bogie wheels of the vehicles were in channel-type tracks, and the tanks were moved forward by powered shuttles in the slot in the diamond-plate steel covers on the floor. Details in the rear of the engine compartment are visible in the M3 in the left foreground. TACOM LCMC History Office*

story addition to the office building would be needed, and a new 50,000 square foot building built for part specifications. Chrysler told the government that if the $20,000,000 expansion was approved by 1 November, the new addition should be ready for occupancy on 15 July 1942. The intent was to begin production of the M4 on the three new lines, and then convert the three old lines from M3 to M4 production.

On 27 October 1941 Supplement 5 to contract ORD-461 was signed, which implemented the previously agreed 6-day workweek, and formalized the production order T-1473 for 1,600 tanks. The supplement also reset the costs of all the tanks previously contracted for:

Each of the first six tanks were $38.349.40
Each of the next 994 were $39,408.40
Each of the next 153 were $34,472.40
Each of the next 1,600 were $36,234.40

All these prices did not include government furnished equipment such as engines, guns, radios, etc.

**Above:** *Three Chrysler workers are guiding a turret ring as it is lowered onto an M3 on 20 June 1941. The bottom of the inner face of the ring is painted white with black azimuth marks in ten-degree increments, for the reference of the 37mm gun crew. Farther forward awaiting installation is a Wright/Continental R-975-EC2 radial engine on a stand. Military History Institute*

The next day the government issued a letter of intent to proceed with the expansion of the tank arsenal as proposed on 11 October.

On 27 November 1941 the 500th tank left the Chrysler assembly line. The next day General Wesson wrote to K.T. Keller saying, 'It was a great pleasure to hear you completed the 500th medium tank at the Arsenal. I sincerely congratulate you on this accomplishment and shall count on you to continue the good work. I also understand that you have finished a Pilot Chrysler tank engine in record time and that has given a good account of itself in operation to date. We will be pleased to consider a proposal from you to install a small number of these engines in medium tanks which can be put in the hands of troops at an early date."

Supplement number 6 to contract ORD-461 was issued on 10 December 1941, formalizing the plant expansion, and also providing in an increase in ground area of the Arsenal from 113 to 160 acres. Twenty days later the final piece of machinery

originally ordered for M3 production arrived at the arsenal. By New Year's Eve the Arsenal had shipped 729 tanks, putting it four months ahead of the original production schedule.

Despite all this, on 3 January 1942 the Government appealed to Chrysler to create a plan targeting production of 1,000 medium tanks per month, plus spare parts, as well as an additional 250 final drives, suspensions, rear idlers and sprockets to be supplied to other tank manufacturers.

By this point the M4 was the medium tank of choice, however the shift in production from one model to the next was very complex. Not only did the materials and components for the M4 have to be placed on order, and those items begin their own sometimes complex and time consuming production process, but also the skilled workforce at the Tank Arsenal had to be kept working, and of course the Allies had to have medium tanks of enemy type to prosecute the war. Chrysler had

**Above:** *In another 20 June 1941, photograph, the M3 assembly line at the Chrysler Defense Plant is viewed from above. Chrysler did not complete any M3s that month, and finished just seven vehicles the following month, but after that, production rapidly increased. Military History Institute*

stated that the most efficient and economical change over point between M3 and M4 production was at 4,000 tanks. The Army of course, wanting the change immediately but recognizing this was not feasible, approved 600 additional M3-series tanks, putting the change over point at 3352. Chrysler's Edward J. Hunt, hoping to gain a little more time, requested that the 109 M3A4s be in addition to the above number, but the army refused and included the 109 M3A4s in the 600-tank addition. Hunt responded that in order to keep the Arsenal operating at least ten M4s would have to be built in June, with a rapid increase in M4 production.

The change over from M3 to M4 was addressed again by the Deputy Chief of Staff for Requirements and Resources on 30 June, not only for Chrysler, but for all manufacturers, when it was written, "1. It is impracticable, from a production

standpoint, to stop the manufacture of Medium Tanks, M-3 on July 1, 1942, and at the same time meet our requirements under Lend-Lease.

"2. The conversion of facilities from the manufacture of the M-3 tanks to the manufacture of Medium Tanks, M-4, has been underway for some time, and the Chief of Ordnance is expediting the change-over as much as possible. It is anticipated that this conversion will be completed by the 1st of September, 1942, with the exception of the Baldwin Locomotive Works, which may continue a limited production into December, 1942.

"3. The entire output of Medium-Tanks, M-3, should be absorbed by Lend-Lease requirements, and the further assignment of this type of tank to our own troops is not contemplated."

**Above:** *By the time this photo documenting M3 production at Chrysler was taken, there were three full lines in operation in the portion of the plant that is in view. An overhead crane spanning all three assembly lines is in the background. Other, smaller overhead cranes spanning single assembly lines are visible at intervals. Military History Institute*

On 13 January Supplemental letter contract 10 was issued, providing for the production of 4,000 additional medium tanks.

Owing to the tremendous increase in production, along with the shift from government furnished equipment to contractor furnished materials for such notable items as engines, armor plate, etc., the demands of the tank plant required more working capital than Chrysler had available. This led Comptroller L.A. Moehring to write to Colonel Crane on 6 February requesting that the government provide more working capital. This was agreed to in the form of a contract dated 17 March 1942.

Chevron-design track shoe manufacture was initiated at Goodyear per Chrysler's request on 2 February 1942, reflecting Chrysler's understanding that Ordnance wanted that style of track on 1,000 M3s. On 15 March 1942 the decision was made that this track would instead be introduced on the first 1,000 M4 tanks. The track, designated T48, is

not known to have been installed on any M3s during production. Rather, the Lees were equipped with T41 track, and the Grants (none of which were built by Chrysler) used WD-212 track.

On 16 March the steelwork for the expansion of the assembly building at the Arsenal was begun. This was the previously discussed effort to raise capacity to 750 tanks monthly. Ten days later a new supplement to contract ORD-461 is entered into between Chrysler and the government to further increase the capacity to 1,000 tanks per month, to be possible in October.

The steelwork begun in March was completed 30 April 1942. By 1 May Chrysler was building half of the total production of Medium Tanks in the US, yet on 16 July Supplement 15 of the tank contract was signed, approving the expansion of the plant in order to hit the 1,000 tanks per month goal. The first expansion, to meet the 750 units per month goal, was completed on 1 August 1942. This would bring the square footage to 1.3 million.

**Above:** *Numerous Medium Tank M3 chassis are viewed from the rear at the Chrysler Defense Plant in this undated photo. The chassis in the center foreground lacks the engine, but engines have been installed in the chassis farther forward. Note the two vertical fuel tanks in the forward corners of the engine compartment of that tank. Military History Institute*

Incidentally, the planned expansion to hit 1,000 tank per month production, called for on Supplement 15 (which was targeted to occur during Sherman production) moved at such a pace that when General Alfred Bixby Quinton, Jr., wired on 18 November 1942 to cancel the expansion, Chrysler Vice-President and General Manager Herman Weckler responded by calling him to state that the work, with the exception of minor finishing, was already done! General Quinton advised Weckler to finish the work.

Dr. J.J. Prendergast, Chrysler Medical Director, attended a meeting at Fort Knox on 27 January 1942, for the Medical Science Division Research Council, at the suggestion of Colonel Kenner of the Armored Force.

"It had been reported to the Armored Force Headquarters that soldiers were becoming ill in the tanks. In the meeting, Colonel Kenner expresses the hope that tests could be made for toxic gases in the tanks in operation. Dr. Prendergast agree for Chrysler to provide technical aids immediately to assist the Army in making these tests."

"The report of the test indicated that no significant toxic effects should be found during the normal operation of either tanks or trucks. Tests were performed January 27, 1942."

The rotor of the 75mm gun, and to a lesser extent the rotor of the 37mm gun, was vulnerable to damage from enemy small arms fire. Small high velocity rounds, while not penetrating, could disturb the surface of the rotor, causing binding of the mount. To address this, auxiliary gun shields were developed. These were not factory installed, and thus far photographic evidence indicates that beyond test tanks, they were only installed on the T10 Shop Tractor (Canal Defense Lights).

At the end of July 1942, Chrysler reported turning out 405 tanks during the month, which were comprised of 330 M3s, 75 M3A4s and 2 M4A4s.

Production of the M3 series tanks were discontinued by Chrysler in August 1942, with 26 M3s and three M3A4s being completed that month, with the final of the group, an M3A4, rolling off the line on 3 August. This brought the total

**Above:** Dignitaries gather on 27 November 1941 as the 500th tank is completed at the Detroit Tank Arsenal. In just less than two months, the total production will have doubled. National Archives

**Left:** This is an official crop of the preceding photo by the Office of War Information, showing closer details of the M3 chassis in the center assembly line at the Chrysler Defense Plant. The engine compartment of the closest vehicle is in view, with an opening in the bottom of the forward bulkhead for the engine's connection with the drive shaft. Visible through the opening for the turret are the driver's instrument panel and a vertical pipe to help support the roof of the fighting compartment. Library of Congress

**Above:** *Chrysler assembly-line workers are guiding a Wright/Continental R-975-EC2 Whirlwind radial engine as it is being lowered into the engine compartment of a Medium Tank M3. The thickness of the armor of the engine-access doors on the rear of the hull is visible. To the left side of the left door is a hole in the armor for the left exhaust. Library of Congress*

**Above:** *A crew of women mechanics is preparing a Chrysler A57 Multi-Bank engine for installation in a Medium Tank M3A4. The rear of the engine is in the foreground; the right side of the forward engine mount is next to the right knee of the woman to the right. Vintage Power Wagons*

number of Lees built by Chrysler to 3,352.

As an aside, all the of turret castings used by Chrysler for M3 production were supplied by American Steel Foundries or Continental Foundry and Machine Company. Also interestingly, while the almost photographically invisible Blue Drab as the specified color used to stencil registration numbers on US military vehicles at the various factories during WWII, Chrysler's specifications called for the numbers applied by them at the Tank Arsenal to be black.

## Tank Committee

The Tank Committee met for the first time on 18 October 1940. The committee included representatives of the Army, American Locomotive Company, American Car and Foundry, Baldwin Locomotive Works, Chrysler Corporation, Lima Locomotive Works, Pressed Steel Car Company,

and Pullman Standard Car Manufacturing Company. Chrysler's E. J. Hunt was elected chairman of the committee. The purpose of the committee was to clarify information in specifications in drawings; discuss change orders received; and to make recommendations involving major improvements through experimental equipment.

One month and one day later, at the third meeting of the committee, Hunt resigned as chairman, citing increased duties, having been named manager of the tank arsenal a dozen days prior. Baldwin's H.S. Colby was elected chairman, replacing Hunt.

The Tank Committee continued to function through the production of the M3, and the free flow of information among the manufacturers was instrumental in facilitating rapid production.

**Right:** *An Army officer and a civilian, apparently a Chrysler executive, shake hands in congratulation in front of the 1,000th medium tank of the M3 family to be completed by the Chrysler Defense Plant. The occasion was on 23 January 1942, and, as the sign proclaims, this tank was built six months ahead of schedule. TACOM LCMC History Office*

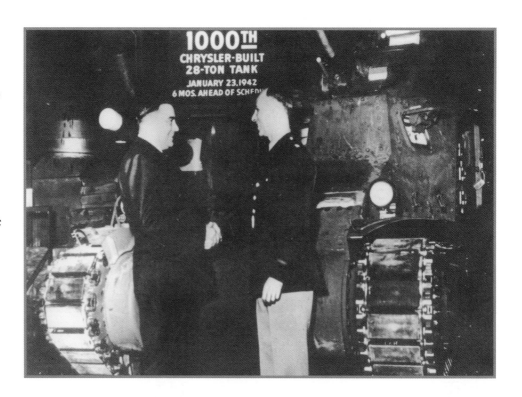

**Above:** *Machining is underway on a center section, or differential housing, of a three-piece final-drive assembly for a Medium Tank M3 at the Chrysler plant on 20 June 1941. Holes have been bored in the flanges on the sides and edges of the casting for attaching the three sections together and then attaching the final-drive assembly to the hull. Chrysler was the only M3 manufacturer to build their own transmissions; and the company also supplied transmissions and transmission components to other firms. Military History Institute*

# The race off the production line

Even before the United States entered the war, Ordnance placed considerable pressure on the contractors to begin production as quickly as possible. The early production medium tanks produced under US contracts were received by Aberdeen Proving Ground for testing as follows:

| Serial Number | Date arrived | Manufacturer |
| --- | --- | --- |
| 1 (pilot) | 21 March 1941 | Rock Island Arsenal |
| 2 | 5 May 1941 | Chrysler |
| 1002 | 5 June 1941 | Baldwin Locomotive Works |
| 1003 | 25 June 1941 | Baldwin Locomotive Works |
| 1689 | 26 June 1941 | American Locomotive Works |
| 1692 | 7 July 1941 | American Locomotive Works |
| 1693 | 7 July 1941 | American Locomotive Works |
| 1694 | 8 July 1941 | American Locomotive Works |
| 3 | 31 July 1941 | Chrysler |

**Above:** Very-early turrets for Medium Tanks M3 are stacked up at the Chrysler plant. These had the extensions for supporting the cupola with an abrupt joint between the bottom and the side of the turret. Soon, the turrets would be designed with a smooth transition between the extension for the cupola ring and the left side of the turret. FCA North America archives

**Above:** Turned upside down, a turret for a Medium Tank M3 is being milled around its base. This was to make the surfaces to precisely fit on the turret ring on the roof of the fighting compartment. More turrets are stacked in the background. The photo is dated 19 June 1941. Military History Institute

**Above:** *A Chrysler Defense Arsenal worker is tightening the screws on a steel plate for attaching the hinges of the two-piece, bifolding hatch cover on a cupola for a Medium Tank M3. On the front of the cupola are the openings for the .30-caliber machine gun and the gunner's sight. Library of Congress*

## The evolution of the design

Although when compared to other tank designs, the M3 series was in production for a relatively brief period, the design did see several improvements through time. These were more prevalent in the Lee than in the Grant, one government report noting that, "During its initial production, when the inevitable 'bugs' were being eliminated, engineering changes were authorized at the rate of three thousand per month."

Some of these evolutions brought about the various models of tanks described in this book, others are more subtle, such as the refinement of the contour of the Lee turret below the commander's cupola.

When production of the M3 began, the tanks were equipped with Hycon hydraulically boosted steering. This system was intended to lessen the amount of effort that the driver had to exert to steer the vehicle. However, this system proved problematic, and was particularly susceptible to vibrations inherent in tank operation. On 19 May 1941 Chrysler started work under a contract to develop double anchor brakes for M3 tanks as a possible alternative.

Aberdeen Proving Ground studied the brake problem, and a 23 August 1941 report compared the Hycon system with a boosterless, so-called "long lever" system and the Chrysler self-energized brake band with the standard steering linkage and without a booster.

These tests indicated that using the standard "short lever" steering gear, without the Hycon boost, required 60 pounds of effort on the part of the driver to execute a 30-foot turn at 5 mph. With the improved Hycon system this effort was reduced to 20 pounds, while the long lever system, without boost, required 24 pounds of steering effort. More significantly, stopping the tank from 20 MPH took

**Above:** *One of the approximately 10,000 members of the workforce of the Chrysler Defense Arsenal is preparing a cupola for installation on the turret of a Medium Tank M3. The hinged cover of the left vision port is installed. The hole on the side of the cupola was for the left trunnion of the machine gun and sight mount; a similar hole on the right side of the cupola accommodated the right trunnion. Library of Congress*

**Above:** *A turret assembly is being lowered onto a Medium Tank M3 chassis on the Chrysler assembly line. The 75mm gun is not installed in its sponson yet. Mounted on the glacis is a storage box for grousers. National Archives*

18-feet longer with the long lever system than the 50-feet required with the Hycon system.

At the time of the report, the Chrysler self-energized brake band had been tested for only 375 miles. Based on the preliminary data, the report opined that "…the only advantage that this system might have over the 'long lever' system is that the brake band adjustment need not be set as closely. On the other hand, it will probably be easier to make the 'long lever' installation than the Chrysler brake band installation."

The report made the recommendation that:

"1. Existing standard Hycon booster systems be modified with the Hydraulically actuated control valves.

2. Future steering installations employ the 'long lever' steering linkage without the hydraulic booster system.

3. Drawings of the 'long lever' system be made at the Detroit Tank Arsenal according to the sketches that have been sent there.

4. Additional tests be made on the Chrysler self-energized brake bands over an extended period of time in order to determine the endurance and reliability of the system."

The US was quick to act on the Aberdeen recommendations, and Chrysler adopted the long lever system in August, with Alco making the change in November.

The British had had some concerns about the reliability of the Hycon system from the outset and had therefore required that the steering levers on the Grants be three inches longer than those of their American counterparts initially. The Dewar files reported in December 1941 that, "U.S. are dispensing with Hycon control and are fitting five (repeat five) inch longer lever on gear-box to increase leverage. This permits steering without

**Above:** *A Medium Tank M3 chassis has come to the end of the conveyor tracks on the Chrysler assembly line. From here on, the vehicle will be rolled forward onto the tracks that are laid out to the front of the vehicle, and the installation of the track assemblies will be initiated. Library of Congress*

**Above:** *Several workers are guiding a 37mm gun mount into its position on the front of the turret of a Chrysler Medium Tank M3. The gun is viewed from the left side, also showing the recoil guard and the elevation hand wheel. Note the white paint overspray on the exterior of the hull around the driver's vision port and the pistol port. Library of Congress*

**Left:** *The Medium Tank M3 in the foreground has been rolled forward on the track assemblies so that all of the bogie wheels are on the tracks. The forward ends of the tracks have been folded back and positioned on the sprockets. Next, those ends of the tracks will be run to the rear over the track-support rollers, and finally the ends of the tracks will be pinned together to complete their assembly process. The front M3 on the other assembly line has its tracks fully installed. Library of Congress*

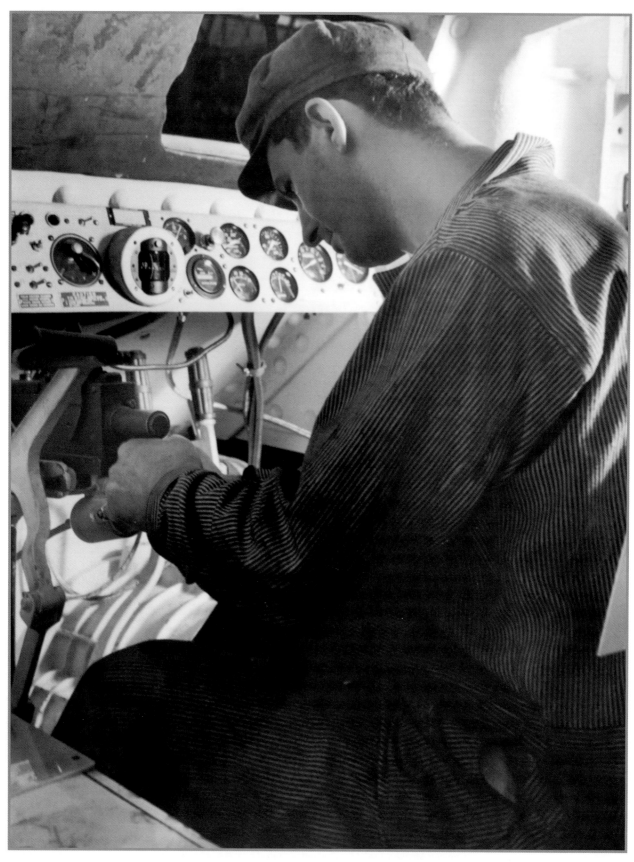

**Above:** *A Chrysler technician is connecting the firing solenoid on the left bow machine gun in an M3 medium tank., To his front is the driver's instrument panel, below which are the grips of the steering-brake levers and the transmission. Library of Congress*

**Right:** *This configuration of auxiliary gun shield was installed on M3A4 number 671 at Aberdeen Proving Ground in July 1943. No evidence has surfaced that these shields were used in the field, but they were installed on the US Canal Defense Lights. Patton Museum*

**Above:** *This auxiliary gun shield was developed in mid-1942 in an effort to prevent small arms fire from burring the gun mount, hampering movement. Above and to the right of the 75mm gun tube can be seen a M15 direct sight telescope, an effort to improve accuracy over that which was achieved with periscope sighting. Patton Museum*

**Left:** *On the assembly line at the Chrysler Defense Arsenal on 27 November 1941, Medium Tanks M3 are nearing completion. The center front vehicle has manufacturer's number 505 in chalk on the glacis, and the tank to the front right is number 510. These vehicles are equipped with their tracks and 75mm guns. The 37mm gun mounts are installed but the gun barrels are not. On the cart in the foreground are two 75mm guns. The recoil surfaces, at the rear of the gun tubes, were left unpainted. National Archives*

**Above:** *A undated, low-angle photo of the final-assembly area at the Chrysler Defense Arsenal shows almost complete tanks in the background, with the huge overhead crane to the rear. In the left foreground is the rear of a Medium Tank M3A4, with its extended rear hull. Library of Congress*

**Left:** *Scores of M3s are in the final-assembly area of the Chrysler Defense Arsenal. The U.S. Army registration numbers have been painted on the sponsons of all vehicles here. Some of the visible registration numbers include W-3028892 on the vehicle in the center foreground; W-3010618 and W-3010654 on the two tanks just beyond the front-center tank; and W-3010713 on the tank to the far right. National Archives*

Hycon." At that time, the British opted to retain Hycon, although with improved valving, however they too abandoned Hycon by February 1942.

The matter of brake systems was revisited by Aberdeen about a year later, in a report of 29 August 1942. That report compared two modifications of the Hycon system with the long lever system, the Chrysler Self-energizing system (which was sometimes known as a fixed double anchor system), a Baldwin Hydraulic system and a Bendix Hydrovac system. That report concluded with the recommendation that the Chrysler self-energizing brake system "...be accepted as the preferred type and be incorporated in the

production medium tanks as soon as possible." Further, the report stated, "The Production Long Lever Brake System be considered second choice and be installed in production medium tanks until such time as Chrysler Self-energizing Brakes can be used in all medium tanks,: and that "No more medium tanks be equipped with booster type brakes and those already produced be changed over preferably to the Self-energizing or Long Lever system as soon as possible."

Ordnance Committee Item 17301 of 9 October 1941 eliminated the side doors from the cast-hull M3A1. In the supporting documentation it was stated that as of 14 July 1941 the patterns for the

**Above:** *The final step of assembly for each Medium Tank M3 at the Chrysler Defense Arsenal was a stop in the paint booth, where it received a final spray coating of Olive Drab paint. Library of Congress*

**Above:** *Recently completed, or nearly completed, Medium Tanks M3 are parked outside of the Chrysler Defense Arsenal on 27 November 1942. Only one of the vehicles has the 37mm gun installed, and that tank also happens to be the only one with the registration number painted on the sponson; it is faint but appears to be W-304537. FCA North America archives*

**Above:** *A Chrysler test driver is operating a brand-new Medium Tank M3 as it leaves the factory. He will put the vehicle through a series of manufacturer's tests to ensure it is ready for delivery. The driver's vision-port cover is in an unusual position, straight up, with no support rod installed. Library of Congress*

cast upper hull were being revised, and that any other changes desired should be made at that time. It also cited 23 June 1941 correspondence from Fort Knox, recommending that the side doors be eliminated, which would strengthen the hull and improve ballistic resistance. It also stated that if the side doors were eliminated, that a bottom escape hatch would need to be fitted, as well as an escape opening in the turret basket and a pistol port with protectoscope installed in the side of the hull near the former location of the side doors.

Records of a meeting on 26 April 1942 include a notation that Mr. Currie of Alco "said that his company had had a problem in the last week of M3 tanks coming in without the side doors and they had to put in an escape door at the bottom." This indicates that it took approximately six months to implement the changes approved by OCM 17301. It appears that the change of the hinge location for the upper hatch happened concurrently with the elimination of the side doors.

The Aberdeen test report on Alco M3 #2322, tested 6 June 1942, makes mentions of various improvements, stating, "This vehicle incorporates a number of modifications not found on previous production vehicles. The vehicle is not provided with side doors in the hull; the air cleaners are mounted to the rear of the engine compartment under the armored hood; and short fishtails on the engine exhaust pipes replace mufflers. A mushroom ventilator was installed in the turret over the 37mm gun; all rivets, except those on the bottom of the hull, are seal welded; and bogie arm spacer studs are replaced by spacers on the gudgeon pins between the bogie arms."

Similar changes were made to the rolled armor M3s in the same time frame. For a period of time, the components, whether rolled plate or hull castings, had been previously manufactured to accommodate the side doors. Those vehicles had the doors, or blanks for the doors, welded in place until such time as the new components became available.

**Above:** *Two late-production Medium Tanks M3 are rolling along a road outside of the Chrysler Defense Arsenal. The vehicle in front has the long-barreled 75mm Gun M3, and both tanks have riveted hulls with the side doors deleted. The bogies are not the ultimate model with the track-support rollers mounted on arms. The 37mm gun mounts haven't been installed as of yet. FCA North America archives*

**Above:** *An apparently new but incomplete Chrysler Medium Tank M3 being taken for a test run. The 37mm gun is mounted; the opening in the thee rotor shield for the 75mm gun has been taped over. Note the light-colored interiors of the covers for the driver's vision port and the pistol port; overspray from this paint is present around the openings. Patton Museum*

**Above:** *With the side of the Chrysler Defense Arsenal as a backdrop, three M3s (the turret of one is visible between the two vehicles in the foreground) are being test-operated. The only armament mounted in the tank to the left is the Browning .30-caliber M1919 machine gun in the cupola. This vehicle has ventilators installed; one is visible on the front left corner of the roof of the fighting compartment. The rear of the vehicle to the right exhibits late-production features: the pepperpot exhausts were removed, box-type air cleaners were installed in their former positions, and fishtail exhausts, faintly visible here, were installed just below the overhang of the rear of the upper hull, between the air cleaners. A ventilator and armored splash guard is visible on the roof of the turret of that vehicle, adjacent to the cupola. FCA North America archives*

Vice-President and General Manager Herman Weckler wrote to Colonel John Christmas 19 February 1942 concerning delays in production. Weckler's letter said, "I am quite sure you are wondering why production has not kept pace with our performance last month and with our schedule. I am attaching an important memorandum from Mr. M. J. Leonard covering changes in the tank which explains this delay.

"We should all realize that any change in production should be thoroughly worked out and a pilot job approved by production people before the change becomes effective."

The attached memorandum, written by Matt Leonard, Tank Arsenal General Superintendent, elaborated, "Tank production has been reduced the past few weeks due to incorporation of stabilizers on 37 and 75-mm guns. The effective period set by Chrysler to make this change effective was 1500 tanks but the government ordered immediate installation."

"A pilot tank previously tested had been found unsatisfactory for mass production but the government took no steps to correct this design. This resulted in units which could not be installed and it became necessary for us to re-work 12 different items to secure clearances and allow parts to operate.

"As of today, there are still 45 items necessary to the operation of the stabilizer which still have not been released by Ordnance engineering. This makes it necessary for us to set up every unit by trial and error to work out lengths of wire, conduit, cables to re-work practice clamps and parts as we go along.

"Installation drawings are not available and some are missing – some parts were released for the 1500 point recommended by Chrysler and consequently are not available."

"On February 11, Westinghouse, in a meeting, agreed to make certain changes. On February 18, they were instructed by the government to make no changes whatsoever. This resulted in our assembly line becoming an experimental stage for the development of this particular unit."

**Above:** *A worker from Department 501 of the Chrysler Defense Arsenal, also called the Detroit Tank Arsenal, is applying sealing materials to a newly completed Lee tank for British service. The sealant will keep out the elements during the long voyage across the Atlantic. In the background, U.S.-type Medium Tanks M3 have been loaded on railroad flatcars for transport. FCA North America archives*

**Right:** *Chrysler workers are making final adjustments to a new Medium Tank M3 on 2 July 1941. None of the armaments have been mounted at this point. The U.S. Army registration number has been painted on the sponson but is not legible. Military History Institute*

**Above:** *The big overhead crane in the Chrysler plant is lifting a Medium Tank M3 for loading onto a railroad flatcar. By installing railroad tracks inside the plant building, the loading of tanks onto flatcars was greatly facilitated. TACOM LCMC History Office*

"As of February 15, extra men were assigned to make by hand necessary wiring, harnessing, conduits, welding, etc. and to re-operate parts where were not usable. Westinghouse also has 4 men in our plants re-operating parts which they furnished. These corrective measures are resulting in current production again approaching the schedule."

The same debacle surfaced again in a letter from K.T. Keller to Mr. A. R. Glancy, Special Assistant to the Under Secretary of War on 27 February. In it, Keller states, "...we received quite a jolt on our tank production on the second ten days of February due to an early introduction of some new features the Army desired, the supplier for which were not ready. We got 22 tanks behind last months shipments, but as of this morning our shipments are 256 tanks against 242 this time in February."

In an effort to address these problems, Ordnance shipped M3 number 382 from American Locomotive to the East Springfield, Massachusetts facility of Westinghouse so that Westinghouse technicians could work with Ordnance representatives to correct the issues.

The gyrostabilizers were also introduced into Grant production, although at a later date. Photographic evidence suggests that the 37mm gun became

gyro equipped in March 1942, with the 75 becoming similarly equipped the next month.

The gyrostabilizers were not the only planned component that was not available when the various plants began turning out M3s. A 9 March 1942 message from Captain Toothacker to Colonel Christmas advised:

"1. To expedite delivery of canvas covers for Medium Tanks, M3, now in the field, a contract has been placed with the Waterhouse Company, Webster, Massachusetts, for 700 sets of covers consisting of the following:

a. Cover, Muzzle, 75 mm., M2, with counterweight
b. Cover, Breech, 75 mm., M2
c. Cover, 75 mm., Gun Periscope Sight, M1
d. Cover, Muzzle, 37 mm., M5, M6
e. Cover, Breech, 37 mm., M5, M6
f. Cover, 37 mm., Gun Plate
g. Cover, Cupola
h. Cover, Door, Indirect Vision

" To fasten Covers 1, C, F, G, and H, to the tanks, steel frames are required. These frames are attached to the tanks by tack-welding. The above contract includes both the canvas covers and frames necessary for fastening covers to the tanks."

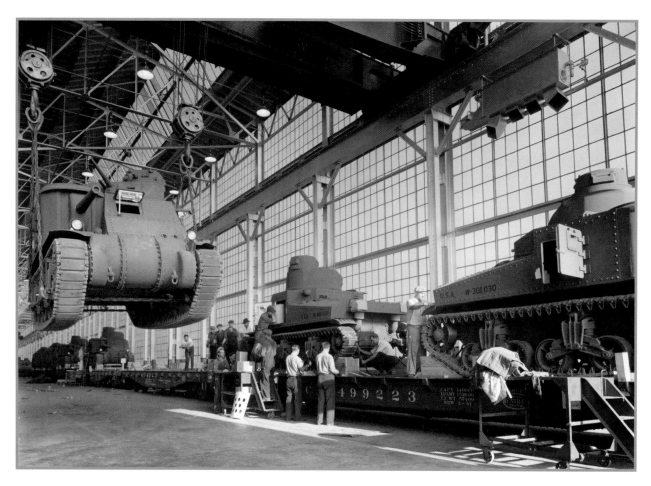

**Above:** *The hoisting of another M3 during a flatcar-loading operation is shown from the front of the vehicle. The hoisting sling consisted of two heavy-duty cables that were routed underneath the hull. To the right, workers are securing two M3s, registration numbers W-301030, right, and W-301039, on a flatcar. Workers are loading boxes of spare parts and supplies into W-301039. FCA North America archives*

**Right:** *Workers at the Chrysler plant are positioning a Medium Tank M3 with a riveted hull and armaments not installed on a flatcar, for delivery to the Army. In these factory photos of completed M3s, there is great variation in how the interiors of the covers of the drivers' vision ports were painted. On this example the interior and the support rod are white. Note the light-colored cover over the 37mm gun barrel. Military History Institute*

**Above:** *A Chrysler worker arranges a tarpaulin over one of the final M3s to leave the production line.*
*Library of Congress*

The memo went on to say, "Deliveries of these covers will begin on or about April 1, 1942. First delivery will be thirty (30) sets per week. Deliveries will be accelerated at the rate of thirty (30) sets per week until the production rate of 100 sets per week is reached."

The specification for the front machine gun installation of the M3 series tanks was changed by OCM 17906 on 6 March 1942, reducing the number of .30-caliber machine guns in the front plate from two to one. At the same time the number of tripods carried as on vehicle equipment was reduced also from two to one. By June the .30 caliber front-mounted machine gun was deleted entirely.

Another matter had Captain Toothacker's attention on 2 April 1942 when he wrote to Lt. Colonel Crawford, who then forwarded the correspondence to Col. Christmas concerning the air cleaner and exhaust installation of the tanks. Concerning the M3, the memo said:

"1. The following report shows when the quick-fix

and production modifications of exhaust muffler and air cleaner installations will be initiated by various tank manufacturers. The quick-fix modification includes outside mounted air cleaners and straight exhaust pipes with no exhaust mufflers. The production modification includes outside mounted air cleaners, modified exhaust collector ring and inside mounted exhaust mufflers.

"Chrysler Corporation  The quick-fix modification was initiated on March 10, 1942, and will be included in 600 tanks. On completion of 600 tanks the production modification will be initiated.

"American Locomotive Co.  First cast steel hull tank having quick-fix modification will be Serial No. 2114, and will be shipped about April 4, 1942. First riveted hull tank with quick-fix modification will be on serial number 2298, and will be shipped about April 3, 1942. All tanks produced thereafter will include the quick-fix modification until Continental Radial Engines with modified exhaust collector rings are received, at which time the production modification will be made.

**Above:** *A recently completed M3 at the Chrysler plant has been prepared for overseas shipment. These measures included removing the cupola and storing it in a box; greasing and sealing all moving parts; sealing areas where moisture and salt can penetrate with tape, 2 to 14 inches in width; greasing and waxing the doors; and spraying the bottom of the tank with soft wax. In addition, silica gel was hung in certain parts of the tank to absorb moisture, and oil, fuel, and other liquids were drained off and replaced with rust-preventative liquids. Military History Institute*

"Pullman-Standard Car Co. The quick-fix modification will be started in the 400th tank produced, which will be shipped about May 1, 1942.

"Pressed Steel Car Co. The quick-fix modification will be initiated in the 400th tank, which will be shipped about April 26, 1942."

A follow up memo from Toothacker to Christmas on 18 April reiterated the change over points provided above, but for providing further clarification regarding Chrysler. The updated information said the company was "Using quick fix now, new installation on tank #2600." This follow up memo also addressed the matter of on vehicle stowage, responding to Christmas's query of "At what time will all medium tanks leave the factory completely fitted for stowage?" Regarding the M3, Pullman and Pressed Steel reported all tanks were equipped, while Baldwin stated all British tanks

were equipped, and US production would start being in June, Chrysler would start at tank 2100, and it was stated that American Locomotive with the introduction of the M4.

However, this proved to be optimistic, as a 13 June 1942 examination of 1,004 tanks shipped by Chrysler revealed 39 line items of equipment were missing. These were not occasional items missing, but rather a wholesale shortage of items. The least frequently missing item was a M1 screwdriver, which was missing from 299 tanks, while all 1,004 tanks were missing the Sight, Bore, 76mm, Bore RF-11AD and the Roll, Tool, M12, with contents. Addressed separately was the matter of small arms-related gear that was missing from these tanks, which included 75 tanks which were each missing the 12 50-round magazines for a Thompson sub-machine gun, and ranged up to 1,000 tanks missing the case with strap for those magazines.

**Above:** *A pair of late production M3s turn down Detroit's Woodward Avenue near Grand Circus Park. This tank exhibits the late production characteristics of roof and turret top ventilators, armored plates at the rear to protect the air cleaners, no side doors and the use of the stamped C85163 roadwheels, rather than the D38501 open spoke roadwheels more typically found on M3 series tanks. Wayne State University*

**Above:** *The last of the Chrysler Medium Tanks M3 were completed in August 1942. As these tanks were being finished, the new Medium Tanks M4 followed them off the assembly line. To commemorate the occasion, the last Chrysler M3-series tank and the first Chrysler M4 were decorated with placards. The one on the M3 stated, "CHRYSLER M-4 TANKS CROWD LAST M-3 OFF THE LINES," while the sign on the M4 read, "CHRYSLER-BUILT M-4 TANK." Horizontal ribs are present between the inner and outer vertical ribs on the D37892 bogie brackets of the M3 and C85163 stamped bogie wheels are used. The M4 following the M3A5 off the line has D47527 suspension assemblies. Patton Museum*

**Above:** *On the left and center production lines in this August 1942 photo are the last of the M3s, with long 75mm guns, grouser boxes, and side doors omitted, while on the line to the right are five of the earliest small-hatch, direct-vision M4A4s. Note the M3 turret assemblies to the lower left and the 75mm guns on the carts in the center foreground. Patton Museum*

**Above:** *The last Chrysler M3 is to the right, with a line of new M4A4s to its rear. All of the vehicles on the center and left assembly lines are M4A4s. Note the two grouser boxes on the M3: one on the glacis and the other to the front of the turret. Next to the upper grouser box is a ventilator. Patton Museum*

**Above:** *This photo was taken a moment apart from the preceding one, showing the last Chrysler M3 to the right and the M4A4 at the front of the center assembly line to the left. Patton Museum*

**Above:** *Pressed Steel Car Company, of the Hegewisch community area of Chicago, completed 501 Medium Tanks M3 between August 1941 and July 1942. The chassis of a Pressed Steel Grant is on a stand in this photo, viewed from the rear, with the armor plates tacked together with nuts and bolts until rivets are installed. This photo was taken on 28 May 1941; PSCC completed its first Grant in July of that year, raising the possibility that this is the company's pilot. Joe DeMarco collection*

**Right:** *A profile view of the same Grant taken in the Pressed Steel plant. Interestingly, the suspension brackets, sans the suspension components, have been installed on the hull in this 28 May 1941 view. Ken Nielsen collection*

**Right:** *To the right of the incomplete M3, men examine the Grant's driver's station, which rests on the floor. To the left, a workman works beneath the floor, preparing the plant for tank production. Ken Nielsen collection*

**Above:** *A Wright/Continental R-975-EC2 radial engine is being lowered into the engine compartment of a Grant tank chassis at the Pressed Steel plant on 1 July 1941. The turret is already installed. Note the exhaust stubs to the sides of the engine-access doors on the rear of the hull. The tracks are the WD-212 "double-I" type. Joe DeMarco collection*

**Above:** *Pressed Steel Car workers are building a Grant tank chassis on or around 1 July 1941. The WD-212 tracks are installed. A worker is visible through the open front of the 75mm gun sponson. Joe DeMarco collection*

**Above:** *In a view inside the Pressed Steel plant in Hegewisch dated 13 July 1941, in the center and in the right background are several Grant hulls under assembly. Lying on the floor to the left of center are several final-drive assemblies. In the left background is a Grant tank with the turret's right pistol port not installed and an American flag attached to the right front of the vehicle. This was almost certainly the same Pressed Steel Grant tank shown earlier in this book in a series of photos outside of the factory, with British and U.S. flags on staffs attached to the front of the tank. Joe DeMarco collection*

**Above:** *The same scene depicted in the preceding photo is viewed from more to the right, showing four Grant hulls under assembly at the center and two more to the right. The hulls are viewed from the front. Note the temporary pipes attached horizontally in the fronts of the lower hulls, to brace the front ends until the fronts of the hulls and the final-drive assemblies were installed. Joe DeMarco collection*

**Above:** *In a photograph printed on 3 September 1941, but possibly taken before that date, a Grant chassis is under assembly to the left, positioned over tracks used for conveying the vehicles. A British turret is lying on the floor to the front of that chassis. To the right are three Grant tanks in a more advanced state of assembly. They have their tracks installed and evidently were able to move along that part of the assembly line under their own power. To the right are track assemblies, stacked one above the other. Joe DeMarco collection*

**Above:** *Three Grant tanks are departing from the Pressed Steel Car assembly plant in a photo printed on 23 September 1941. The armaments remain to be installed. The company had completed its first Grant the preceding month; in September the company built 18 tanks. On the center of the final-drive assembly of the first Grant is a sign reading, "CAUTION TESTING." Joe DeMarco collection*

**Above:** *In another photo printed on 23 September 1941, the 37mm guns have been mounted in the turrets of the two nearest Grant tanks. The first Grant has placards with the number 12, presumably the manufacturer's vehicle number, on the 75mm gun sponson and below the side door. Joe DeMarco collection*

**Above:** *A Grant tank has paused during evaluations on a test course outside of the Pressed Steel Car plant on or before 14 November 1941. The course includes a patch of sand in the right foreground. The barrel of the 75mm gun is wrapped with a taped cover, and sealant material is on areas such as the bow machine-gun ports, the gun sponson, and the gunner's sight port on the turret. Joe DeMarco collection*

**Above:** *Negotiating a steep ramp at the Pressed Steel Car factory is a Grant tank, evidently the same one in the preceding photo. This vehicle was painted in a dark color, likely Olive Drab, as used on U.S. M3 medium tanks. Joe DeMarco collection*

**Above:** *The same Grant is beginning to ascend a steep ramp at the Pressed Steel Car plant, on or around 14 November 1941. The extreme compression of the front bogie wheel and arms is testimony to the amount of weight that was borne on the front end when the tank was in this attitude. Joe DeMarco collection*

**Above:** *Assembly is underway on two lines of Grant tanks at the Pressed Steel Car factory in a photo printed on 8 December 1941. Placards are in view containing what apparently were manufacturer's numbers: on the line to the left, the first tank has the number 78 attached to its forward bogie assembly, with 84 visible on the fourth tank in line. A placard with the number 77 is either on the first vehicle in the line to the right, or on the floor behind it. Final-drive assemblies have not yet been installed on these vehicles. Joe DeMarco collection*

**Above:** *Pullman-Standard completed 500 Medium Tanks M3 (Grant) at its Hammond, Indiana, plant between August 1941 and July 1942. In this photo taken on 21 October 1941, Pullman-Standard workers have begun construction of an M3 lower-hull assembly. The hull is viewed from the front left. National Archives*

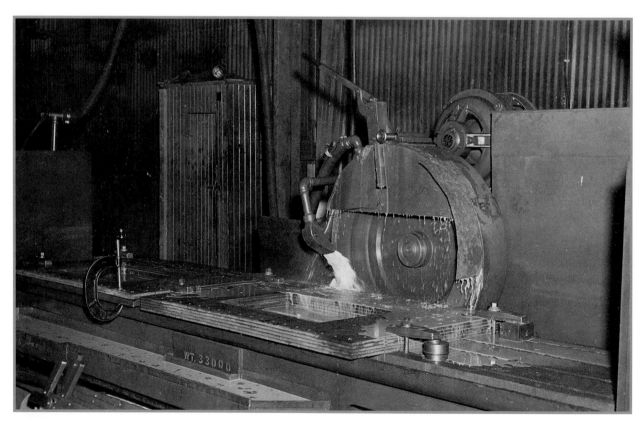

**Above:** *A grinder is trimming armor plates for M3s to size at Pullman-Standard. Five plates were clamped together and ground at the same time. Grinding coolant is pouring along the cutting edge. National Archives*

**Above:** *Finished armor plates for the construction of Medium Tank M3s are stacked on the Pullman-Standard factory floor on 27 November 1941. Wooden sticks are placed between the plates. National Archives*

## The British Tanks

A 27 February 1942 notation in the Dewar files explains the process by which the British were able to achieve a level of customization for their tanks, stating as follows:

"In the event of our wishing to have any modifications incorporated in the design of a tank, or any additions, such as sand guards, the procedure is as follows:

(1) Complete drawings have to be made of the modifications or addition.
(2) These have to be submitted to the U. S. Ordnance for approval.
(3) The need for them has to be explained.
(4) After approval has been obtained the drawings for the modification are issued by the Ordnance Department through the District Ordnance Office.

"Our own contractors have always been most helpful as regards modifications, but, with the end of direct British contracts, modifications will become more and more difficult, particularly as all the big producers are under pressure to get the greatest output, and consequently resist every change in design.

"The U.S. Ordnance have agreed to establish Depots, which will be operated under their control, for making modifications to the standard design of the tank, to suit the agreed requirements for various Lease Lend 'Customers'. The first of these Depots, which is going to be run by the Ford Motor Company in Pennsylvania, should commence operations in the near future."

However, given the war situation, there were some changes that were needed prior to implementation of the Depot system, and which the manufacturers were either unable or unwilling to make prior to shipping the tanks directly to the combat theater. To remedy these deficiencies, the Mechanisation Experimental Establishment (Middle East) in December 1941 began releasing a series of

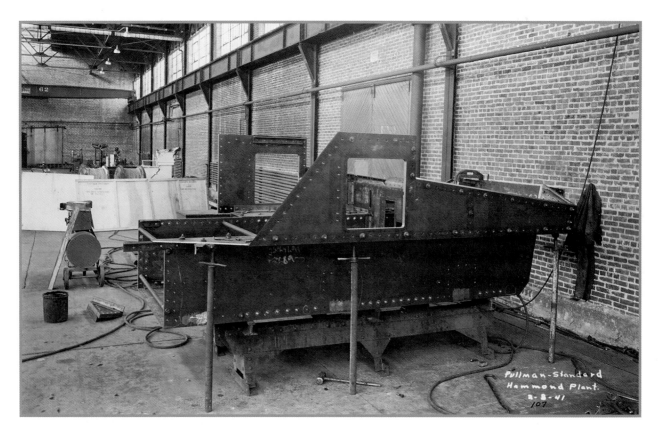

**Above:** *The first Pullman-Standard Grant tank for British service is under construction on 8 February 1941. Liberal use was made of bolts and nuts to temporarily join the armor plates together until they were riveted. The assembly was seated on a stand made of angle irons, with screw jacks supporting the sponsons. National Archives*

**Above:** *A Pullman-Standard mechanic is using a riveter on the upper hull of an M3 chassis. The cast-armor sponson for the 75mm gun is in place, in the front of which the horizontal rotor for the gun has been installed. Pivoting inside the horizontal rotor is the rotor shield, which has swung down 90 degrees from its zero-elevation position. National Archives*

**Above:** *Machinist Harold Ward of Pullman-Standard in Hammond, Indiana, is overseeing an industrial planer that operates on up to seven side doors for Grant and M3 tanks in one operation. The 8 July 1941, photo shows six of the doors clamped down to the carriage, which would move the doors, one after another, under the cutters. National Archives*

"Modifications of Medium Tank, M3." As these modifications were approved and the materials became available, the No. 5 Base Ordnance Depot at Tel-el-Kebir, Egypt began performing the required work. The earliest of this work was done in January 1942, and involved the "Fitting of sandshields." Also in January stowage racks and ""Ds" and straps for securing blankets, etc." were installed. Internally, work was done to improve the fire control system. While approval had been given for the "Fitting of mantlet dust cover to 75mm gun," those dust covers don't appear to have become available for several months, and its installation required the relocation of the stowage rack mounted, per earlier modifications, ahead of the 75mm gun.

The War Diary of the 4th Base Ordnance Workshop (WO 169/6122) records the retrofitting of locally manufactured A.A. mounts for M3 medium tanks in the Middle East as follows:

"29 January 1942.

A pilot pattern for an anti-aircraft mounting for a 'flexible' Browning Machine Gun suitable for the M3 Medium Tank at M.E.E. to be produced. Authority:- U.M.CR/ME/35305/3 (D.M.M.) dated 18/1/42.

"15 February 1942.

After pilot model A.A. mounting for the flexible M.G. has been approved, manufacture of 200 mountings to be arranged. Authority:- U.M.CR/ME/35305/3 ) (D.M.M.) dated 14/2/42"

In April, a month after US Army Ordnance made a similar change, MEE (Middle East) ordered the "Removal of twin Browning guns and plugging of holes." This modification coincided with the installation of the armored ammunition stowage bins discussed elsewhere in this volume. The plugging of the holes was done in a variety of ways, with some tanks apparently being plugged inside, while others had lengths of steel rod welded in place, suggesting to the enemy that the guns were still present.

**Above:** *The progress of work on a Pullman-Standard Medium Tank M3 chassis is documented in a 28 March 1941, photograph. The final-drive assembly is installed; above it is the opening for the fairing for the machine guns. All rivets for the armor are installed. The right rear bogie bracket has been installed. Indiana Historical Society*

**Above:** *The same M3 hull depicted in the preceding photo is observed from the left front. The splash guards around the sides and bottoms of the driver's vision port and the pistol ports were formed from bent strips of steel that were welded in place, with very smooth weld beads around their outer sides to make a beveled finish. Indiana Historical Society*

**Above:** *A Pullman-Standard worker is mounting an open spoke D38501 wheel on the suspension arms of a bogie assembly for an M3 medium tank on 8 July 1941. When the wheel is positioned correctly, he will drive the spindle home with a mallet. Next to the worker are stacks of bogie wheels. Indiana Historical Society*

## Uniquely Grant changes

Of course, the turret is the most instantly noticeable differentiating characteristic between the Grant and the Lee. However, even after the new turret design was approved, just as with US vehicles, service experience caused an evolution in the M3 design as production wore on, and further, numerous depot-level and field modifications were made as well.

The prototype Grant turret was available for inspection in mid-December 1940, and was installed by 30 December. The turret at that time called for a rectangular loader's hatch, as well as an aperture for a 2-inch smoke bomb projector. While the loader's hatch did not see production, General Steel Castings' initial pattern included provisions for this hatch. The pattern was modified to omit the hatch, but the "ghost" of that hatch remained, as well as the clearly defined mounting points for the hatch hinges. Photographic

evidence shows that some of the early castings were supplied to Pullman Standard. However, relatively quickly the pattern was "cleaned up,' or more likely remade, eliminating all traces of the planned loader's hatch.

Unlike the loader's hatch, all the Grant turrets were cast and machined to accept the "2 inch Mortar Mk III (smoke)" on the upper right of the turret face. Inside, the turrets were equipped with the mounting fittings for the mortar, as well as a rack which would hold 14 rounds of "2 inch (smoke)" bombs. Unfortunately, production of the smoke mortar lagged behind production of the tanks. A 28 February 1942 telegram in the Dewar files reports, "No shipments of Grants yet with bomb throwers. First 110 bomb throwers being shipped to U.S.A. from Canada for Grants in March." Until the mortars could be installed at the factory, in their place a 1-inch thick piece of armor, formed in the contour of the turret, was welded over the aperture. This plate was referred to as the "Hood Plate."

**Above:** *Mr. W. Boese, left, welding supervisor at Pullman-Standard, supervises the operation of a device of his own design: a machine for flame-hardening a cluster of 20 sprockets in one operation. The photo was dated 8 July 1941. Indiana Historical Society*

Beyond the turret, another readily identifiable feature of most Grants were the sand guards over the return track run. While they were not supplied on Grants initially, they were quickly put into production, reportedly beginning with the 32nd Pullman-built tank, completed in September 1941. In Dewar's files, it is noted that as of "28Nov41...Sand guards for Grants now in production by one firm, other two start shortly." Prior to factory introduction of the sand shields, the Grants were equipped with Lee-type rubber rear fenders. The Dewar Files also note that, "Pressed Steel shipped 63 tanks deficient of sand guards, Serial Numbers 24689 to 24750 (sic). Baldwin will produce sand guards by Feb. 1 approx. 160 their tanks will be deficient and deficiencies will not (repeat not) be made up. No General Lee will have sand guards until depot is formed. Date of this is uncertain. Pullman and Pressed Steel are shipping immediately 94 sets to cover deficiencies their tanks. If M.E. have equipped these tanks already, surplus can be used on Baldwin or Lease Lend tanks arriving without."

In the interim, the sand shields, which were essential in the Middle East, were installed as field modifications according to M.E.E. [Mechanisation Experimental Establishment] patterns 112A & B.

Factory installed sand shields are of a slightly different pattern than the field modifications, and can be distinguished by the shape of the leading edge. British sand shields have a smooth curve over the leading edge, whereas factory installed sand shields are angular. When viewed in profile, the factory applied sand shields slope upwards at a point about half-way back on the drive sprocket, while the British shields don't turn upward until well to the rear of the drive sprocket. At the rear of the flank of the tank, the British shields have a steep upward angle ahead of the idler, while factory sand shields have a gentle slope beginning at the approximate midpoint of the rearmost suspension assembly.

**Above:** *The interior of a British Grant chassis is viewed from the front at Pullman-Standard on 2 May 1941. With the glacis, final-drive assembly, and 75mm gun yet to be installed, construction details are visible. National Archives*

**Above:** *Over 20 M3/Grant chassis are under assembly in the Pullman-Standard plant in Hammond, Indiana, on 6 August 1941. A Grant tank with the turret installed is in the right background. In the right foreground are stacked armor plates and side doors. National Archives*

**Above:** *In a view taken from a similar perspective to that in the preceding photo but over three months later, Grant tanks are under assembly on 28 November 1941. Three turret baskets, painted white and ready for installation, are on the floor to the left. Starting with the fourth tank in the line to the right, British turrets have been installed. More British turrets are on the floor in the middle background to the right. National Archives*

In the same general area, but less obvious, is the British use of a different rubber block track. Whereas tanks produced on US contracts used the T41 track, the British used a track of their own design, sometimes known as the "Double I" track, which was optimized for operation in the sand. This track, the WD-212 (sometimes known as the WE-210, which is the part number for a four-link assembly), shared a 16-inch width with the T41, but was about 1-inch thicker. The T41 had 1-1/8-inch track pins, whereas the later, similar appearing T51 Sherman track used 1-1/4-inch track pins, and were 9/16-inch wider.

A cypher telegram from the British Purchasing Commission on 28 November 1941 advised "For your information installation of the no. 19 set in medium tank M-3 with British turret has now been finalized and the necessary modifications to the tank are being introduced in production lines." Prior to this the British radios, either number 11 or number 19, were installed in the field.

The US Armored Force Board had looked into jettisonable external fuel drums as early as August 1941. This topic was taken up again with regard to the M3 and M4 medium tanks beginning in October 1941. The objective at that time was "to develop suitable mountings and release devices for auxiliary fuel drums carried exposed on the exterior of the tank and designed to meet the following requirement:

a. Capable of disconnection by control from the interior of the tank.

b. Capable of being jettisoned by control from the interior of the tank at the will of the tank commander, whether full or empty, and of sufficient durability to withstand the shock of jettisoning without impairing the re-use value."

The tanks developed by this later effort, which were produced by B.F. Goodrich, met all the parameters above, plus were additionally of self-sealing construction and did not interfere with the normal operation of the tank. Although a British Purchasing

**Above:** *As seen in a photo taken at Pullman-Standard on 27 November 1941, a special fixture was employed in mounting the 75mm gun, consisting of a large, C-shaped piece of steel on a hoist, with a fitting on the lower end that was inserted in the gun breech. The right rear panel of the fighting compartment was screwed on, not riveted, so that gun installations and removals could be accomplished. Two 75mm guns are on sawhorses, and a carriage and recoil mechanism assembly is on the floor to the left. National Archives*

Commission telegraph of 16 January 1942 said "U.S. propose fitting auxiliary fuel tanks to all tanks. 3 medium tanks will be fitted within six weeks. They will be supplied retrospectively", no evidence has yet surfaced indicating that US Ordnance procured these tanks in quantity for the M3, but the British adopted a similar design that extended the range of the tank about 30 miles. These tanks were included in a Department of Tank Design modification package. The British jettison tanks can be seen in occasional photographs of both Grants and Lees in British service in the United Kingdom.

Inside the tank, it appears that the Grants came factory-equipped with a 60 round 37mm bin, "adjacent left door," in the space that was occupied

by the radio on the Lee. This was not armored ammunition stowage.

A telegram from the British Purchasing Commission on 13 November 1941 advised George Usher of the British Tank Board that the Grant tanks would be painted Coranado Tan, "specification same color as Canadian Ford vehicles that being shipped to M.E."

On 23 December the Ministry of Supply reversed this, requesting that the vehicles return to being painted Khaki Green No. 3. This request was acknowledged, with the stipulation that the manufacturers of the Grant would return to that color when their present supplies of Coranado Tan is exhausted.

**Above:** *Once a basic turret was cast or welded, it was necessary to machine areas such as the hatches and the bases, to perfect the surfaces. This casting is being machined on a horizontal boring mill at the Pullman Standard plant on 7 May 1941. Interestingly, just above the "4" scrawled on the side (believed to be the General Steel Castings serial number) can be seen the ghost of the hinge mounting pads for the aborted loader's hatch, which the British had advocated. National Archives*

## Adapting the Lee for British use

Following the passage of the Lend Lease Act on 11 March 1941, the British were allocated a certain number of tanks from US contracts, these being in addition to the tanks which the British Purchasing Commission ordered.

The Lees, of course, were not built to British standards, and thereby had to be modified to better fit the Royal Armoured Corps requirements. A British Purchasing Commission document hand-dated 9 May 1942 listed the changes required. These included:

| | |
|---|---|
| LIM-1A | Remove US Cupola, provide and install upper turret ring and doors |
| LIM1B | Periscope for Commander |
| LIM1C | Mount AA gun |
| LIM1D | Reel Brackets for stowing extra reels for AA gun, under Commander's seat, two reels per spindle on ammunition rack |
| LIM2 | Install sand Guards |
| LIM3 | Provide and install ventilating system, blower fans at pistol port in hull and pistol port in turret. |

**Above:** *Two Grant turrets are on a stand, receiving additional machining, on 7 May 1941.*

| | |
|---|---|
| LIM4A | Install British Radio |
| LIM4B | Install British Aerial and wiring harness |
| LIM4C | Remove present slip ring box and provide and install WD-549 slip ring box |
| LIM5A | Provide and install splash guards at side door pistol ports |
| LIM5B | Provide and install splash guards at pistol port left of driver |
| LIM5C | Provide and install splash guards at pistol port rear hull |
| LIM5D | Provide and install splash guards at driver's vision door |
| LIM5E | Provide and install splash guards at side doors |
| LIM5F | Provide and install splash guards at turret ring |
| LIM5G | Provide and install splash guards at 75mm mount |
| LIM5H | Provide and install splash guards at 37mm mount |
| LIM6A | Provide and install periscope for driver |
| LIM7A | Provide & install compass, if tank is equipped with a compass, replace with WC-755 |
| LIM7B | Provide & install compass corrector |
| LIM7C | Provide & install compass bracket |
| LIM8 | Provide and install water tanks |
| LIM9 | Provide & install oil primer pump |
| LIM10 | Provide & install 4" smoke discharger mount |
| LIM11 | Provide & install parts for stowage of driver's lookout lever C84814 |
| LIM12 | Provide & install closures for bow gun apertures (details later, do not remove junction box on bow gun firing circuits) |
| LIM13 | Drill 75mm gun guard to permit withdrawal of actuating shaft (details later) |
| LIM14 | Install map case per drawing WA-219 |
| LIM15 | Install cooker per drawing WA-220 |

**Above:** *Two workmen are guiding a turret onto a Grant tank chassis at the Pullman-Standard plant on 23 October 1941. The rough texture of the armor of the turret is evident. Indiana Historical Society*

**Above:** *Wright Whirlwind radial engines on work stands are being prepared for installation in M3 medium tanks at the Pullman-Standard factory in this undated photograph. For the convenience of the engine technicians, the work stands had hand cranks for tilting the engines to the desired angle. Library of Congress*

**Above:** *Two inspectors are checking over a Wright Whirlwind engine at the Pullman-Standard plant. Note the fan and the shroud on the engine in the foreground. Library of Congress*

**Above:** *A 15 April 1941, photo shows the rear of a Grant tank with the engine-access doors open. The lower elements of the engine accessories are visible through the open doors. Instead of the WD-212 tracks often seen on Grants, this vehicle has the T41 tracks. National Archives*

**Above:** *The same Grant tank is viewed with the engine-access doors closed. The hinges were welded, not screwed, to the doors and the hull. Exhausts and pepper pot mufflers are to each side of the doors. National Archives*

**Above:** *Although information is not available on the circumstances of this photo, it depicts a Pullman-Standard Grant tank on the manufacturer's test ground, and evidently the tank had driven over and destroyed the mashed car to its side. Allen County Historical Society*

**Above:** *A newly completed Pullman-Standard Grant tank is being steam-cleaned on a wash rack at the factory on 29 November 1941. Tape has been applied over the screws attaching the removable panel on the right side of the rear of the fighting compartment. National Archives*

**Above:** *A Grant tank is being driven up a ramp onto a railroad flatcar for shipment in the Pullman-Standard plant on 28 November 1941. A cord is holding the side door open. Sealant material has been applied to the 75mm gun and its sponson. National Archives*

**Above:** *Blocking has been secured against the WD-212 tracks of a Grant tank being readied for shipment from the Pullman-Standard plant at Hammond, Indiana, on 21 November 1941. Note the solid-steel tie-down attached to an eye on a steel plate bolted to the lower part of the forward bogie assembly. Indiana Historical Society*

# M3 Production ends

As recorded in "Official Munitions Production of the United States," published by the Civilian Production Administration, 1 May 1947, the M3 series tanks were delivered as follows:

| 1941 | |
|---|---|
| July | 26 |
| August | 80 |
| September | 193 |
| October | 249 |
| November | 309 |
| December | 475 |
| 1942 | |
| January | 545 |
| February | 586 |
| March | 622 |
| April | 684 |
| May | 691 |
| June | 738 |
| July | 624 |
| August | 203 |
| September | 58 |
| October | 74 |
| November | 80 |
| December | 11 |
| Program complete total | 6,248 |

The figures above omit the two Lees built by Baldwin in June 1941, as well as the 8 M3s assembled by Alco the same month, which raises the total to 6,258. Of these, Lend Lease shipments accounted for 4,337 vehicles broken down as: British Empire 2,855; Brazil 96; and USSR 1,386, although 410 of the latter were lost in transit.

Of these, the British Purchasing Commission (BPC) ordered 1,685 Grants. Ultimately 123 of the tanks ordered by the BPC were ultimately completed under US production order numbers (Baldwin T-4155 for 89 tanks and Pressed Steel T-3751). A further 150 tanks were finished not as tanks but at T5 Tank Recovery Vehicles.

**Above:** *Workers are preparing to secure the last of the Pullman-Standard Grant tanks to a railroad flatcar in the Pullman-Standard factory. Under the overhang on the rear of the hull box-type air cleaners are mounted directly over the fishtail exhausts. Fewer than 100 of the Grants built by Pullman-Standard left the factory with this arrangement. The muzzle of a 2-inch Mortar Mk. III (Smoke) is visible in the aperture on the right front of the turret roof. Three more Grants with sealant material installed are on flatcars in the background. Allen County Historical Society*

**Above:** *A switcher locomotive is coupled to a flatcar about to transport Grant census number T-24238 from the Pullman-Standard plant. This is one of the 19 Grant tanks completed by Pullman-Standard in October 1941.*

**Above:** *Several early-production Medium Tanks M3 are about to depart from the factory on flatcars. Tarpaulins have been thrown over the three forward tanks, and the nearest M3 is still being secured to its flatcar. Indiana Historical Society*

**Right:** *The fuel tank was designed such that it could be released from inside the tank, and could withstand the hazards of dropping whether full or empty. It was intended that the tank could be recovered and reused. National Archives*

**Above:** *B. F. Goodrich fabricated this self-sealing, jettisonable fuel tank for the M3. National Archives*

**Above:** *The fuel tank is shown with the releases tripped to allow the drum to fall free. Aberdeen recommendd that these tanks become standard equipment. However, the US forces did not accept this recommendation. The British, however, were much more interested. National Archives*

As has been noted, production of the M3 was scarcely underway when it was known it would be replaced by the M4. Thus, it is not surprising that Ordnance Committee item 17202 of 11 September 1941 recommended that the M4 be classified as Required type, Adopted type, Standard article and be placed into production also recommended that the M3 be reclassified as Required type, Adopted type, Substitute Standard item.

The M3 was further downgraded to Limited Standard in April 1943, and while some of the tanks were used for instructional purposes at Engineer training centers or Ordnance Evacuation centers, many were dismantled, with the usable parts salvaged and the remainder of the vehicle scrapped. A list published on 11 September 1943 listed 279 tanks of the M3 series in the continental United States.

**Above:** *A number of people pose with a fresh-appearing Pressed Steel Car Grant that had been equipped with many of the modifications recommended by the Department of Tank Design. Visible along the suspension are mud chutes, and an auxiliary fuel tank has replaced the factory-installed right-side stowage box. Just ahead of the "auxiliary petrol tank" is a stowage bin which was to contain the gun cleaning gear and an array of other equipment. At the rear of the tank, above the rear fender, is another stowage bin, this to contain the 75mm gun cover and mounting. Atop that bin is a bracket for a fire extinguisher. A similar bin, also topped with a fire extinguisher, on the other side of the tank contained a bivouac cover, poles and pegs. David Fletcher*

The types and distribution of those tanks were as follows:

| | |
|---|---|
| 8 | M3 |
| 18 | M3A1 |
| 1 | M3A2 |
| 9 | M3A3 |
| 108 | M3A4 |
| 315 | M3A5 |

The largest concentrations of these tanks were 103 M3A4 at Red River Army Depot, Texas; 76 M3A5 at Letterkenny Ordnance Depot, Pennsylvania, and a further 224 M3A5 at Camp Cook, California.

The tanks were recommended for reclassification as Obsolete on 19 February 1944. Concerning the M3s, Colonel Christmas observed, "We are beginning to run into the motor car dealer's problem. Our customers, the fighting men, want only the latest models."

**Above:** *Late production M3s, part of a Lend-Lease shipment to Britain, are loaded on flat cars prepared to leave the Richmond (California) Tank Depot. The tanks have been modified to meet British standards, with the cupolas removed and sand shields added. National Archives*

**Right Above:** *From this angle, the crates of On Vehicle Material and spares stowed on the rear decks of the M3s can be seen. Throughout the war shipping space was a critical factor in the prosecution of the war and considerable effort went into developing packaging to minimize space. The British census number of the nearest tank, T-26024 can be seen, and faintly visible below it, the original US registration number, 3058041, which identifies the tank as July 1942 production. National Archives*

**Right:** *M3 T-26057 shows off the supports used for the 75mm tube during transport. Faintly visible above the rotor is a periscope, swathed in packing material for the overseas voyage. National Archives*

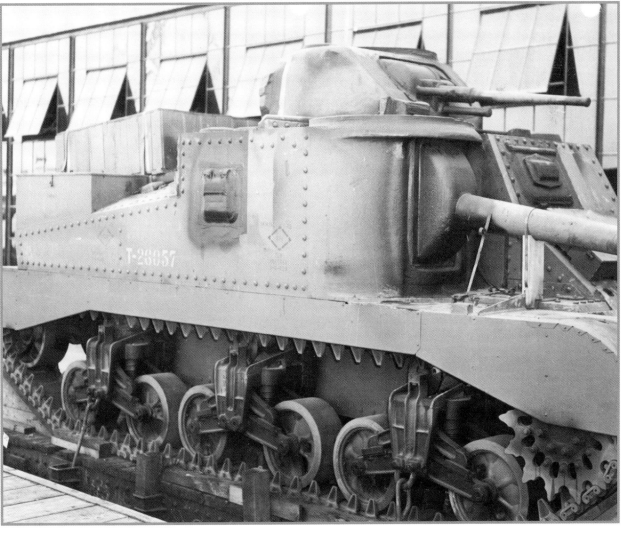

**Above:** The first production Medium Tank M3A4, registration number W-309733, was accepted in June 1942. Like all M3A4s, it is armed with the long-barreled 75mm Gun M3 and is equipped with solid-spoked bogie wheels. The bogie assemblies are the type developed specifically for the M3A4, and later used on Shermans, with the track-support rollers mounted on arms jutting to the rears of the bogie brackets. Series-produced M3A4s had all the late M3-series improvements, such as lack of side doors and a counterbalance mounted under the 37mm gun barrel, as well as a ventilator with an armored splash guard on the front left corner of the fighting-compartment roof. Patton Museum

**Above:** As seen in a right-side photo of M3A4 W-309733, the pistol port was retained on the right side of the upper hull. Near the rear of the top of the sponson is the oblong shape of a new feature: the cover for a grouser compartment. A ventilator is toward the rear of the fighting compartment roof adjacent to the turret. Patton Museum

# Chapter 8
# M3-based conversions

Armored combat vehicles are expensive to produce, and as seen, manufacturing of such vehicles can be a time-consuming process. Further, in addition to the cash investment, in wartime – especially the early years – there was a sizeable investment of scarce resources in each M3 produced. Thus, as the Sherman eclipsed the M3 as the primary medium tank, it not surprising that other useful roles were found for the redundant Lees.

## T2/M31 recovery vehicles

At the same time, the need an armored vehicle for battlefield recovery was becoming apparent. Toward that end, on 21 September 1942 the Headquarters, Ground Forces, directed the Commanding General, Service of Supply to take steps to develop and procure an initial quantity of 108 recovery vehicles based on the M3.

The developmental example of this vehicle, designated the Tank Recovery Vehicle T2, was

built by Baldwin Locomotive Works, Eddystone, Pennsylvania, in October/November 1942. Immediately after the vehicle's test run it was shipped to Fort Knox for testing by the Armored Board.

The conversion process involved the removal of both the 37mm and 75mm guns. The mount and armored shield for the 75mm gun was removed as well, being replaced by an armored door to which a dummy gun was affixed. The side doors were welded shut, and an escape hatch was installed in the bottom of the tank.

A winch, driven by chain from the tank drive shaft in the bottom of the tank, was fitted beneath the turret. The wire rope from the winch could be fed either beneath the tank for straight pulls or through the turret and to the boom for lifting.

The turret basket was removed, and the 37mm mounting plate was replaced with a special boom mounting plate, to which a fourteen-foot long girder-type boom was mounted. The normal

**Above:** *The first of the M3-based tank retrievers is shown here loaded on a flatcar at Baldwin Locomotive Works ready for shipment to Fort Knox for evaluation. This pilot T2 was converted from Medium Tank M3A3, registration number 305373, an August 1942 production tank. The 75mm gun was deleted; in its place was a fake cannon barrel mounted on a door attached to the front of the gun sponson. The boom jacks have been secured to the floor of the flatcar, to support the boom during transit. Baldwin Locomotive Works*

247

**Above:** *This left rear view of the pilot vehicle reveals that indeed is Diesel-powered. Once the M3-based recovery vehicles were standardized, this configuration of Diesel-powered, welded hull retrievers was designated M31B1. Note the positioning of the bracket for pinning the foot of the right boom jack, which has been moved from the right to the center of the angled plate on the rear of the upper hull. Baldwin Locomotive Works*

traveling position of the turret was with the boom to the rear, and accordingly a dummy 37mm gun barrel was welded to the former rear of the turret. The boom could be elevated to approximately 45-degrees. It was intended that the manual traversing mechanism would allow the turret to rotate 360-degrees, and it could swing 5-tons with a free boom, lift and carry six tons when the boom was supported to the hull, or lift 15-tons static with the boom jacks extended to ground.

**Above:** *The name "Katrinka" was stenciled on the T2 during the Armored Board tests at Fort Knox. When the boom jacks were positioned on the ground, as seen here, the crane could lift a load of 30,000 pounds. National Archives*

However, testing by the Armored Force Board revealed that the vehicle could not successfully lift and swing five tons, and when supporting 6-tons over the rear of the vehicle, the rear volute springs were considerably overloaded.

Despite these deficiencies, the Board felt that the T2, while needing certain modifications, was superior to recovery vehicles previously seen.

When production of the T2 was authorized it was envisioned that 500 such vehicles with gasoline engines would be procured, as would be 150 of the vehicles powered by Diesel engines, with the intent being to distribute the vehicles to units utilizing like-type fuel (such as M10 units, whose vehicles were also powered by the GM 6046).

Three variants were planned, with the following nomenclature assigned:
- M31, built on the M3 chassis
- M31B1 built on the welded M3A3 chassis
- M31B2, built on the riveted M3A5 chassis

It was decided that production of 100 of the gasoline-powered versions, along with 8 of the Diesel

vehicles, was to happen between 1 December and 20 December 1942, with the production to be completed by 1 April 1943. In reality, only 10 of the gasoline-powered vehicles and 2 of the Diesel units were delivered by the end of 1942.

The official Ordnance history of the program states "The M31B2, based on the Medium Tank M3A2 (sic), riveted hull and G.M. 6046 Diesel engine was never built." This is consistent with the information reported in the Ordnance Report of Acceptances Tank-Automotive Material 1940-1945," which records only M31 and M31B1 vehicles, yet has the proper total. The same can be said for the totals shown in the "Recapitulation of Facility Expansions of Tracked & Wheeled Vehicles from 1940 to July 15, 1945."

These leads this author to believe that for reasons unknown, the M31B2 designation was abandoned, and that all Diesel-powered M31s were designated M31B1 regardless of hull fabrication technique, and the following text reflects that position.

Ultimately Baldwin, the sole builder of the recovery vehicle, produced 509 M31 recovery vehicles and

**Above:** *In this left front view of "Katrinka" the tapered tube representing a 37mm gun which has been welded to the front (formerly the rear) of the turret can be seen. The armor for the hull of M3A3 chassis upon which this vehicle was based had been fabricated with cutouts for side doors, but that feature had been eliminated by the time the tank was assembled. Accordingly, armor plates were welded over the door openings. Patton Museum*

296 M31B1 vehicles which utilized either the M3A3 or M3A5 Diesel chassis. Plans were in place to produce a further 226 vehicles, but the supply of Lee hulls was exhausted before the goal was met. Of the 296 M31B1 vehicles produced, 150 of these were new-built vehicles, while 146 were remanufactures and conversions of completed tanks. The final M3-based recovery vehicles were completed in December 1943, when 28 M31s were completed, along with a single M31B1 built on a remanufactured chassis. Of these 805 recovery vehicles, ultimately 671 were deployed overseas, with the 146 rebuild-based vehicles being supplied to the Soviet Union under Lend-Lease.

The M31 family of recovery vehicles were classified as Limited Standard on 7 November 1943.

It was March 1944, three months after production was completed, before an example of the production vehicle was shipped to Aberdeen Proving Ground for testing. The resultant report was extremely harsh, with most of the problems being related to design deficiency, rather than production defect.

Some of these deficiencies could be corrected by Field Modification, such as the lack of a shear pin and lack of published information on capacities; flimsy construction of the battery cover, allowing it to drop onto the battery terminals; tow bar breakages as a result of too small of a lunette; lack of holding device for steering levers, the result of which was the driver had to be in dangerous proximity of the winch line to hold the brakes during winching operations.

**Above:** *In this front view of "Katrinka" the dummy 75mm gun can be seen, along with the door upon which it was mounted. The dummy gun and door assembly replaced the gun mount and rotator found in this location on combat tanks. Mounted to the final drive housing is a towing pintle. Centered on the glacis is a grouser stowage box. Patton Museum*

**Above:** *This vehicle, which has Diesel engines and a riveted hull, should be classified as a M31B2, but no vehicles with that designation were officially logged as produced. Wearing registration number 4096599, this T2 was the second such vehicle delivered to the Armored Force Board in early 1943. Spare wheels are stored on the glacis, and tow cables are on the side of the upper hull. Storage boxes are on the front of the roof of the fighting compartment. It is shown here using its Gar Wood crane to lift the front end of a Medium Tank M3 with the aid of boom jacks on 5 December 1942. The side doors of this vehicle have been welded in place. US Army Transportation Museum.*

RA PD 347125

**Above:** *This heavily retouched photo, intended for publication in the vehicles' Technical Manual, also shows a T2 in M31B2 configuration. A 10,000-capacity Gar Wood Model 10-Y 5500 crane was mounted on the front of the turret, while a dummy gun barrel was attached to the rear of the turret. Inside the fighting compartment was a Gar Wood winch, rated at 60,000 pounds. Rock Island Arsenal Museum*

RA PD 4836

**Above:** *Another Tech Manual image of a Tank Recovery Vehicle T2 based on a Medium Tank M3A5 chassis illustrates the vehicle viewed from the left rear, showing details of the crane, the extra-tall storage boxes with spare track sections stored on their rears, and the sand shields. A tow bar and a crowbar are stored on the rear plate of the upper hull. The tube next to the lower part of the crane boom is the left boom jack; another boom jack was on the right side of the boom. A bracket for securing the foot of each boom jack is on each side of the angled plate above the rear vertical plate of the upper hull. National Archives*

RA PD 457

**Above:** *This comparison view of a production M31 clearly shows the differences between the rear plate of the gasoline-powered vehicles such as this one, and the Diesel-powered version shown previously. National Archives*

Problems which could not be fixed through a Modification Work Order, but rather that were inherent with the design included inadequate armament; turret brake inadequate and unable to hold turret; poor routing of winch cable; poor visibility from the winch controls; and inadequate suspension.

It was recognized that many of these troubles stemmed from the vehicle being a rushed expedient, but they were nevertheless problems. Thus, it is little surprise that OCM 21935 of 20 September 1945 declared the M31 and M31B1 obsolete recommending that one of each be retained at Aberdeen for historical purposes, with the remainder to be slated for disposal.

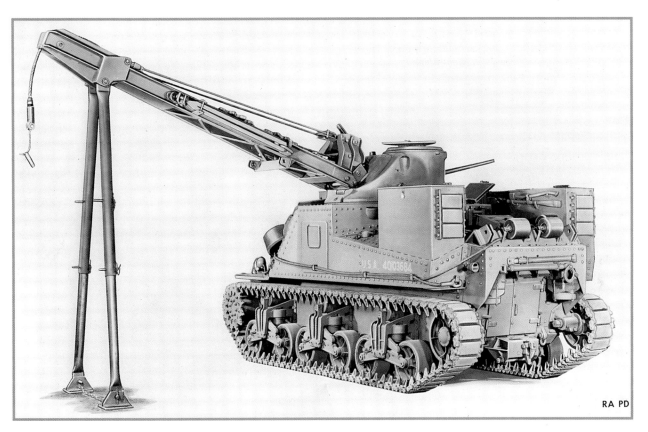

**Above:** *The turret and boom arrangement of the T2 was originally designed to pivot under load. It was later found that the turret race and traverse mechanism were inadequate to do so while under moderate load, although the turret could be rotated under no load or light load conditions. For lifting the heaviest loads, it was necessary to support the load with boom jacks, as shown here. National Archives*

# Leaflet – the Canal Defense Lights

During WWII, night fighting by armor was in its infancy. The British devised a scheme whereby tanks would be equipped with narrow-beam, high-intensity searchlight which could be used to both illuminate targets and to dazzle and blind enemy troops.

The development of this weapon, which was first mounted on a Matilda tank, was given the code name "Canal Defense Light," today often shortened to CDL. However, such an installation left the tank without its main armament. For that reason, the decision was made to mount the special Canal Defense Light turret on the M3 medium tank chassis, which while losing the 37mm turret in the process, nevertheless retained the sponson-mounted 75mm main gun. Ammunition

stowage for the 75mm gun on CDL tanks was increased to 77 rounds.

The specially designed turret housing the light on the Matilda was designated the Type A turret. The Type A turret type was later transferred to the M3 chassis. Later, those turrets were rebuilt, with the access hatch being welded up, spall deflectors added inside of the vents and a dummy gun being installed. At that time they were redesignated Type D turrets.

Inside the turret was a 13-million candlepower carbon arc lamp. A separate compartment in the turret housed the operator, who also controlled the turret-mounted 7.92mm Besa machine gun. The light was exposed through a 2-3/8 inch wide by 24-inch tall slit, with an internally mounted shutter made of armor plate. The shutter could be operated either manually, or electrically, in the latter case being selectable between two rates of

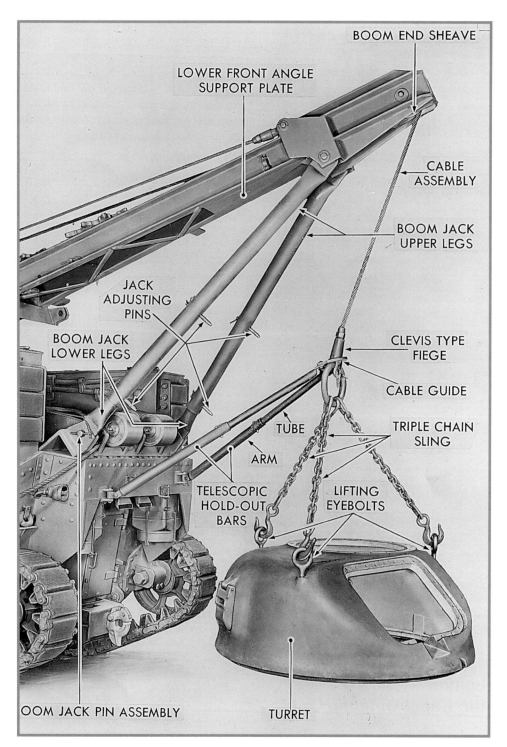

BOOM END SHEAVE

LOWER FRONT ANGLE
SUPPORT PLATE

CABLE
ASSEMBLY

BOOM JACK
UPPER LEGS

JACK
ADJUSTING
PINS

CLEVIS TYPE
FIEGE

BOOM JACK
LOWER LEGS

CABLE GUIDE

TUBE

TRIPLE CHAIN
SLING

ARM

TELESCOPIC
HOLD-OUT
BARS

LIFTING
EYEBOLTS

OOM JACK PIN ASSEMBLY

TURRET

**Left:** *When supporting a heavy load to the rear of the vehicle while traveling, boom jacks were again used, this time being supported by the rear deck of the vehicle. Telescopic hold out bars prevented the suspended load from swinging into the rear of the tank. National Archives*

speed, the intent being to dazzle enemy troops through the flickering high intensity light. Colored filters were provided for the lights, which could be use to mask the distance to the tank.

British troops were trained in the use of the CDL tanks primarily at Lowther Castle, although a smaller school was also operated briefly at Rafah, Egypt. A portion of the British CDL conversions were also performed in Egypt. The tanks converted in Egypt came from British supplies there, while those converted in England were a mix of turned in Canadian tanks and new tanks arriving from the US. Photographic evidence indicates at least some of the British M3 CDL tanks were converted from General Lees, and this author suggests that

given the British preference for the Grant-type turret, most CDLs were probably Lee-based.

The first large scale demonstration of the CDL occurred at Lowther Castle on 5 May 1942, with Viscount Alan Brooke and Earl Louis Mountbatten attending.

In September 1942 the British demonstrated their new secret weapon to a group of senior US officers, including Generals Eisenhower, Clark, and Barnes, sparking immediate interest on their part. On 24 September Brigadier General John Darlquist, Deputy Chief of Staff, approached General Weeks of The War Office concerning the possibility of adopting the British CDL for use by

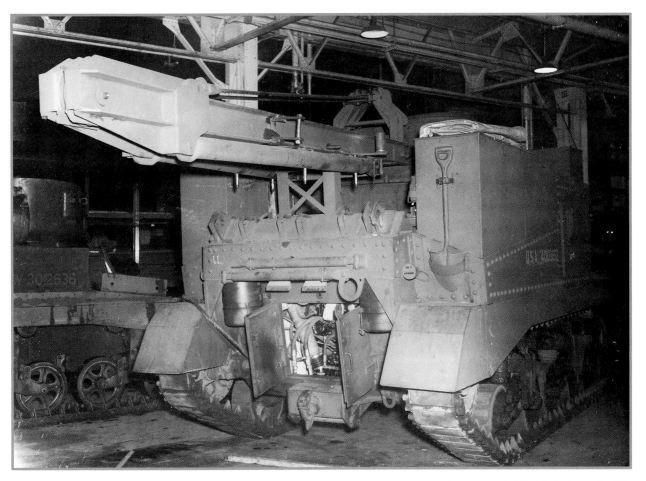

**Above:** *Photographed at the Chester Tank Depot, T2 registration number 40103652, likely the first M3-based retriever, is shown. Once standardized, the M3 to retriever conversions were designated M31. Later production vehicles had three spare track links stowed on the rear vertical surface of the extra-height tool boxes. National Archives*

the US Army, as well as to produce the equipment in the US. In order to do so, complete drawings and specifications would need to be supplied by the British, along with one or more complete sets of equipment and a technical liaison.

By 22 November 1942 negotiations had been completed for six complete sets of CDL equipment along with accessories and auxiliary equipment to be shipped to the United States. The power take off unit, necessary to drive the generator which provided the current for the carbon arc, was in short supply, and only two of those were shipped with the notation that "Additional power take-off units will have to be made in the United States." The shipment was comprised of approximately 20 boxes, with a total weight of 24 tons and occupying 1,554 cubic feet. Three sets of the equipment were to be shipped by the first available fast boat, the remaining equipment on the next available boat. The shipment was split as a precaution against loss. Technical specifications and plans were to be sent the same way, or by air.

The British placed some conditions on this transfer of equipment and knowledge, including stipulating that: "That the equipment shall not be used in action by United States Forces in the first instance

without prior reference to and agreement by the War Office.

"That the manufacture of any C.D.L. equipment in the United States shall be undertaken by different firms in order to maintain secrecy, the various components being finally assembled under Military supervision, as is the case at the British C.D.L. school."

On 4 March the request was modified to include ten complete sets of CDL equipment (less power take offs), 3 glass matrices to be used for the production of the mirrors in the United States, 200 flat reflectors, 200 mirrors, 500,000 sets of carbons and 10 spare lamps. Just over a week later the request for carbons was dropped to 300,000 sets. The conversion of the first six tanks to CDL configuration in the United States was done at Aberdeen Proving Ground, inside of a specially erected enclosure in the Engineering Building. Five of these vehicles were shipped to the Special Training Group, Fort Knox upon completion, for use as training articles pending the completion of US production units. The sixth was dismantled and its subassemblies used as examples for manufacturers of the components.

**Above:** *The supports for the three spare road wheels can be seen in this view of 40103652. The M31s were fitted with sand shields above the tracks which were similar in design to those that Baldwin installed on British Grant tanks. National Archives*

**Left:** *The documents originally accompanying this photo refer to the vehicle as a "T2," despite the fact that it was among the last of the vehicles produced. The vehicle, serial number 597, was photographed at Aberdeen Proving Ground on 28 December 1943. Faintly visible ahead of the sealed side door is evidence that prior to conversion to a recovery vehicle it featured functioning doors. National Archives via Joe DeMarco.*

Work toward series production of the vehicles in the US began in March 1943 when representatives of the Rochester Ordnance District met with American Locomotive Company to discuss their involvement in the project, which consisted of remanufacturing the chassis. For security purposes, the vehicle was designated the "Shop Tractor, T10." On 6 March 1943 Research and Development Order 799 was issued for the design and engineering work on two of the T10 vehicles, at a cost of $32,000.00. In late March, M3 serial

number 2289 was released to American Locomotive for conversion. On 17 July 1943, order 799 was superseded by R&D Order 199-1, with a value of $44,260.00.

Per the agreement with the British, manufacture of the components was spread to a diverse array of companies.

The turret, which was designated the "S" turret, was produced by the Pressed Steel Car Company,

**Right:** *From this angle a number of the updates made to 597 during its conversion to recovery vehicle configuration are visible. Among them are the disc type idler wheel and the British-style sand shields. With the exception of but two, all T2s built after this one were subsequently converted to M33 prime movers. National Archives via Joe DeMarco.*

**Above:** *T2 597 exhibits one of the shortcomings of this series of recovery vehicles while coupled to a composite hull M4. The boom extending over the glacis of the tank provides ample opportunity to collide with either the gun of the Sherman or the glacis of the tank, including the lights and guards, any of which would cause damage. To combat this, many crews operated the vehicle with the boom in an elevated position. National Archives*

Chicago. Purchase Order T-6925 dated 23 February 1943 was issued for the engineering and production of two pilot turrets. On 23 March purchase order T-7541 was issued for "485 Turrets, Coast Defense (S Turrets)." This was amended on 1 May to include four additional turrets for training purposes, to be sent to the Special Training Group, Fort Knox.

Consistent with US practice, whereby the Corps of Engineers contracted for searchlights, the Corps ordered the 24" H.C.D. lamps, the parabola-ellipse mirrors, flat reflectors and switchboards. For the lamps, production order T-7867 was issued to the

Mole-Richardson Company of Hollywood, California, a firm whose primary business was and is the production of stage lighting equipment.

In this area, rather than duplicating the British components, the decision was made to adapt Corps of Engineers beach lights for use in the CDL. The beach lights were already in production at Mole-Richardson, and were a more modern design than that which the British had used, further the major components were not only already in production, but also in the military logistics chain. The mirrors, one of the more challenging items to produce, were originally purchased from England

**Above:** *The problem is clearly illustrated in this 22 January 1944 photo taken at Aberdeen Proving Ground. The potential for damage to boom, tow bar, tow lugs and lights exists even with the towed tank's turret traversed to the rear. National Archives*

**Above:** *The crew of this T2 has elevated the boom to prevent it from colliding with captured German StuG III in tow behind the vehicle. An improvised rack made of steel rods on the rear of the upper hull of the M31 is holding a row of U.S. five-gallon liquid containers. Due to the inadequacies of the British style turret hatch with machine gun mount, the crew of this vehicle has added a ring mount for a .50-caliber antiaircraft machine gun (not mounted) above the vehicle. Army Engineer School History Office.*

*Right: The British developed the high-intensity, carbon-arc Canal Defense Light (CDL) as a means of illuminating battlefields at night. A number of Medium Tanks M3 and M3A1 were converted to CDL tanks: some 195 by the British, and 497 by the Americans.*
*Patton Museum*

**Above:** *A British Grant CDL nicknamed GIRAFFE, census number T-39481, is viewed from the left rear. The large, round door on the side of the turret for the light operator/machine gunner, a feature of the early British CDL turret, has been removed and a form-fitting armor plate has been welded over the opening. On the storage box on the left rear of the hull is the insignia of the 79th Armoured Division.*
*Warehouse Publications*

**Left:** *This M3 CDL was converted by the British, and the turret is the early style, with a round vision port above the machine gun on the left front. Between the 7.92mm Besa machine gun and the dummy gun on the right front of the turret is a vertical slot, the aperture for the CDL. David Fletcher*

**Above:** *The British tanks were equipped with what was known as the 'Type D' turret. The Type D featured 60mm armor on the turret walls, and were the result of rebuilding Type A CDL turrets, originally installed on Matildas, to incorporate additional spall protection inside the turret as well as welding the access hatch shut. At the same time, the dummy gun was installed. David Fletcher*

**Right:** *The same Canal Defense Light, now with textured camouflage. Although rarely used, the concept behind the CDL was proven, although weather and dust conditions could marginalize the effectiveness of the Top Secret weapon. David Fletcher*

**Above:** *An American CDL based on a Medium Tank M3A1 chassis exhibits a common feature of the U.S. version of this vehicle: a supplemental armor shield on the 75mm gun barrel. The vertical aperture of the searchlight is on the center front of the turret. Pressed Steel Car Company manufactured the American turrets, which were designated the "S" or so-called coast-defense turret. The American machine-gun mount on the left front of the turret was a ball design. Sealant material has been applied to various areas of the vehicle to prepare it for shipping or storage. The tracks are the T48, with rubber blocks with chevron grousers. Patton Museum*

**Above:** *Another U.S. Army CDL is based on a late-production, riveted-hull Medium Tank M3. A good view of the right side of the CDL turret is offered. The bogies are the late style, with track-support rollers on trailing arms. The vehicle also has the supplemental gun shield, driver's periscope; and D47366 "economy," or solid, sprockets. Note the tape over the searchlight slot and the ball mount for the machine gun on the turret, and on the side door and pistol port. Patton Museum*

on reverse Lend-Lease, until such time as production could be undertaken by the War Department Searchlight Mirror Plant, Mariemont, Ohio. The metal reflectors were produced by the Crouse-Hinds Company from rolled Alclad, an aluminum alloy covered with pure aluminum in order to produce high reflectivity.

The cradle was made by American Car and Foundry in Berwick, PA, through purchase order T-7550. The conversion of the tanks was done by American Locomotive Company under purchase order T-7551. As part of the conversion, the tanks were fitted with auxiliary armored shields for the gun mounts, and the tanks were refitted with heavy duty Sherman suspension units with the trailing return rollers.

Because of delays, it was not possible to test the design until the after the first two production units were complete. Per the Tank Automotive Command, the test and pilot vehicles were to be serially numbered as production vehicles 496 and 497.

The British had recommended that due to the Top Secret nature of the project that final assembly take place at a government installation. The Army obliged, tasking Rock Island Arsenal with the final production of the vehicles. This was accomplished via a 13 May 1943 letter from Brigadier General John K. Christmas to the Commanding General at Rock Island.

Both the British and the US governments code named the training programs involving the Canal Defense Lights "Project Cassock." As mentioned, the British training was at Lowther Castle and Rafah, Egypt, while the initial US training took place under very tight security in a remote area of Fort Knox, Kentucky before moving to Camp Bouse in the California-Arizona Maneuver Area (formerly known as the Desert Training Center).

Initially, it was planned that six medium tank battalions would receive the Cassock training, the 701st, 736th, 740th, 748th, 749th and 750th. Ultimately, the 749th and 750th were replaced by

**Above:** *A corporal is sitting on the roof of a U.S. Medium Tank M3A1 CDL. To disguise the true purpose of these vehicles, the U.S. Army referred to them as Leaflet Tanks and also as Shop Tractor T10. Steve Zaloga*

**Left:** *Two soldiers with horns are having a jam session on a U.S. Medium Tank M3A1 CDL. A tarp is draped over the turret, secured in place by a continuous rubber-band half-track track. Another half-track track is lying on the engine deck. The U.S. CDLs saw little use in combat, the main example being during the Rhine River crossings in early 1945. Warehouse Publications*

**Left:** *Five Grant CDLs display the wedge-shape beam of light each were capable of emiting. In addition to pure illumination, it was intended that the high intensity light would blind and disorient enemy troops. David Fletcher*

the 738th and 739th. The training was undertaken with strict security, with the assigned troops restricted from all outside contact for the first two months of training, thereafter for some time they could only leave post in groups, five men per group at first, later reduced to pairs. The intent was that no man was ever to be left alone.

By late June 1943, Colonel Thompson, commander of the Special Training Group, noted that only five tanks were on hand, with two pilot tanks equipped with American-made CDL equipment about July 7 for test and training purposes.

Ten of the T10 Shop Tractors, less turrets, were expected to arrive at Fort Knox on or about 15 July, 1943 where the Special Training Group would install the British training turrets. These may have been the ten turrets requested on 4 March.

Secrecy of the operation was so tight that no one could be transferred out, attend another service school, or even be discharged. In the event of a medical condition which would normally require discharge, the man had to be retained in service. As their operational training completed at Fort Knox, the units were transferred to Camp Bouse, Arizona for tactical training, beginning to arrive there in August 1943.

Ultimately, the 701st, 736th and 748th Medium Tank Battalions (Special) were deployed to Europe, first to Wales, adjacent to the British CDL units, and in August 1944 they were moved to the Avranches area. In time, both the US and British CDL units turned in their special tanks, dubbed 'Gizmos' by the troops. The 738th and 739th became mine exploder units and the 740th a standard tank unit while still in Britain.

**Right:** *The Grant CDL now faces the lights of the four other CDLs shown earlier. A shutter mechanism in the turret allowed the lights to be flashed rapidly, further disorienting enemy troops. David Fletcher*

**Right:** *Four Grant CDLs, each with a 13-million candlepower carbon arc lamp, demonstrate their battlefield illuminating power. David Fletcher*

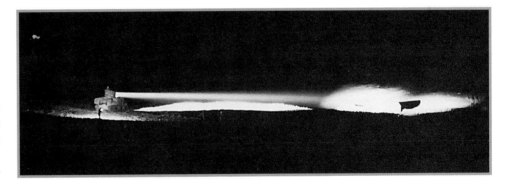

**Right:** *A Grant CDL illuminates a distant barn. The slot through which the light is emitted is very slim, and when combined with the intensity of the light, even without using the flicker, made strategists feel that the crew was safe from incoming small arms fire. David Fletcher*

However, in preparation for crossing the Rhine, 64 of the American CDL tanks were brought to the front. They were used to protect bridges. The vehicles were sufficiently effective that 60 of the vehicles and their crews were returned to the US in preparation for redeployment to the Pacific, the Tenth Army requesting 18-20 of the vehicles for use on Okinawa. However, those tanks did not arrive until the fighting was over on that island.

The 11th and 42nd RTR were initially deployed, as Matilda CDL units, to Egypt. As noted previously, both units were converted to Grant-based CDLs while in Egypt, with some of the vehicle conversions being performed in country.

Two British CDL units, the 11th and 49th RTR, moved onto the continent and were located near the Carpiquet airfield outside Caen until they were converted to other duties in October, while their 200 CDL tanks were shipped back to Lowther Castle. Some of the 11th's men were called back to CDL duty and along with 28 of the vehicles were brought forward to the Rhine in March 1945, albeit at that time forming the B Squadron of the 49th Armoured Personnel Carrier Regiment. Their last combat use appears to be in crossing the Elbe River near Lauenburg.

Similarly, the British sent 36 CDLs to India with the 43rd RTR, the last British unit trained with the

**Above:** *Because of delays in production of the High Speed Tractor M6, the Army contracted with the Chester Tank Depot, in Chester, Pennsylvania, to convert a number of Tank Recovery Vehicles M31 to Prime Movers M33. This stopgap measure was accomplished by removing the turret and crane. Seen here from above is a Prime Mover M33, registration number 40704051. A ring mount for a .50-caliber antiaircraft machine gun was installed on top of the former 75mm gun sponson. A fake 75mm gun was mounted on a door on the front of that sponson. A heavy-duty bracket for a tow pintle was on the final-drive assembly. Grousers are piled up on the roof above the driver's station. Visible inside the opening where the turret was removed are a winch and cabinets and drawers for tools and spare parts. Patton Museum*

vehicle. They arrived in Bombay on 2 August 1945, only two weeks before the war ended.

## M33 Prime Mover

As noted earlier in this chapter, the T2/M31 had some serious deficiencies as an armored recovery vehicle. Concurrently, production of the M6 High Speed Tractor was lagging badly behind. As the M32 recovery vehicle became increasingly available, the Chester Tank Depot began converting 109 M31s, the bulk of the final three month's production, into M33 Prime Movers. This work began in December 1943, just as M31 production was winding down, and continued through February 1944. Sixty of the conversions

were completed in December 1943.

These vehicles were used in pairs to move the 240mm Howitzer. One M33 towed the gun, while another towed the gun carriage. The majority of the vehicles were assigned to the 4th Service Command, although some went to Italy, and then on to the European Theater.

The conversion involved removing the turret and boom, and adding an air compressor to supply the service brakes on the artillery pieces. A commander's hatch ring with machine gun mount, similar to the D51050 mount used on some Shermans, was installed above the former 75mm sponson.

**Right:** *Carriers for three spare bogie wheels were on the glacis of the Prime Mover M33. This example has the late-production bogie assemblies and T62 steel tracks, with curved chevron grouser and three large rivets. Above the rear of the vehicle is what appears to be a crane, possibly on an adjacent vehicle that is out of view. Patton Museum*

**Above:** *A Prime Mover M33, registration number 40104071, is towing a 240mm Howitzer M1 gun barrel across rough terrain. The side door is welded shut, and a .50-caliber machine gun is installed on the ring mount over the former 75mm gun sponson. The tops of the two storage boxes on the right rear sponson formed almost a straight line with the top of the fighting-compartment roof. National Archives*

## Grant ARV Mk. I

Although the British designated the T2 recovery vehicles that they received through in-Theater transfers as "Grant ARV Mk II," in fact they were all converted in the US from M3 Lee tanks. There was in fact only one Grant-based ARV, and that was the solitary Grant ARV Mk. I, T-23673. After trials, it was ultimately decided that a recovery vehicle based on the lower profile Churchill tank was preferred, and no further Grant ARV MK Is were produced.

## Australian ARV

The Australian Directorate of Armoured Fighting Vehicle Production was compelled to create an armored recovery vehicle to support its rapidly growing tank force. The pilot vehicle, which was initially designated Tank, Tank Recovery, was based on a M3 Grant, which was stripped of its armament, although the turret itself was retained. A hinged observation flap covered the former location of the mantlet, and a hinged door replaced the 75mm mount in the sponson.

**Above:** As Grant tanks became redundant following the introduction of the Sherman tank, the British considered converting quantities of their Grants to armored recovery vehicles (ARVs). The pilot ARV I, converted from Baldwin-built T-23673, is displayed here, featured a detachable jib crane with a chain hoist, which could be installed on the front of the vehicle. Mounts for the feet of the boom have been welded to the fronts of the final drives. The turret was removed, and provisions for twin Bren machine guns were installed in the opening. The 75mm gun was removed and its opening in the sponson plated over. Note the sheave for the boom to the front of the former gun sponson. *Patton Museum*

**Above:** The Grant ARV I, T-23673, is viewed from the right side. Storage boxes were mounted on the right fender. Pioneer tools are stored on the side of the sponson, and a tow cable is secured to the side of the upper hull. *Patton Museum*

**Above:** *On the rears of the sponsons of the Grant ARV I were what appear to be boxes for spare track links, although on close inspection, what appear to be track end connectors inside the boxes actually aren't. A tow bar is stored on the side of the sponson. Patton Museum*

The spacious fighting compartment, bereft of the usual combat equipment, became the home of massive 28,000-pound capacity winch, which was powered by its own Canadian Mercury V-8 engine. The 120-foot 1-inch wire rope of winch exited the vehicle through the bottom of the vehicle passing around a roller before extending to the rear of the vehicle. A rear ground anchor was fabricated which was raised and lowered by manually operated winch.

Following initial testing, the pilot was sent for troop trials with the 1st Australian Armoured Division. Following trials, the vehicle, with some modification, was placed into production, with an initial order for 16 conversions. It was specified that these conversions would be performed on M3 Lee tanks, allowing the nation to retain the preferred Grant types as combat vehicles.

The production vehicles, designated Armoured Recovery Vehicle (Aust.) No. 2, differed from the pilot in several details. Chief of these was the inclusion of an auxiliary winch driven from the main drive shaft. This was used to raise and lower the ground anchor rather than the manual winch of the pilot. The cable for this winch ran through the flap in the turret.

Large tool boxes containing recovery and repair gear were mounted on the engine deck.

**Above:** *The arrangement of the hatch, doors, and Bren machine gun mount on the roof of the Grant ARV I is depicted. The sheave assembly for the boom is on the right fender. The boom was not included on this vehicle. Patton Museum*

Six production vehicles were completed in August, at which time the decision was made to delete the Mercury engine, and instead power the main winch via a power take off from the main tank engine. This change was made in September with the 7th production vehicle. The improved vehicle was designated the Armoured Recovery Vehicle (Aust.) No. 3, and the total order was increased to 24.

One vehicle was sent to New Guinea for trials in jungle warfare, where it did not perform well. In 1946 all of these vehicles were declared obsolete, although remarkably in 1950 a M3A5 was converted to a Beach Recovery Vehicle. This vehicle served until 1970, when it was retired to a museum.

**Above:** *Following a trial conversion of a Grant, the Australian Army converted 24 of its Lee tanks to armored recovery vehicles. The first production model of this vehicle was designated Armoured Recovery Vehicle (Aust.) No. 2. The armaments were removed, and a winch powered by a Ford Mercury V-8 engine through a gearbox was installed inside the fighting compartment. A rear spade also was mounted. This example was ARV (Aust.) No. 2 registration number 25959. Patton Museum*

**Above:** *As seen in a photo of number 25959, on the Australian Lee ARVs, an armored door with two hinges on the inboard side was installed on the front of the former 75mm gun sponson. A grouser box was under the driver's vision port. The purpose of the drum-shaped extension on the top of the former gun sponson is not clear, although in some photos of this vehicle, a tow cable may be seen coiled up inside the drum. Patton Museum*

**Above:** *As seen on Australian ARV registration number 25959, storage boxes lined the sides of the engine deck, and a tailgate with four hinges on the bottom spanned the space between the boxes. The storage boxes had hinged lids on top and hinged doors on the rears. Note the port for the spade-operating cable to the upper side of the winch operator's vision port on the turret. Patton Museum*

**Above:** *Australian ARV 25959 is viewed from the left side. On the roof next to the turret is the muffler and tail pipe for the Ford Mercury V-8 winch motor. The original side door has been replaced with a plain piece of armor with no pistol port. On the top center of the spade, the sheave for the spade-operating cable is in view. Patton Museum*

**Above:** *A final photo of ARV (Aust.) No. 2, registration number 25959, shows the vehicle from the front. Plugs have been tack-welded into the ports for the two bow machine guns. The muffler for the winch motor is visible on the roof next to the turret. Patton Museum*

**Above:** *The vehicle shown here was an Armoured Recovery Vehicle (Aust.) No. 3, which varied from the No. 2 model by deleting the separate engine for the winch and instead powering the winch by a power take off. The winch-motor muffler and tailpipe on the left side of the fighting-compartment roof, as seen on the No. 2 vehicles, were thus deleted. The spade is secured in the travel position. Above the spade is a frame holding winch rollers, used for guiding the winch cable when raising and lowering the spade. The turret was fixed in a rear-facing configuration, and the former gun port was equipped with a hinged armor flap and was used as a vision port by the winch operator. Patton Museum*

# Chapter 9
# North American Use

With every indication showing that war was inevitable, the US Army had begun a major expansion as noted earlier in this volume. Part of this expansion included the creation of an experimental Armored Force on 10 July 1940, and concurrently, the activation of the 1st and 2nd Armored Divisions.

From 1920 to 10 July 1940, in the US Army "tanks" had been the property of infantry. Cavalry, who desired tanks, but were forbidden from having such vehicles by the National Defense Act, had "combat cars" – which looked just like tanks. The 7th Cavalry Brigade (Mechanized), Colonel Adna R. Chaffee, Jr commanding, which was organized at Fort Knox in the 1930s, became the prototype combined arms mechanized force. Ultimately it included two cavalry regiments, an artillery battalion and even observation aircraft and an attached infantry regiment.

The unit consistently demonstrated its effectiveness in small-scale maneuvers, to the extent that when the 1940 Louisiana Maneuvers were planned, three of the four field armies wanted the 7th Cavalry assigned to them. Ultimately, the 7th was assigned to the Third Army, Lt. General Stanley Embick commanding. Embick also got the Infantry's Provisional Tank Brigade, Brigadier General Bruce Magruder commanding, allowing the two units to be merged, creating the Army's first provisional mechanized division.

The overwhelming success of this unit is what led Generals Chaffee, Magruder, Patton and Brigadier General Frank Andrews to appeal directly to General George C. Marshall to create the Armored Force, which he placed under the command of General Chaffee.

In order to prevent a continuation of old inter-

**Above:** *Infantrymen in a trench, manning a Browning M1919 .30-caliber machine gun, watch as a Medium Tank M2 prepares to cross the trench during field maneuvers at Fort Benning, Georgia, in February 1940. National Archives*

**Above:** *A Medium Tank M2A1 with the late-type vision ports with armored covers, numbered A7 on the turret, is driving onto a treadway bridge at Fort Benning, Georgia, during a test of the bridge's ability to support the tank sometime in 1940. The A7 vehicle code also is painted on the rear of the turret, and an Army Air Corps-style recognition insignia, likely consisting of a white star with a blue circle in the center, over a red circle, is on the rear of the fighting compartment. National Archives*

**Above:** *A crewman is aiming a Browning M1919 .30-caliber machine gun on a pintle mount on the right side of the turret of a Medium Tank M2 from the 67th Infantry Regiment during Third Army maneuvers in 1940. The tank is registration number W-30446, and it has a tactical symbol of a triangle with a number 5 on it on the glacis and on the side of the upper hull. The driver is visible through his side vision port. A good view is available of the ribbed final-drive gear housings. National Archives*

**Above:** *A column of six Medium Tanks M2 from the 67th Infantry Regiment is on a road march during Third Army maneuvers in 1940. The lead tank is registration number W-30458; it bears a tactical sign of a number 1 inside a circle. Note the chrome-plated sirens on these vehicles, above and inboard of the right headlights. Dust covers are installed over the barrels of the sponson and bow .30-caliber machine guns. National Archives*

**Above:** *The same column of M2s shown in the preceding photo, except with only five in view, is seen from the other side of the road, with the tank marked number 1 still to the front. On the tank to the front, note that the left hatch door on the roof of the fighting compartment is hinged on the rear, while the right door has hinges on the front.*

**Above:** *The last in the series of photos of Medium Tanks M2 from the 67th Infantry Regiment during maneuvers of the Third Army in 1940 includes this view of registration number W-30458 climbing a road embankment. The number 1 on a circle is visible on the side door. Attached to the armor above that door is a small placard with the crossed-rifles symbol of the infantry. National Archives*

**Above:** *Medium Tank M2 W-30457 has paused during the crossing of a creek on a pontoon raft operated by the 16th Engineers during 1st Armored Division maneuvers in March 1941. Note the crewman looking out of the pistol port on the rear of the turret. National Archives*

**Above:** *On very close inspection, several of the crewmen of this Medium Tank M2 are identical to ones in and on the tank in the preceding photo. Before crossing this bridge, the tank had been operating in muddy ground, as the front end is heavily covered in muck. National Archives*

**Above:** *The entire pontoon raft ferrying a Medium Tank M2 as depicted in the preceding two photos is in view during a creek crossing in 1st Armored Division maneuvers in March 1941. The raft consisted of a truss-type treadway-bridge section resting on shallow-draft boats equipped with outboard motors. Crewmen on the boats also are using long oars to maneuver the raft. National Archives*

**Above:** *During the annual visit of the First Class of the United States Military Academy to Aberdeen Proving Ground, on 15 May 1941, cadets are riding over a test course in a Medium Tank M2A1, registration number W-30816. Clear views are available of the interior of the side door and the front of the machine-gun mount on the left rear sponson.  National Archives*

**Above:** *A Medium Tank M2A1 is in the front of a column of three tanks at Aberdeen Proving Ground on 16 May 1941. The second tank is an M2A1 with the 37mm gun removed and a cover installed over the opening for the gun in the front of the turret. The third vehicle is a Medium Tank M2. National Archives*

**Above:** *Visiting USMA cadets are enjoying a check-out ride in a Medium Tank M2A1, evidently the same tank seen in the preceding photo with a cover over the gun port on the turret. This tank is registration number W-30445. No machine gun muzzles are present in the two ports near the lower corners of the glacis. National Archives*

branch politics, Chaffee placed General Magruder (Infantry) in command of the 1st Armored Division, which been created around the 1st Armored Brigade (itself formerly known as the 7th Cavalry Brigade). Major General Charles Scott (Cavalry) was initially placed in command of the 2d Armored Division, which included the 2d Armored Brigade (the Infantry's old Provisional Tank Brigade). He was succeeded by Brigadier General George Patton in December 1940.

From the outset, it was planned that there would be additional maneuvers in Louisiana in 1941.

The 1940 maneuvers were considerably hampered by equipment shortages, with only 18 medium tanks (M2) available, along with 400 light tanks. The 1941 maneuvers were a little better equipped, with the M3 becoming available, albeit in limited numbers. Thus, in some cases the M3 light tank was used as a substitute, with large "Ms" painted on their sides to designate them as faux medium tanks.

By September 1941, the government had leased or secured trespass rights to over 30,000 square miles of land extending from Shreveport south to Lake Charles and from Jasper, Texas, to the Mississippi River. On this mass of land there

would initially be pitted Lieutenant General Ben Lear's 130,000-man "Red" Second Army north of the Red River against Lieutenant General Walter Krueger's 270,000-man "Blue" Third Army north of Lake Charles. While it may seem that there was wide disparity in the armies, Lear had Magruder's and Patton's armored divisions.

Five days later, and the armies clashed again, now with Headquarters, I Armored Corps, and Patton's 2nd Armored Division assigned to the Blue Army.

As expansive as the 1941 Louisiana Maneuvers were, they were not the only such training exercises carried out. In October and November 1941 additional maneuvers were carried out on a 9,375 square mile parcel formed by a rough triangle defined by Charlotte, North Carolina, on the northwest; Fayetteville, North Carolina, on the east; and Columbia, South Carolina, on the south. Clashing in the Carolinas would be two more blue and red armies, with the 195,000-man "Blue" First Army under command of Lt. General Hugh Drum, pitted against the motorized and armored, but smaller at 100,000-man "Red" Army (IV Corps) under command of Major General Oscar W. Griswold.

The next major maneuvers were the Tennessee Maneuvers, which began on 2 June 1941. These

**Above:** *A trainload of M3A4 medium tanks has just arrived in Louisiana for Third Army training maneuvers on 28 August 1942. Markings for vehicle 17 of Company D, 68th Armored Regiment, are on the final-drive assembly. Two ventilators are present on the roof of the fighting compartment, and the trademark of the Continental Foundry and Machine Company, East Chicago, Indiana, a capital H inside a capital C, is on the cupola. National Archives*

**Above:** *Troops from the 27th Division, New York National Guard, are clambering over and investigating medium tanks after a mock battle during Second Army maneuvers in Louisiana on 9 September 1941. The closest vehicle is a Medium Tank M2A1, with "E-1" and the insigina of the 1st Armored Division on the glacis. The next tank also seems to be an M2A1, based on what little is visible of the vertical side of its turret. Next are another M2A1, followed by a Medium Tank M2, with its angled turret plates. National Archives*

**Above:** *A Medium Tank M2A1 rolls past the Castor, Louisiana train station during a mock attack on a neighborhood during the Third Army maneuvers in northwestern Louisiana on 11 September 1941. As a modification, a raised rack has been positioned over the engine deck, to hold a number of five-gallon liquid containers. Note the bullet deflector to the rear of the upper hull. National Archives*

**Above:** The code "F-2" is painted on the side of the turret of a Medium Tank M2A1 from the 2nd Armored Division, advancing from a protective smokescreen during maneuvers in October 1941. Another M2A1 is to the right side of the photo. Both of the tank crewmen are wearing a prewar style of tanker's helmet.  National Archives

**Above:** Soldiers and local civilians watch as a Medium Tank M3 numbered D-6, of Company D, 69th Armored Regiment, 1st Armored Division, is being driven down ramps from a flatcar on 2 November 1941, during preparations for the Carolina Maneuvers held during that month. Although the location of the photo was not identified, the "Victoria Cotton Mill" sign on the water tower in the right background was a clue to establishing the location as Rock Hill, South Carolina. Half-tracks are loaded on the flatcars to the right. National Archives

**Above:** *The M3 numbered D-6 from the 69th Armored Regiment, 1st Armored Division, is being driven away from the railyard as another M3, numbered D-7, is being driven from the flatcar at Rock Hill, South Carolina, on 2 November 1941. The insignia of the 1st Armored Division is on the glacis of each tank. National Archives*

**Above:** *At least 15 Medium Tanks M3 are being transported on flatcars during a deployment of the 69th Armored Regiment, 1st Armored Division, to the Carolina Maneuvers in November 1941. Conducted on the eve of the United States' entry into World War II, these were a series of wargames to increase the readiness and proficiency of the U.S. Army and the Army Air Corps. The lead tank has "C-16," indicating the 16th vehicle of Company C, painted on the front, over the insignia of the 1st Armored Division. Two five-gallon liquid containers are stored on the right side of the engine deck of this vehicle. National Archives*

**Above:** *In a view taken at the same time and location as the preceding photo, the nearest M3 is marked "1-HQ-1" next to the driver's vision port. National Archives*

**Above:** *A Medium Tank M3, registration number W-301043, fords a creek outside of Winnsboro, South Carolina, during the Carolina Maneuvers in November 1941. The number 6 is painted on the rear of the right sponson, and equipment is tied down on top of the engine deck. Note the light-colored rectangles painted at intervals on the bottom of the turret. National Archives*

**Above:** *Medium Tanks M3 from Company C, 69th Armored Regiment, 1st Armored Division, are on a road march outside of Rock Hill, South Carolina, during the Carolina Maneuvers, on 3 November 1941. The nearest vehicle is marked "C-11" on the front of the hull. Three more M3s are visible behind the first tank. National Archives*

**Above:** *During maneuvers at Fort Benning, Georgia, on 18 December 1941, a Medium Tank M3 is crossing a treadway pontoon bridge as other M3s prepare to cross the bride to the rear. These tanks have identification stars on the glacises: a white star with two points on top, on a red circle, with a blue circle at the center. The guidon on the lead tank's left mudguard is not clearly legible, but it seems to have the number 67th, which makes it likely that this tank was assigned to the 67th Armored Regiment, part of the 2nd Armored Division, which was based at that time at Fort Benning. National Archives*

**Above:** *During the First Army's Carolina Maneuvers, on 20 November 1941, the weight of a Medium Tank M3 has caused the plank surface of a bridge to collapse, leaving the tank incapacitated. The site was at Monroe, North Carolina. National Archives*

**Above:** *A cargo truck has parked alongside the incapacitated M3 on the bridge at Monroe, North Carolina, while a soldier crouching to the left assesses the situation. National Archives*

**Above:** *The same M3 is viewed from the rear on the bridge. Freeing the tank from its predicament would likely entail the services of a tank recovery vehicle or heavy wrecker; it would also entail repairs to the bridge, courtesy of the U.S. Government. National Archives*

maneuvers, originally planned to span nine counties, ultimately expanded into 21 counties in Middle Tennessee. One reason this area was chosen was because of the similarity of the train to that found in Belgium, France and Germany. The Tennessee Maneuvers employed the VII Corps of the Second Army as well as the 2nd Armored Division. During three of the four exercises comprising the Tennessee Maneuvers, the 2d Armored Division under Major General Patton, emerged victorious, in one achieving victory in a mere three hours.

The importance of these maneuvers cannot be overstated. In addition to a much-publicized weeding out of deficient officers, the war games also provided real-world experience for drivers, maintenance men, and significantly, the consumption of spare parts in field conditions.

M3s rumbled through towns, along roads, through forests and across dusty fields in five states during these maneuvers, adding to the lessons being learned at Fort Knox, Fort Hood and what grew to be the 18,000-square mile Desert Training Center situated on the California-Arizona border.

In January 1942, Patton said in a speech to his troops: "The war in Europe is over for us. England will probably fall this year. Our first chance to get at the enemy will be in North Africa. We cannot train troops to fight in the desert of North Africa by training in the swamps of Georgia. I sent a report to Washington requesting a desert training center in California. The California desert can kill quicker than the enemy. We will lose a lot of men from the heat, but training will save hundreds of lives when we get into combat. I want every officer and section to start planning on moving all our troops by rail to California."

**Above:** *Sergeant William Meek, of Company D, 67th Tank Battalion, gives some attention to a small puppy on the barrel of the 75mm gun on a Medium Tank M3 during First Army maneuvers in the Carolinas, on 24 November 1941. Below the sergeant's feet on the glacis is the insignia of the 1st Armored Division. A covering is wrapped over the muzzle and the forward several feet of the 75mm gun barrel, and another one is wound around the unpainted part of the barrel to the front of the rotor shield.*
*National Archives*

**Above:** *Two M3s with a Jeep between them are crossing the Pee Dee River on a pontoon bridge during field maneuvers of the 1st Armored Division in the Carolinas in November 1942. Crewmen in both tanks are waving what appear to be white flags. A small tactical symbol consisting of a T with a short L next to it is on the center section of the final-drive assembly. Note the cloth recognition band around the turret, and the two men manning a Browning .30-caliber M1919 machine gun on one of the pontoons. National Archives*

**Above:** *Four Medium Tanks M3 and several more vehicles to their front, all from the 1st Armored Division, are crossing a pontoon bridge over the Pee Dee River in November 1942. The weight of the vehicles has caused the pontoons under the second M3 from the rear to become awash. National Archives*

**Above:** *Tanks number 10, left, and 8, of Company D, 67th Armored Regiment, are part of a force of M3s advancing across a field at Fort Benning on 27 February 1942. Note the large recognition stars, with one point at the top, on the glacises, and the smaller recognition stars on the sponsons. National Archives*

**Above:** *Crewmen of M3s with markings for Company E, 67th Armored Regiment, 2nd Armored Division, are conducting a field exercise at Fort Benning, Georgia, on 6 February 1942. The company-vehicle codes on the turrets lack the hyphen between the letter and the number as seen on Company D vehicles. These tanks also lack recognition stars. National Archives*

**Above:** *The same M3 numbered E7 that is seen in the preceding photo, registration number W-304705, is facing the sun during a training exercise at Fort Benning on 27 February 1942. The registration number is painted with black paint, characteristic of Chrysler M3 production. National Archives*

**Above:** *A motorcyclist is accompanying a column of M3s assigned to the 2nd Armored Division during a road march at Fort Benning on 27 February 1942. These tanks have the Armored Force recognition stars on the rears of the turrets and on the sponsons. The rear overhang of the upper hull of the nearest M3 is mud-spattered, but a white number 1 and a letter D are discernable on the plate, indicating this is the first vehicle of Company D, presumably of the 67th Armored Regiment. A letter that appears to be an A is on the right side of the rear of the next tank in line. National Archives*

**Above:** *M3 W-304433 is climbing an embankment onto a road during a field exercise at Fort Benning on February 29, 1942. The turret is marked "I 7," indicating the 7th vehicle in Company I. Again, it is assumed this was a 67th Armored Regiment tank and crew. National Archives*

**Above:** *One percent of the 300 cast-hull M3A1 tanks produced by Alco are visible in this photo. The number "1988" is scrawled in blue on the flank of the tank nearest the camera. Two of the three M3A1s lack their 75mm main gun, and the tank in the distance has the chevron-style track. Although arguably the most combat-capable of the Lees owing to their lack of rivets and ballistically superior shape, no M3A1 saw combat; rather, all were relegated to training like this. In the distance can be seen one of the new M4 Shermans. Library of Congress*

**Above:** *In a posed scene seemingly out of a Hollywood movie, the crew of an M3 at the Armored Force School, Fort Knox, Kentucky, pose with their small arms alongside and on top of the vehicle during June 1942. American tank crews were trained to fight under a variety of conditions, including dismounted if necessary. Five of the crewmen are wielding service revolvers, while the man to the front on the ground is aiming a Thompson M1 .45-caliber submachine gun. Library of Congress*

**Left:** *Wearing gas masks, the crew of the same M3 portrayed in the preceding photograph demonstrate an extravehicular charge during a training exercise at Fort Knox in June 1942. This tank bore the marking "D-R B-3" on the center of the final-drive assembly. Two other M3s are in the right background. Faintly visible on the recognition stars on the turrets of the tank in the foreground and the one to the right are the letters, "AFS," standing for Armored Force School. Library of Congress*

**Left Below:** *The crewmen of the Medium Tank M3 marked "D-R B-3" are posing with their individual weapons during a June 1942 training session. Details of the Protectoscope on the driver's vision-port cover are in view. Library of Congress*

**Above:** *Crewmen in two Medium Tanks M3 use their hands to signal halt by raising their right arms during training at Fort Knox in June 1942. The crewmen of the nearest dust-covered tank are clearly wearing herringbone twill overalls, tanker's helmets, and goggles. Library of Congress*

**Above:** *The muzzles of both cannons as well as the cupola and coaxial machine guns of this Fort Knox-based M3 have dust covers fitted. The covers for the machine gun muzzles are leather, while the cannon muzzle covers are canvas. Notably, leather covers can also be seen tied onto the muzzles of the hull-mounted machine guns. Library of Congress*

**Above:** *Also seen at Fort Knox, Kentucky, during June 1942, this M3 was possibly completed during the late 1941-early 1942 37mm gun shortage. Within the yellow star on the turret has been stencilled in "AFS," for Armored Force School, in black. Library of Congress*

**Above:** *The muzzle covers for the hull-mounted machine guns can be clearly seen in this view of another M3 advancing along a dusty Fort Knox tank trail in June 1942. Unfortunately, no registration numbers are visible to aid in identifying when the tank was built or by whom. Library of Congress*

**Left Above:** *During a training exercise on 29 May 1942, at the Desert Training Center, in the Mojave Desert at Indio, California, Sergeants Kuka and Cowan fry a couple of eggs on the griddle-hot roof of their Medium Tank M3. National Archives*

**Left Below:** *At Fort Knox, Kentucky, in June 1942, two soldiers are greasing the right center track-support roller of a Medium Tank M3. The man to the right is operating the foot pedal of the grease tank. The bogie tire is grooved, a modification that was applied for a short time in an attempt to reduce overheating. Unfortunately, instead the grooves caused damage to the tires when rocks were caught in them. Library of Congress*

**Above:** *A Medium Tank M3 nicknamed ACHIEVEMENT is advancing during training maneuvers at the Desert Training Center on 1 June 1942. The 75mm gun is not mounted. In the absence of roof ventilators on this early-production M3, the crew has opened the side and rear pistol ports to admit some fresh air. National Archives*

On 5 February, General Leslie McNair, Army Ground Forces Commander concurred, and ordered Patton to survey the area with an eye toward selecting the disposition of the training elements.

The Desert Training Center, later known as the California-Arizona Maneuver Area, was established in March 1942. Its purpose was to provide an area where US troops could be trained in conditions comparable that which was expected in North Africa, where they would face the Germans. The wide-open desert allowed for unrestricted maneuvers, and the climatic conditions were also much more like the desert than had been Louisiana, the Carolinas or Tennessee.

Though vegetation was sparse, temperatures could reach 120 degrees in the shade, and rainfall averaged less than 3 inches per year.

One soldier stationed at the Center related, "Water in Lister bags sometimes reached 90 degrees. After you have been inside the tanks for a while, water even at 90 degrees seemed cool."

**Above:** *Wearing tanker's overalls and helmet, Sergeant George Rapich, of Company C, 752nd Tank Battalion, takes a long swig from a canteen in front of a Medium Tank M3 at the Desert Training Center on 2 June 1942. The rubber treads of the T41 tracks are worn down to the metal cores. National Archives*

**Above:** *On June 16, 1942, a Medium Tank M3 is operating in the field at the Desert Training Center, Indio, California. A cover that appears to be of cloth is installed over the entire length of the 75mm gun barrel, and the same treatment appears to have been given to the 37mm gun barrel and the barrels of the coaxial machine gun and the cupola machine gun. National Archives*

**Above:** Brush has been piled up for camouflage on the front of a Medium Tank M3 parked in an area of scrub brush at the Desert Training Center on 16 June 1942. The muzzle plug for the 75mm gun is of a type that had a hollow center with what looked like a large hex nut on its front. A similar muzzle plug has been observed in photos of other M3s. National Archives

**Above:** During maneuvers in the Carolinas in July 1942, a Medium Tank M3 churns up dust as it proceeds along a dirt road. A small portion of a band painted around the lower part of the turret is visible below the gunner's sight port on the front of the turret. National Archives

**Above:** Vehicles marshaled in a clearing at Fort Benning, Georgia, during training maneuvers in April 1942 include, in addition to the half-track in the foreground, ten visible Medium Tanks M3. Some markings are visible on certain tanks. Those with turrets visible have recognition stars as well as bands painted around the turrets. The nearest M3 has the nickname EUREKA painted on the sponson to the rear of the side door. On the tank to the far right, "D-5" was painted or chalked freehand on the right side of the rear plate of the upper hull. On the tank to the left of that one, a blue drab registration number is faintly visible: W-305964. National Archives

**Above:** Two crewmen are standing in the hatches of an M3 rolling down a dusty road during 1942. The muzzles of the 75mm and 37mm guns have covers on them to keep out dust and foreign objects. A band of fabric material is wrapped around the lower part of the turret as a recognition device for wargames. National Archives

**Above:** *Soldiers sitting on the ground in the shade to the right and the crew of a Medium Tank M3 take a break during training maneuvers at Fort Benning on 29 April 1942. Note the rag stuffed in the 37mm gun muzzle and the cloth muzzle cover on the 75mm gun barrel. National Archives*

**Above:** *Several tanks are paused in the entrance to a pine forest at Fort Benning in April 1942. The tank to the left has the nickname GEYSER on the sponson, to the rear of which is the registration number W-304890. National Archives*

**Above:** *While on maneuvers at Fort Benning, the crew of an M3 have emplaced the vehicle in a concealed position under a heavy canopy of pine trees. During actual fighting, such a position would constitute a reasonably safe one from aircraft attack. A crewman in the roof hatch is scanning the sky through binoculars. National Archives*

**Above:** *M3s are advancing from a clearing into a pine forest during maneuvers at Fort Benning in April 1942. At least the front tank on the left and the tank to the far right have the style of bogie brackets with two horizontal ribs on the sides. National Archives*

**Above:** *Six crewmen are scrambling into their Medium Tank M3 during an exercise at Fort Benning in April 1942. They are equipped with gas-mask pouches. On the sponson to the rear of the side door is the nickname IRRESISTABLE. National Archives*

**Above:** *A column of six M3s is tightly parked on a road at Fort Benning during training maneuvers in April 1942. The nickname I'M A FOOLIN is painted in small letters on the sponson to the rear of the side door on the closest tank. Similarly, a nickname is visible but not legible on the same area of the second tank. National Archives*

**Above:** *Using a smokescreen for cover, infantrymen are on the advance to the rear of a Medium Tank M3 in August 1942. These forces were part of the Demonstration Regiment at Fort Knox, Kentucky. The recognition star on the tank turret has the "AFS" marking of the Armored Force School, and the vehicle's nickname, BULL-FROG, appears to the rear of the side door. National Archives*

**Above:** *BULL-FROG, from the Demonstration Regiment of the Armored Force School at Fort Knox, surmounts a manmade earthen barrier during an August 1942 exercise. The marking "D-R B-2" is on the final-drive assembly. National Archives*

**Above:** *Tanks, including a Medium Tank M3A4 in the foreground, from the 68th Armored Regiment, 6th Armored Division, are being offloaded from a railroad flatcar during maneuvers of the VIII Corps, Third Army, in August 1942. An early form of U.S. Army unit markings is on the center section of the final-drive assembly: "68" for the regiment number, "E" for the company, and "5" for the vehicle's number in the unit's line of march. A figure, apparently a 6 standing for the 6th Armored Division, is partly visible on the recognition star on the turret. National Archives*

**Above:** *M3A4 medium tanks from the 6th Armored Division, VIII Corps, are being unloaded from flatcars in preparation for Third Army maneuvers at Boyce, Louisiana, on 28 August 1942. The number 6 is painted on the recognition stars, signifying the division number. The tank to the far right, nicknamed DIABLO, is registration number W-3058027, while unit markings are visible on the final-drive assembly of the second tank, 68, for the 68th Armored Regiment, and D, for Company D. National Archives*

**Above:** In another view taken on the same occasion as the preceding photo, more M3A4s from Company D, 68th Armored Regiment, are being prepared for unloading from flatcars at Boyce, Louisiana. The tank to the far right has a registration number that appears to be W-3058054. The next two tanks have order-of-march numbers 2 and 3, respectively, on their final-drive assemblies. Seventeen tanks in all are visible on the flatcars. National Archives

**Above:** A late-production M3 has just arrived by railroad flatcar at Camp Polk, Louisiana, for Third Army maneuvers in August 1942. The tank has the long-barreled 75mm Gun M3, the late-style bogie assemblies, and lacks the side doors. On the final-drive assembly are a number 1 followed by a letter D and the number 17, while on the sponson, the nickname DIABLO is faintly discernible. National Archives

**Above:** *By the summer of 1942, the Medium Tank M3 and its crews were undergoing trials and training exercises at the Desert Training Center, located in Southern California and an adjacent area of Arizona. Here, a Medium Tank M3 is loaded on a Heavy Tank Retriever M19 during a testing operation by the 302nd Ordnance Regiment at Camp Young, part of the Desert Training Center, in September 1942. The Heavy Tank Retriever M19 consisted of the Truck, 12-ton, 6x4, M20, designated the Model 980 by the manufacturer, Diamond T; and the Trailer, 45-ton, M9. The M20 truck derived its power from a Hercules DXFE diesel engine with a displacement of 893 cubic inches. A 40,000-pound Gar Wood winch, driven by the power takeoff, was mounted to the rear of the cab. National Archives*

**Above:** *A loading procedure in which a disabled M4 is winched onto a Heavy Tank Retriever M19 from the 302nd Ordnance Regiment is documented in the following series of photos taken at Camp Young, Desert Training Center, in September 1942. Here, the 45-ton Trailer M9 has been backed up toward the tank, and cables from the Gar Wood winch on the Diamond T prime mover have been secured to tow shackles on the final-drive assembly of the M3. National Archives*

**Above:** *Two cables from the Gar Wood winch are drawing the disabled M3 up the loading ramps to the runways of the Trailer, 45-ton, M9. The registration number of the tank is indistinct but appears to be W-304506. Note the faint shape of a recognition star on the turret, which has been painted over to reduce its visibility. National Archives*

**Above:** *This photo was taken within a moment of the preceding one, from a higher perspective. Note the line of half-tracks parked in the right background. National Archives*

**Above:** *A moment after the preceding photo was taken, a photographer snapped this image of the same M4 being winched onto the trailer. Now, the track is taut, and the previous sag on the upper run is now straight. Lying on the ground by the trailer is a chock block. National Archives*

**Above:** *The prime mover has been uncoupled from the M20 trailer holding the Medium Tank M3 at the Desert Training Center in September 1942. On the front of the trailer is the drawbar, with a lunette ring on the front end for coupling to the prime mover. The steerable front axle was equipped with eight wheels. The tandem rear axles had eight wheels each. National Archives*

**Above:** *A Medium Tank M3, seemingly the same one depicted in the preceding photos, has been brought on the M9 trailer to a base camp at the Desert Training Center in September 1942. National Archives*

**Above:** *In a 1942 photograph taken at the Desert Training Center, a Medium Tank M3 with the nickname CYCLOPS painted on the right sponson is embarked on a Heavy Tank Transporter M19. Although the M3 would be retired soon enough, the M19 transporter would remain in use by the U.S. Army and the British Army throughout World War II. National Archives*

**Above:** *A Medium Tank M3 is entering a roadway as another M3 comes up behind during desert training maneuvers near Rice, California, on 21 September 1942. These tanks were assigned to the 33rd Armored Regiment. On close inspection, more M3s are on the road in the right distance.*

**Above:** *Heavily caked with fine dust, a Medium Tank M3 from the 33rd Armored Regiment leads the way as several more M3s follow during desert training maneuvers near Rice, a town in the southern part of the Mojave Desert in California, on 21 September 1942. Despite the heavy dust in the air, the vision and pistol ports are open to admit air, as the early M3s lacked roof ventilators for the fighting compartment and the turret. National Archives*

**Above:** On 21 September 1942, an M3, registration number W-304854, assigned to the 2nd Tank Group, 191st Armored Battalion, is negotiating rough and rocky ground while towing a trailer during training maneuvers outside of Rice, California. These exercises were to acclimate the troops to operations in desert conditions in advance of the forthcoming Operation Torch invasion of North Africa. *National Archives*

**Above:** In a frontal view of a Medium Tank M3 during desert training maneuvers in Southern California in September 1942, a canvas water bag is hanging by a cord from the 75mm gun barrel. Local camouflage in the form of pieces of scrub brush have been arranged on the tank. *National Archives*

**Above:** *Evidently the soldier in the foreground is motioning the driver of a Medium Tank M3 to place the sprockets into drive, in order to move the tracks, during a track-replacement operation. Markings for the ninth vehicle, Company F, 33rd Armored Regiment, are on the final-drive assembly of this M3. The number 3, indicating the 3rd Armored Division, is painted on the recognition stars on the turrets of all three tanks. National Archives*

**Above:** *Third Armored Division vehicles, including different types of M3 medium tanks as well as half-tracks and cargo trucks, are lined up at Camp Iron Mountain, California, in September 1942. At least part of these vehicles were assigned to the 33rd Armored Regiment. In the foreground is a mix of riveted-hull M3s as well as cast-hull M3A1s. Many more M3s are in the background. National Archives*

**Above:** *A Medium Tank M3 assigned to the Red Army is operating cross-country during wargames in the Iron Mountains of the Mojave Desert, on September 20, 1942. The vehicle commander is standing in the cupola, which is traversed to the left; in his right hand is his microphone, sometimes nicknamed the "pork chop." National Archives*

**Above:** *A recovery crew is preparing to extract a Medium Tank M3 from the ditch into which it went astray at the Desert Training Center in September 1942. Markings on the bow are for the third vehicle, Headquarters Company, 191st Tank Battalion. The rubber of the tracks is worn down almost to the steel frames. National Archives*

**Right Above:** *Two engine mechanics are working on a Wright/Continental R-975-EC2 Whirlwind radial engine for an M3 tank, possibly the one in the background, at an unidentified base in September 1942. The man on the left is grasping the electric starter. National Archives*

**Right:** *The crew of an M3A4 from Company H, 68th Armored Regiment, 6th Armored Division, is engaged in Sixth Army maneuvers out of Camp Polk, Louisiana, on 6 September 1942. Note the cloth recognition band around the turret. This vehicle was numbered 6 on the final-drive assembly. The recognition star on the turret is marked with the number 6, indicating the number of the armored division. Note the late-style bogie assemblies, the roof ventilator, and the lack of a side door. National Archives*

**Above:** *Medium Tank M3A4 number 1 of Company H, 68th Armored Regiment, pauses at a creek crossing while two more Lee tanks move up in the right background during Sixth Army maneuvers in Louisiana on 6 September 1942. The recognition band around the turret of the closest tank almost covers the recognition star. National Archives*

**Above:** *An M3 assigned to Headquarters Company, 7th Armored Division, speeds along through a dusty clearing during the Louisiana Maneuvers during midafternoon on 2 October 1941. A counterweight is under the 37mm gun barrel; the 75mm gun is not mounted, and the opening for it in the rotor shield has been covered neatly. Note the long covers over the two bow machines, the muzzles of which normally were approximately flush with the glacis. National Archives*

**Above:** *The crew of a Medium Tank M3 from Headquarters Company, 7th Armored Division, moves out of a bivouac area in Louisiana during Army maneuvers on 1 October 1942. The checkerboard pattern on the 75mm rotor shield appears to have been a piece of white material with dark-colored tape criss-crossing it, to close off the opening for the gun. The band of cloth around the turret evidently was a recognition device; similar cloth bands are often seen on the turrets and cupolas of M3s photographed during Army maneuvers in the early 1940s. National Archives*

**Above:** *A Medium Tank M3A1 churns up dust while advancing on a dirt road during Army maneuvers in Tennessee in October 1942. The counterbalance for the 37mm gun is a style with an extra weight on the center of it. On the engine deck is a rack for equipment and baggage. National Archives*

**Above:** *Mechanics are removing a Wright/Continental Whirlwind engine from a Medium Tank M3A1 during Second Army maneuvers in Tennessee on 12 October 1942. The crane of a wrecker is doing the heavy lifting. The tank was assigned to Company H, 37th Armored Regiment, 4th Armored Division. National Archives*

**Above:** *In a photo presumably related to the preceding one because of their consecutive negative numbers, mechanics from the 4th Armored Division are loosening connections on a Wright/Continental R-975-EC2 Whirlwind radial engine during maneuvers in Tennessee. Good views are available of the vertical fuel tanks and filler caps in the front corners of the engine compartment, the open hatch to the far left, and the bowl-shaped antenna bracket to the left of center. National Archives*

**Above:** *During Second Army maneuvers near Shelbyville, Tennessee, on 13 October 1942, a track-changing operation is underway on Medium Tank M3A1 number 22 from Company H, 37th Armored Regiment. A powered cable is pulling the upper run of the track to the rear, and it will soon be connected to the lower run of track. A unit marking, 37-H-22, is on the rear of the upper hull. National Archives*

**Above:** *Markings for the 9th vehicle of Company G, 37th Armored Regiment, are painted on the final-drive assembly of an M3A1 parked tightly between trees during Army maneuvers in Tennessee on 15 October 1942. The muzzle cover for the 37mm gun has a retainer cord, tied to the counterweight. Note the nuts and screw threads on the bottom of the left mudguard, for securing the headlights, blackout lights, and brush guards. National Archives*

**Above:** *The vehicle commander of a Medium Tank M3A1 is giving a hand signal to the commanders of the following tanks during a cross-country advance, part of U.S. Army maneuvers in Tennessee on 16 October 1942. The side door of the lead tank is welded shut and a blank plate is welded over the original opening for the pistol port. National Archives*

**Above:** *During the Tennessee Maneuvers on 16 October 1942, an M3A1 exhibits a raised rack for equipment, covered with a tarpaulin, over the engine deck. A band, for recognition purposes, has been painted roughly on the turret, right up to and possibly over the recognition star.*

**Above:** *This is one of the Medium Tanks M3A1 photographed during U.S. Army maneuvers in Tennessee on 16 October 1942. This vehicle has a functional side door and pistol port. The rubber treads of the tracks have been driven nearly to disintegration. National Archives*

**Above:** *Markings for Company H, 37th Armored Regiment, 4th Armored Division, are on, respectively, the final-drive assembly and the recognition star of an M3A1 photographed during maneuvers in Tennessee on 10 October 1942. This is one of the later M3A1s with the side doors omitted. National Archives*

**Above:** *With a Ward LaFrance M1 wrecker standing by in the background, a tank-recovery crew is gathered around the front of a Medium Tank M3A1 during U.S. Army maneuvers in Louisiana in October 1942. The tank has markings on the rear of the upper hull for the first vehicle of Company D, 31st Armored Regiment, 7th Armored Division. The flags on the front of the tank and on the rear mudguard may indicate that the vehicle was declared "knocked-out" during mock combat, or it is possible the tank suffered a mechanical breakdown. National Archives*

**Left Above:** *M3A1, vehicle number 23 of Company H, 37th Armored Regiment, is poised in a clearing in Tennessee during Army maneuvers on 10 October 1942. This vehicle lacks side doors and has the early-style bogie assemblies with open-spoke wheels. National Archives*

**Left:** *The soldier in the foreground is observing the movement of an M3A1 as it drives into a dip in the ground and prepares to surmount the slope in the foreground. Unit markings in the style of those seen on U.S. Army military vehicles for the remainder of World War II and beyond are on the final-drive assembly, with symbols for, left to right, the 7th Armored Division, 31st Armored Regiment, Company E, and an indistinct order-of-march number that appears to be a 5. National Archives*

**Above:** *Members of the crew of a Medium Tank M3A1 are enjoying the sunshine while crossing a treadway bridge during Army maneuvers in Tennessee, on 3 November 1942. This tank was assigned to Company D, 37th Armored Regiment, of the 4th Armored Division. The unit marking on the center of the final-drive assembly is 37-D-16. National Archives*

**Left Above:** *Corporal J. D. Quinlan, a member of the 302nd Ordnance Regiment, is cleaning his mess kit with sand to the front of a Medium Tank M3 at the Desert Training Center, California, on 6 October 1942. Lying in the sand to the front of him are his tanker's helmet and goggles. National Archives*

**Left:** *Corporal Quinlan makes a reprise appearance in this photo of him, left, and Pfc. I. B. McGhee digging a slit trench in the sand next to Medium Tank M3 serial number W-304480, at the Desert Training Center on 6 October 1942. The vehicle's nickname, BINGO, is painted on the sponson to the rear of the side door. National Archives*

**Above:** *A Medium Tank M3A1 is fording a stream in Tennessee during Army maneuvers on 3 November 1942. A raised casting number, 218, is visible on the side door below the pistol port. Counterweights are present on the 75mm gun muzzle and below the 37mm gun barrel. National Archives*

**Right Above:** *The "37-H-15" unit marking on the final-drive assembly of this Medium Tank M3A1 indicates that it was the 15th vehicle in the order of march of Company H, 37th Armored Regiment. The vehicle was photographed during the Tennessee Maneuvers on 9 October 1942. The vehicle commander is standing in the cupola hatch, and the driver's face, with goggles over his eyes, is in view inside his vision port. Note the covers over the service headlight lenses. National Archives*

**Right:** *This view of an M3A1 (foreground) and a M3 (distant) during maneuvers in Tennessee on 9 October 1942, offers an excellent view of the counterweight on the barrel of the 75mm gun. The counterweight consisted of two halves, secured with four nuts and bolts. Casting numbers are visible but not legible on the fronts of both halves of the counterweight. National Archives*

**Above:** M3A1 number 15 from the 37th Armored Regiment, seen in a preceding photograph, is crossing a treadway bridge at night during the Tennessee Maneuvers, on 15 October 1942. The driver's head is protruding through his vision port, and he is not wearing head protection. National Archives

**Above:** After the engine of this late-production Medium Tank M3A4 stalled out during an exercise at Camp Chaffee, Arkansas, on 10 November 1942, the Ward LaFrance M1 wrecker took it under tow back to base. The wrecker is using a single, heavy-duty tow chain to pull the tank. The registration number is faintly visible on the side of the sponson of the tank and appears to be W-3058018. National Archives

**Above:** *Using the boom on a 10-ton wrecker, members of the Maintenance Company of the 33rd Armored Regiment are removing the Wright/Continental R-975-EC2 Whirlwind radial engine from a Medium Tank M3. A small number 3 is on the center of the recognition star on the turret, signifying that the tank served with the 3rd Armored Division. National Archives*

**Above:** *Medium Tank M3 registration number W-304696 is shown while undergoing testing of an installation of Signal Corps radio equipment at Fort Monmouth, New Jersey, sometime during 1942. The vehicle commander is in the cupola, speaking into a handheld microphone. A single whip antenna is mounted on the bracket on the left rear of the fighting compartment. Library of Congress*

**Left:** *The same Medium Tank M3 depicted in the preceding photo is viewed from a closer perspective during testing of the installation of Signal Corps radio equipment at Fort Monmouth in 1942. Library of Congress*

**Left:** *A woman technician at the Signal Corps General Development Laboratory, Fort Monmouth, New Jersey, is servicing radio equipment inside a Medium Tank M3 in 1942. The radio set has been moved to the position shown in the photo for ease of access. Based on the pattern of wear marks on the sponson, this is the same tank depicted in the two preceding photographs. Library of Congress*

**Above:** *An instructor is giving troops instructions in defending against mechanized attacks, using a mid-production Baldwin M3A5 Medium Tank with welded in place side doors as an instructional tool. The instructor has an oversized leaf sight to his side, as a training aid. The sign, which reads, "Defense Against Mechanized Attack," features an owl with a helmet and rifle, advising, "Better wise up, soldier!"*

*Quartermaster Museum*

# Chapter 10
# The M3 in British Isles

Thankfully, there was no tank combat in the British Isles during WWII. This, combined with the pressing need for tanks in North Africa as the M3 was leaving the assembly lines, meant that relatively few of M3 tanks touched English soil during the early stages of the war.

The first M3s to land on English soil were three Grants that arrived in late September 1941, which is after other British M3s had been shipped to the Middle East. The vehicles landing in England were used for testing and training, including the very first M3 built by Pressed Steel Car Company, census number T-24689, which underwent testing at Lulworth. Also arriving in September were Pullman-built T-24193 and T-24195.

British, Canadian and US troops in England used the M3 for training as well as potentially protecting the island from a feared Nazi invasion. During the summer of 1942, Chester Tank Depot shipped 252 reconditioned M3 Lee tanks to the UK. These were used primarily for training, with some ultimately being converted to Canal Defense Lights (see Chapter 8).

## Canadian M3 Grant/Lee use

The Canadian Army began planning to put an M3-equipped armored division in England in December 1940. Canadian Colonel James Ralston, former Minister of Finance, and since July 5, 1940 Minister of National Defence, along with General Harry Crerar went to England in November 1940 for extensive meetings.

One of those, on 17 December, was with Anthony Eden, who at that time was Britain's Secretary of State for War (five days later he became Secretary of State for Foreign Affairs, essentially Churchill's deputy). Eden told Colonel Ralston he "would like the Canadian Government to provide an armoured division as soon as possible, to be equipped with M.3 (sic) tanks ordered by the U.K. in the U.S.A."

**Above:** *This tank, T-24689, was one of the first three Grants to actually be shipped to England. This tank was the first tank built by Pressed Steel Car Company and it is suspected that this is the tank now on display at the Tank Museum in Bovington. Patton Museum*

**Above:** *As can be seen, T-24689 was shipped without sand shields over the tracks, and it has M3 Lee-type rear fenders instead. Residue of the tape used for sealing during overseas shipping is visible around the side door and the visor. Patton Museum*

**Right:** *T-24689 was subjected to extensive testing at the British Tank Proving Ground at Lulworth, where this photograph was taken in March 1942. From this angle it can be seen that the smoke bomb thrower is absent, and a heavy armor plate has been welded in place to blank off the aperture in the turret. Patton Museum*

**Above:** *The census number on the rear of the tank was likely applied by the British military, as it is in a markedly simpler style than the numbers on the sides of the tanks, which are in an elaborate serif-style lettering commonly used by railway equipment builders of the era. Patton Museum*

**Above:** *Members of the Canadian 10th Armoured Regiment (The Fort Garry Horse) conduct a training exercise in a Lee tank that has an illegible U.S. Army registration on the sponson. The Fort Garry Horse trained on the Lee tanks in the United Kingdom from at least February to June 1942. Patton Museum*

**Above:** *To mark this Lee tank in Canadian service as assigned to a headquarters unit, the crew wrote "HQ" in chalk on the turret. Patton Museum*

**Above:** *Wearing overalls, helmets, and low-slung, British-style pistol holsters, the Canadian crew of a Lee tank scramble to mount their vehicle during a training exercise around early 1942. It isn't clear if the letter C chalked on the turret refers to a C Squadron vehicle, or if it is a vehicle-identification letter.*

**Above:** *A Lee tank crewed by members of the Fort Garry Horse is surmounting a rise during a training exercise at an unspecified location. Library and Archives of CanadaPatton Museum*

**Above:** *A buttoned-up Canadian Lee tank, census number T78861, has paused on an embankment during training maneuvers, probably around the early spring of 1942. This vehicle has the built-up, smoothened fillet between the left side of the cupola ring and the side of the turret. Library and Archives of Canada*

**Above:** *A Canadian Lee, possibly the same one as in the preceding photo, based on the proximity of their negative numbers, negotiates a downhill slope during a training exercise. This tank has the T41 tracks, with smooth shoes, which were not as effective on soft ground as the British WD-212 tracks, with their "double-I" treads. Library and Archives of Canada*

**Above:** *A Lee tank crewed by Canadian trainees is negotiating very rough ground at an unidentified location. The vehicle is devoid of visible markings. The object on the roof to the front of the turret is a tree branch. Library and Archives of Canada*

**Above:** *Lee T78661 takes on a soft-earth slope. The rear of the track seems to have churned up much dirt, and it is not clear if this tank is going to win its contest with the embankment. Library and Archives of Canada*

On 2 January 1941 further discussions were held with Captain David Margesson, who had replaced Eden as Secretary of State for War. Margesson continued the plea for an armored division, explaining that Britain was trying to raise nine armored divisions, as a result of Churchill's telling the cabinet on 15 October, "At present we are aiming at five armoured divisions, and armoured brigades equivalent to three more. This is not

enough. We cannot hope to compete with the enemy in numbers of men, and must therefore rely upon an exceptional proportion of armoured fighting vehicles. Ten armoured divisions is the target to aim for to the end of 1941...."

Canada was being asked to provide one of these divisions at a time when the Canadian armored force was in its infancy. Only on 13 August 1940

**Above:** *A Lee tank in Canadian service is viewed from the upper left front in a sand pit during a training exercise in early 1942. Storage boxes are not mounted. Library and Archives of Canada*

**Above:** *Tankers of the Fort Garry Horse are taking a break during a training exercise in England in February 1942. The first tank has "HQ" chalked on the turret, while the second one has the letter "A" chalked on its turret. Patton Museum*

had the Minister of National Defence approved a recommendation of the Chief of the General Staff for creating a Canadian Armoured Corps, leading to the creation of 1st Canadian Armoured Brigade. The Brigade was formed at Camp Borden in October, with Colonel F. F. Worthington in command. Worthington had previously commanded the Armoured Fighting Vehicles Training Centre, which itself had only been established in September 1939, also at Camp Borden.

In long term, Margesson told the Canadians that the British desires were:

"(a) The War Office are particularly anxious that the personnel of a complete Canadian Armoured division should be formed ready for despatch to the

**Above:** *Members of the 3rd Armoured Regiment (The Governor General's Horse Guards) of the Canadian Army trained on Lee tanks, and a group of them are shown here manning their Lees. Five Lees are in line, with two Stuart tanks to the far right. Note the storage box to the front of the 75mm gun sponson on each Lee. The forward end of a mud chute is to the rear of the sprocket on the closest tank. Patton Museum*

**Above:** *Two Canadian Lee tanks are preceding two Stuart tanks on a road march during training. A mud chute is present on the closest Lee, above the bogie wheels. The second Lee has a triangular tactical sign on the side of the turret, indicating a B Squadron vehicle. Patton Museum*

**Above:** *Pressed Steel Car Company M3 T-25064 was just six months old when it was photographed in front of the Dyke Hotel, in the Devil's Dyke area of West Sussex. The region was home of the 5th Canadian Armoured Division's training efforts. Just visible on the engine deck of the Grant is the mounting bracket for the Auxiliary Petrol Tank. Library and Archives of Canada*

United Kingdom by the early Autumn of 1941. They anticipate that equipment from British orders (either U.S.A. or U.K.) would be available to equip the division, which would thus be completely trained and available for employment during the first quarter of 1942.

"(b) If in addition to the above, and without slowing up its formation, a Canadian Army Tank Brigade, for inclusion in the Canadian Corps, could also be raised, equipped with Mark III Tanks now being made in Canada, and despatched to the United Kingdom in the Summer of 1941, this would be most welcome to the War Office. For this purpose

the United Kingdom Government were entirely agreeable to Canada having priority on Canadian production of Mark III (edit: Valentine) tanks and to assist if necessary by provision of I (edit: Infantry) tanks from United Kingdom production."

On 5 January Ralston cabled Canada recommending changes in the Canadian Army plans in order to accommodate the British request. He suggested that during 1941 Canada should send to England, among other units, an army tank brigade and a complete armored division. This plan was approved by the War Committee on 28 January.

**Above:** *Canadian tankers confer in front of two Lee tanks during training. The closer tank has a very faint "HQ" painted or chalked on the side of the turret. The cupola is rotated to the rear, with the bifolding hatch door open. Library and Archives of Canada*

**Above:** *A lone Lee tank manned by a Canadian crew was photographed from a roadside ditch during a training exercise around early 1942. No visible markings are on the vehicle. Library and Archives of Canada*

**Above:** *Two Lee tanks being employed in the training of Canadian tank crews exhibit several British/Commonwealth modifications, including storage boxes to the fronts of the 75mm gun sponsons, mud chutes, and revised storage boxes on the sponsons, with three present on the left side. The tank to the left has a triangle indicating B Squadron on the turret, while the vehicle to the right has a diamond, representing a Headquarters vehicle. That diamond straddles a bracket for mounting two smoke-bomb dischargers. Patton Museum*

**Above:** *On these two Lee tanks being used by Canadian tankers for training, the closer vehicle has, on very close inspection, a U.S. Army registration number on the sponson, while the farther tank has a census number which is partially visible: either T78862 or T78962. Patton Museum*

**Above:** *TIn this photograph of five Canadian tank crews training with Lee tanks around early 1942, the closest tank and its vehicle commander are identical to those in the foreground of the preceding photo. This tank definitely has "U.S.A." and a U.S. Army registration number on the sponson, but here again, the number is not fully legible: only "W-3058" is discernible. The second tank and crewmen are also present in the preceding photo. Census numbers are present on the sponsons of the two farthest Lees: the number on the one to the far right is T78849. Patton Museum*

**Above:** *Five Lee tanks crewed by Canadians are maneuvering through a training area, probably in England, around early 1942. Canadian armoured regiments gained experience training in these tanks, which would be of much value as they transitioned to Sherman tanks. Library and Archives of Canada*

**Above:** *A Canadian-crewed Lee tank splashes into a mudhole on a training course. The crew has put in place the glass windshield, with wiper, ahead of the driver. Library and Archives of Canada*

**Above:** *Two Lee tanks manned by Canadian crews are negotiating a flooded roadway as part of their training. The two crewmen in the lead tank are wearing overalls and the Helmet, Crash, Royal Armoured Corps, made of three sections of riveted fiber material, with a thick crash pad on the front. Patton Museum*

**Above:** *Lee T78864 displays late modifications, including mud chutes, right-fender storage box with a sloped top, storage box and auxiliary fuel tank over the right sponson, and storage box on the rear of the right sponson. Patton Museum*

**Above:** *A crewman wearing heavy gauntlets and black tanker's beret polishes the detachable windshield of a Lee tank. Just below his hand is the windshield wiper motor. Library and Archives of Canada*

**Above:** *Two Canadian tankers confer on a Lee tank during training. The view is from above the right rear of the fighting compartment, with the turret to the left. A close view is available of the Helmet, Crash, Royal Armoured Corps, with the ear flaps attached for headphones. Library and Archives of Canada*

**Right:** *A photo of a tank crewman checking the tightness of a screw on a track end connector includes an excellent view of one of several types of helmets worn by Canadian tankers: the Helmet, Crash, Tank Battalion. This type was fabricated from cloth-covered cork, with several rubber vents as well as a frontal crash pad and a leather "scrum" that held the headphones. Library and Archives of Canada*

**Above Left:** *The Canadian driver of a Lee tank is at his position, with the 75mm gun and mount to the right and radio equipment and the interior of a pistol port to the left. To the right of the driver's head are the elevating handwheel for the 75mm gun and the crash pad for the gunner's periscope. Library and Archives of Canada*

**Left:** *A crewman makes an adjustment to a bogie assembly on the left side of a Lee tank. Shown in close-up detail are a bogie wheel, the bogie bracket, the front vertical-volute spring, and the track-return roller. Library and Archives of Canada*

**Above:** *A crewman wearing overalls and a knit cap makes adjustments with a screwdriver while holding open the left engine access door of a Lee tank. Details of some of the engine accessories and the interior of the right door are displayed. Library and Archives of Canada*

Accordingly, the 1st Canadian Army Tank Brigade was formally organized in February 1941. The 1st Canadian Armoured Brigade was not directly converted into the Tank Brigade, but two of its regiments became tank battalions.

July 1941 saw the 1st Armoured Division redesignated the "5th Canadian (Armoured) Division," more popularly written without the parenthesis. The Division moved to the United Kingdom, with the bulk of the force arriving on Convoy T.C. 15 on 22 November 1941. Shortly thereafter the M3 medium tanks began to equip the unit, with the 1st Army Tank Brigade, equipped primarily with Churchill tanks, also receiving some of the M3s.

Tank deliveries were slow, and by mid-June the 5th Canadian Armoured Division had only 112 tanks of all types. In large part this was because the Canadians were to draw their tanks from the British, and the fighting in the Middle East was absorbing most of the tanks available to Britain.

The Canadians began training in West Sussex, in the Devil's Dyke area at an installation established as the South Downs Training Area. The training operations would carry on almost two years, during which time the M3s were replaced by M4s.

Most of the M3s supplied to the Canadians were Lees, although they did get a few of the 97 Grants which were shipped to England as well. All were gasoline-powered. The Canadians never used either type in combat, but they were invaluable in training.

Additional M3s were returned to England from the Mid-East, where they, along with some former training tanks, were slated for conversion to Canal Defense Lights as described in chapter 8.

**Above:** *Three Canadian tank crewmen confer over a book held open over the cupola of a Lee tank. All three are wearing U.S. Army Rawlings Pattern tanker's helmets, introduced in early 1941. Library and Archives of Canada*

**Above:** *The 1st Armored Division conducted training in Northern Ireland in the summer of 1942. Shown here are infantrymen wearing gas masks operating with a force of Medium Tanks M3 at a training site in Northern Ireland on June 28, 1942. The vehicle commanders in the cupolas also have put on their gas masks. A censor has scratched out the tactical signs on the 75mm gun sponsons. The closest tank is registration number W-309554. Patton Museum*

**Above:** *A Medium Tank M3 of the 1st Armored Division presents its front to the photographer during a training exercise in Northern Ireland in 1942. The driver is visible behind the detachable windshield. The headphone lead wire and jack are dangling from the helmet of the crewman in the fighting-compartment hatch. The white patch on the right side of the final-drive assembly evidently was made by a censor to cover a marking. Patton Museum*

**Left:** *In the foreground of a line of M3 Lee tanks is one nicknamed BABY BOY, registration number W-309689, equipped with a wooden rack over the storage boxes, and armed with a 75mm Gun M3. The next M3 was nicknamed BART and bears registration number W-309839. Both tanks have the bogie brackets with two horizontal ribs, and solid-spoked bogie wheels. Patton Museum*

**Above:** *Two long lines of M3 medium tanks from the 1st Armored Division are poised to advance across a hilly field in Northern Ireland during a training exercise in 1942. The second tank, a late, riveted-hull M3, registration number W-3028826, bore the nickname BUTURLINOVKA III on the sponson. Patton Museum*

**Right:** *A column of six tightly spaced M3s is paused during maneuvers in Northern Ireland in 1942. A military censor scratched out the recognition star on the turret of the first tank but neglected to blot out the markings on the upper right corner of the final-drive assembly: 0190-L (likely the first part of the number is hidden by the right mudguard) and two horizontal bars. The bars and numbers are visible on the same positions on at least the next two tanks in the column. National Archives*

## United States

The RMS *Queen Mary* brought many of the men of the US 1st Armored Division from New York across the Atlantic, leaving on 11 May 1942 and arriving at the Firth of Clyde, Scotland on 16 May. Two days later they were in Northern Ireland. Some 200 of the unit's tanks, which had left the US earlier, arrived in Northern Ireland on 12 May. On 10 June the balance of the unit's men arrived via the Oriente, which had sailed from New York on 31 May. The 1st Armored Division personnel would

occupy Dundrum Bay, Ballykinler and Newcastle in County Down. The last of the Division's tanks did not arrive until 13 June, and they were M3s. The Medium Tank units trained heavily with the M3. In early September the 1st Armored Division began moving to England, with the first portion, Combat Command B, being the first to go, taking with them their M3 light tanks. By 29 October 1942 the entire division had moved to the English moors, where they remained for just under two months before going to North Africa.

**Above:** *Crewmen from the 1st Armored Division are assembled to the fronts of their tightly parked M3 medium tanks at a training ground in Northern Island in 1942. The tanks are armed with a mix of the short-barreled 75mm Gun M2 and the long-barreled 75mm Gun M3. The crewmen are wearing overalls and a mix of headgear: mostly the Helmet, Combat, Winter, while a few are wearing tankers' crash helmets or herringbone twill caps. Patton Museum*

**Left:** A late-production M3, W-3010752, advances across a field in Northern Island. The nickname STUD is on the sponson, below which is a small depiction of a horse's head. A larger sketch of a horse's head has been chalked onto the armor to the front of the pistol port. Camouflage netting is lying on the engine deck. Patton Museum

**Left:** This riveted-hull Medium Tank M3 assigned to the 13th Armored Regiment was photographed at a very muddy Camp Ballykinler, Northern Ireland, in the summer of 1942 while that regiment was engaged in training for combat there. The 13th Armored passed through the Port of Belfast during their transit to Camp Ballykinler, and while their tanks were being processed through the port, dockhands broke into many of the vehicles, stealing tools, equipment, and personal items. National Archives

**Above:** *Another Medium Tank M3, registration number W-309381, is being shipped from Ordnance Depot O-640 following repairs. The tank is on a Warwell flatcar, which was made especially for transporting medium and heavy tanks. Note the wooden cross being used as a makeshift travel lock for the 75mm gun. National Archives*

**Above:** *Three repaired Medium Tanks M3 are on Warwell cars at Ordnance Depot O-640, ready for shipment. The crates on the engine decks each contains 20 U.S. five-gallon liquid containers. The nearest vehicle is registration number W-309549. Military History Institute*

**Left:** *Around mid-April 1943, a Medium Tank M3 that has been repaired is about to leave Ordnance Depot O-640, Tidworth, Wiltshire, England, on a flatcar. Shipping stencils are on the forward panel of the upper hull. The bogie wheels are the solid-spoked type. National Archives*

# Chapter 11
# Combat debut
# North Africa

**Above:** *Doors and ports sealed against the elements, and extra grease applied to moving parts, Grant tank T24466 is being hoisted for transport by ship. This vehicle was completed by Pullman-Standard in February 1942. Library of Congress*

**Above:** *A Grant tank on a hoist is about to join other Grants on the deck of a transport ship in this 1942 photo. Sealant material has been applied over the engine-access doors on the rear of the hull and also on the bottom of the hull of the tank being hoisted. Note the heavy application of grease on the suspension of the Grant in the foreground. Library of Congress*

**Above:** *A cargo handler or inspector is checking the fixtures securing a Grant tank to the deck of a cargo ship. Shackles with turnbuckles are attached to the tow eyes on the final-drive assembly and to padeyes attached to the deck. Library of Congress*

## Commonwealth use

WWII came to North Africa in June 1940, initially pitting the British against the Italians. Following the defeat of the Italian 10th Army by British troops under General Archibald Wavell during Operation Compass, Hitler dispatched a small expeditionary force consisting of the 15th Panzer Division and the 5th Light Division to reinforce the Italians. These units, which together he dubbed the Deutsches Afrika Korps, were placed under the command of Erwin Rommel.

Following the decision by London to send transfer three divisions from the Middle East to Greece, the fighting pushed across North Africa to Tobruk. Garrisoned by 36,000 troops under Australian Lt. General Leslie Morshead, Tobruk stubbornly held on. The port city was completely encircled by Axis forces except for the sea-lane.

Seeking to break the virtual siege, General Archibald Wavell launched Operation Battleaxe.

The British, equipped with Light Tank Mk VI, Crusader and Valentine tanks, planned to launch a three-pronged attack on 15 June. The resulting battles, which were spread over three days, cost the Germans 12 tanks, 93 men killed, 350 wounded and 235 missing, and the Italians lost 592 men. But the price paid by the British was high, with 122 killed, 588 wounded and 259 missing, and losing 98 tanks, including 65 Matildas. The tank losses represented almost half of the British tanks in the operation, many of which had been brought to the region in a daring convoy run in May. The failure of Operation Battleaxe also cost Wavell his command.

If that weren't bad enough, in November there was another British effort to relieve Tobruk, Operation Crusader. While deemed a British victory, and indeed the Commonwealth forces succeeded in breaking through to Tobruk, the cost was heavy. Against German losses of 100 Panzers through 22 November, the British had lost 530 tanks.

**Above:** *The M3 medium tanks had their debut in combat in the form of the Cruiser Tanks General Grant that served with the British Eighth Army in North Africa. British units in that theater began receiving Grants in early February 1942, and they entered combat during the May 1942 battles along the Gazala Line. Shown here are two columns of Grant tanks, with a General Stuart, based on the U.S. Light Tank M3, second in line on the left. Imperial War Museum*

The heavy British losses led to a deliberate effort to supply British forces in that theater with M3 medium tanks as quickly as possible. The Grants began to arrive in North Africa in August 1941, when Pullman-built T-24190 through T-24192 arrived. However, deliveries were slow, in part hampered by the shortages of components mentioned in Chapter 4, but also the less than optimal production rates described in Chapter 7. By 16 December 1941 only 10 of the M3 Grants had arrived, and half of those were not yet combat ready. In an effort to bolster the campaign, M3 Lees began to be shipped from the United States to British units in North Africa in mid December.

Evaluation of the three initial tanks pointed to the need for some modification to make the vehicles better suited for this combat theater. This work, authorized by the British Mechanisation Experimental Establishment (Middle East), included among other things, the installation of sand shields along the upper track run. These modifications were carried out by the No. 5 Base Ordnance Depot at Tel-el-Kebir, Egypt. These

field-installed sand shields differed slightly in design from those that began to be installed at the factories in November, notably by having curved front fenders.

Grants began to be issued to the 3rd & 5th Royal Tank Regiments (RTR) near the end of January 1942, with the 5th RTR listing 32 on strength at the beginning of February. In March the British began camouflage painting their tanks.

The British continued modifying the vehicles both before and after issue, with the vehicles being cycled through workshops. In April the "Removal of twin Browning guns and plugging of holes" was approved, making it likely that none of the British M3s saw combat with the bow guns installed. At the same time, the ammo load and stowage of the tanks were modified. The original load was 50 75mm rounds and 182 37mm rounds, but the modification changed this to 80 of each, with the 75mm rounds housed in British-designed armored ammo stowage boxes, as were the bulk of the 37mm rounds.

**Above:** *Using a bore-cleaning staff, two members 3rd Royal Tank Regiment are cleaning the barrel of a Grant tank, at a bivouac area in North Africa on 20 February 1942. Imperial War Museum*

**Above:** *September 1941 production T-24205 was a Pullman-built Grant of C Squadron 6th Royal Tank Regiment. The tank, named Fanny, is shown here on 17 February 1942. Australian War Memorial*

**Above:** *Grant tanks assigned to the 3rd Royal Tank Regiment are spread out on a particularly barren plain in the Western Desert of North Africa on 24 March 1942. During that month, the British Army had approximately 340 Grant and Lee cruiser tanks in Egypt. The Grant in the foreground is marked with census number T-24210; this vehicle was completed by Pullman Standard in September 1941. Imperial War Museum*

Early in May, C Squadron, 3rd RTR assembled and tested a sighting device resembling the vane sight that was over a year later adopted for use on the Sherman.

While in January 1942 the "Fitting of mantlet dust cover to 75mm gun" had been recommended and approved, this modification does not appear to have begun until mid-year, and did not become commonplace until fall 1942. The British-added stowage rack directly ahead of the 75mm gun mantlet had to be repositioned to accommodate the dust cover installation.

Records appear to indicate that the Grant was first used in combat on 27 May 1942; the second day of the Battle of Gazala. During this action, the 15th Panzer Division engaged the 4th Armoured Brigade of the 7th Armoured Division, which consisted of the 8th King's Royal Irish Hussars, as well as the 3rd and 5th Battalions of the Royal Tank Regiment. The M3s were mixed with other types of tanks in units. The 7th Armoured Division typically fielded a regimental mix of 24 Grants and

20 Stuarts, while the 1st Armoured Division normally fielded regiments consisting of 36 Crusaders and 12 Grants.

The 3rd RTR reported that the Germans had a force of over 100 Panzer II and Panzer III tanks, and that the Germans were surprised by firepower of the 75mm gun-armed Grants.

However, the British were outnumbered, and were forced into a fighting withdrawal toward El Adem and spent the night near the Belhamed supply base east of the El Adem airfield. During the day's action, the 3rd RTR lost 16 Grants and 3 Stuarts, while the 8th Hussars lost all but 3 of their Grants. Despite these losses, the Grants had proven to be rugged and battleworthy. One Grant took 31 hits, with only three of them (two by 50mm guns and one by 37mm) causing any real damage. Another absorbed 12 hits without penetration. However, 105mm howitzers and the dreaded Flak 88 were lethal, and those weapons accounted for three of the losses.

**Above:** *A Pullman-built Grant tank, census number T-24243, from C Squadron Headquarters, 3rd Royal Tank Regiment, 7th Armoured Division, is being driven up a ramp in order to board a railroad flatcar for shipment to the front lines in the North African desert, on 29 March 1942. A cartoon character is painted on the hull to the immediate front of the side door. The tank is equipped with factory-installed sand shields, readily identified by their beginning an upward slope at a point nearly centered on the drive sprocket. A neatly folded tarpaulin is tied with ropes to the top of the sponson storage box, and a bedroll and camouflage netting is strapped to the fender. A dark, splotchy camouflage pattern has been sprayed over the stone base color of the tank. Imperial War Museum*

**Right Above:** *Two British Grant tanks and two scout cars of an unidentified armoured brigade are parked in a headquarters camp in the Western Desert on 31 May 1942. Crew's knapsacks are secured on the fender to the front of the 75mm gun sponson of the nearer tank. Note the covers over the openings for the smoke-grenade mortar on the front of the turret roof and the coaxial machine-gun port on the 37mm gun's rotor shield. A roll of camouflage netting is on the storage box toward the rear of the hull. "The nearest tank is a command vehicle, identifiable as such by the brace supporting the dummy 37mm gun, which itself is mounted at an unusual angle compared to a live gun mounting. It is also notable in lacking a coaxial machine gun." Imperial War Museum*

**Right:** *A Grant tank passes a smoldering German PzKpfw I tank, on 6 June 1942, probably during the Battle of Gazala. The Grant has a wavy camouflage-paint pattern, and a triangular tactical symbol on the turret. The tank's 37mm and 75mm guns were more than a match for the lightly armored Panzer I. On the Grant's turret is a bracket holding a solar compass, a navigational aid often seen on British tanks in North Africa. Imperial War Museum*

**Above:** *At a site in Libya on 4 June 1942, two crewmen are loading 75mm ammunition into a Grant tank. The rail mounted on brackets along the lower part of the side of the upper hull was used for installing bows for supporting a special cover to disguise the Grant tank as a transport vehicle, to deceive the enemy. Below the rail is part of a sand skirt. The faintly visible census number, T-23632, identifies this Grant as part of Baldwin Locomotive Works' January 1942 production. Imperial War Museum.*

**Right:** *In a desert in North Africa, members of a Grant tank crew are loading the vehicle with ammunition from a lorry, on 18 June 1942. Packing tubes for 75mm ammunition are on the ground to the rear of the lorry. Note the gouge in the right final drive from a nonpenetrating hit from an artillery projectile. Imperial War Museum*

**Right:** *The same ammunition-loading operation depicted in the preceding photo is viewed from another perspective. The rack made of steel strapping on the right fender, for storing liquid containers, was an often-observed modification on the Grant tank. On the roof of the turret is a bracket with a sun compass attached; this also was a frequently used accessory and was invaluable for navigating on the vast deserts of North Africa. Imperial War Museum*

**Left:** *To deceive enemy observers about the nature of the Grant tank, the British developed a so-called "sun shield" to disguise it as a tracked lorry. A Grant tank is shown in the desert with that cover installed in June 1942. Supporting the cover were bows attached to pockets on a rail on each side of the vehicle, just above the sand shields. Imperial War Museum*

**Above:** *A vehicle commander poses in the cupola of a Lee tank serving with C Squadron, 4th (Queen's Own) Hussars, 2nd Armoured Brigade, during the First Battle of El Alamein, in Egypt, on 7 July 1942. A dust cover is fitted over the 75mm gun, and a rack with two U.S. five-gallon liquid containers is on the rear of the upper hull. Imperial War Museum*

**Above:** *A Grant, left, and a Lee tank from C Squadron, 4th (Queen's Own) Hussars, 2nd Armoured Brigade, are parked side by side during the First Battle of El Alamein, Egypt, on 7 July 1942. The stone-colored paint on these tanks appears to be in virtually new condition. Note that the Grant has WD-212 tracks, while the Lee appears to have T41 tracks. Imperial War Museum*

**Above:** *In a photo evidently taken at the same time and location as the preceding image, a Grant, left, and a Lee, assigned to C Squadron, 4th (Queen's Own) Hussars, 2nd Armoured Brigade, are being prepared for action at the end of the first week of the First Battle of El Alamein position, Egypt, 7 July 1942. Racks for holding liquid containers are on the right fenders of both vehicles. Imperial War Museum*

**Above:** *At Foukah, a railroad station near El Alamein, an Afrika Korps photographer snapped this view of a destroyed British Grant tank along a railroad track on 11 July 1942, during the First Battle of El Alamein. Whether the vehicle struck a mine or was knocked out by a German antitank or high-explosive round, the resulting explosion collapsed the right suspension and blew off the roof of the fighting compartment, including the turret. Bundesarchiv*

The Battle of Gazala wore on into June, and in the end it would be considered Rommel's greatest victory, culminating in the fall of Tobruk and the capture of 35,000 Commonwealth troops on 21 June. Beyond that, while the Afrika Korps was down to only 55 tanks, having lost about 400, the British had lost 1,188 tanks in 17 days. During that time, the German forces had lost 3,360 men, and the Commonwealth lost 15,000 men killed, wounded or captured, in addition to the previously mentioned 35,000. British tank strength at the end of the battle stood at 185 operational tanks.

However, the Battle of Gazala had been difficult for both sides, and both the British and the Axis spent July recovering, repairing and restocking.

The armies next clashed at what is now known as the First Battle of El Alamein, with the British under the command of General Claude Auchinleck. At the beginning of the battle the 8th Army had 137 serviceable tanks, with a further 42 en route from workshops, while 902 more waited to be repaired. Following the defeat at the Battle of Gazala, the British had withdrawn to a more defensible position near El Alamein on the Mediterranean coast. The First Battle of El Alamein took almost the entire month of July, raging from 1 July until 27 July, and resulted in a hard-fought stalemate, although it did halt Rommel's advance.

This was followed by the Battle of Alam el Halfa (August 31 - September 5, 1942), with the British forces under new leadership, Lt. General Bernard

**Right:** *A soldier, likely a tank mechanic, identified only as "Smitty" is standing between an assortment of combination wrenches and the right side of a Grant tank. Visible through the open door of the tank is the British-designed armored ammunition bin which was field-installed beginning in April 1942. Military History Institute*

Montgomery. In this action, among the 713 tanks in British forward-deployed units were 164 M3s. The British fought from well-developed defensive positions, with the M3s often dug in to reduce their silhouette. However, the Germans had augmented their panzer force with the Panzer IV Ausf. F2, which sported a high-velocity 75mm gun, comparable to that of the M3. The battle cost the British 31 of their Grants, but 13 were salvaged.

After the fall of Tobruk, Churchill made his famous plea to Roosevelt for Shermans, which he got, but

along with them the first Diesel-powered Grants to enter the campaign were shipped. Between June and September 1942, a mixture of 164 M3A3s and M3A5s were sent to North Africa, with the first arriving with the Shermans and Priests in September.

The second, and decisive, battle of El Alamein began on 23 October 1942. British armored units, bolstered by the recent arrival of 270 Shermans, 252 of which were ready for battle, still included a mix of older types, including 210 M3s.

**Left:** *An officer crouches to look at the work being performed on the track of a Grant tank by a mechanic identified only as "Coleman." The census number on the sponson is T24752. Military History Institute*

**Below:** *The crew of Grant T-24527 are rigging a shelter on the right side of their vehicle in the Egyptian desert in August 1942. Several of the tankers are preparing their bedrolls. A faint triangle representing B Squadron is on the side of the turret.*

**Above:** *Crewmen of a Grant tank are eating a meal on and alongside their vehicle in a North African desert. Splotches of dark paint have been sprayed on the stone base color for camouflage. Bedrolls are secured to the fender.*

**Above:** *Looking out for their health and hygiene, crewmen of a Grant tank are brushing their teeth and shaving. They have dug a pit in the foreground for building a small fire to heat water.*

**Above:** *Members of a tank squadron are receiving a briefing in the Western Desert on 9 September 1942. The officer standing to the rear of the side door is using a light-colored area of the vehicular paint to sketch a map or diagram with a pencil. The four-color camouflage used by the 22nd Armoured Brigade has been painted on the tank. Note: it's difficult to see, but there is a white line alongside the black in the camouflage. Note the droopy dust cover for the 75mm gun and the Browning .30-caliber M1919 machine gun installed on a nonstandard mount atop the turret. Imperial War Museum*

The Second Battle of El Alamein was launched by a heavy British artillery action, during which time 882 guns fired over a half-million rounds over 6 hours, while engineers and infantry attempted to clear 24-foot wide paths through the thick German mine fields. The mine fields were in some places 5-miles thick, and by dawn on Saturday the 24th they had not yet been breached.

At dusk, the 15th Panzer Division, joined by the Italian Littorio Division, left the shelter of Hill 28 to attack the British 1st Armoured Division. Although the fighting was heavy, with half the tanks involved knocked out, the lines remained the same. To the south, the 131st Infantry Brigade had breached the minefield, but when the 22nd Armoured Brigade attempted to pass through the gap, they were brought under withering fire and 31 tanks were disabled.

The Germans had planted vast minefields containing roughly three million mines in the El Alamein region. Rommel had dubbed these the "Devil's Garden," and of course the British had to breach these. Hoping to speed this process, they developed a series of "Scorpion" mine flails. Twenty-five of the initial version, based on the Matilda tank, were used in the Second Battle of El Alamein, and while they proved the theory, were found deficient in several areas, leading to the development of subsequent models, the Scorpion II (also based on the A12 Matilda) and the Scorpion III and IV, both based on the Grant, but these later vehicles did not see use until April 1943 in Libya.

By Sunday 25 October the British had made a 6-mile wide, 5-mile deep penetration into the Axis line. The Axis forces launched a series of probing attacks, looking for a weakness in the British line,

*"(text continued on p.411)"*

**Above:** *ATLANTA II was the nickname on the turret of this Grant tank from A Squadron, Royal Gloucestershire Hussars, photographed in the desert on 10 September 1942. This vehicle has an identical .30-caliber machine gun mount on the turret roof as the tank in the preceding photo. The census number on the sponson is T-24344, which was assigned to a vehicle completed by Pullman Standard in January 1942. Note the muzzle of the smoke mortar projecting through the upper front corner of the turret, and the modification of the driver's vision port cover with a strip of steel that evidently was a swing arm to facilitate opening and closing the heavy armored cover. Imperial War Museum*

**Above:** *During the war in North Africa, the U.S. Army established an Ordnance repair depot at Heliopolis, near Cairo, Egypt, where tanks were repaired and reconditioned. Among tasks carried out there was the repair of battle-damaged British Grant and Lee tanks, such as this Grant, which took a penetrating hit from a German 75mm round on the lower part of the glacis in September 1942. National Archives*

**Right:** *A German 75mm armor-piercing projectile made a mess of the 75mm gun sponson of a British Grant tank. The shell penetrated the armor on the lower outboard side of the 75mm gun barrel, tearing away some of the dust cover for the gun and also carving a notch in the rotor shield. The driver's visor also was torn off its mounting and is leaning against the right brush guard. National Archives*

**Above:** *Another Grant tank photographed at Heliopolis exhibits a penetrating strike from a German 75mm projectile on the upper-right corner of the center section the final-drive assembly. National Archives*

**Above:** *One of the Grant tanks at Heliopolis that was beyond repair was used in tests of the effectiveness of various types of German antitank guns against the Grant's armor. In this photo taken in October 1942, the effects of a 5cm projectile against the armor just below the driver's vision port are documented. National Archives*

**Above:** *Three members of a Grant tank crew present an interesting study in British tankers' dress as they advance to the front during the decisive Second Battle of El Alamein, on 29 October 1942. The man sitting in the fighting-compartment hatch is wearing a V-neck sweater; all are wearing black tankers' berets and goggles. The right mudguard is severely crumpled. Imperial War Museum*

**Above:** *A Lee tank, census number T-30252, in the Western Desert during the lead-up to the Second Battle of El Alamein, on 2 October 1942, displays considerable baggage on the left fender. Crew knapsacks are secured to the rail along the side of the vehicle. Note the antenna locations on the forward part of the fighting-compartment roof. The vehicle commander has his head out of the cupola hatch and is scanning the terrain to the front through binoculars. Imperial War Museum*

**Left Above:** *The crew of a Grant tank, members of the Staffordshire Yeomanry (Queen's Own Royal Regiment), 8th Armoured Brigade, gather for a meal to the side of their tank, census number T-24357, on 24 October 1942. This regiment participated in the Second Battle of El Alamein, and the photo was taken on the second day of the battle. The piece of fabric over the turret likely covers a Browning .30-caliber antiaircraft machine gun. Imperial War Museum*

**Left:** *While the bulk of the Grants in North Africa were M3s, about 164 Diesel-powered Grants saw action there as well, including this M3A5, T-23924, one of 25 to arrive in September. Australian War Memorial*

**Above:** *A Grant tank, a Jeep, and lorries are negotiating a road flooded by recent heavy rain while in pursuit of the retreating Germans on 10 November 1942, the day before the conclusion of the Second Battle of El Alamein. The number 86 is painted on the left mudguard of the Grant, which has been camouflage painted. Imperial War Museum*

**Above:** *Also photographed at Souk El Arba on 23 November 1942, was M4 W-309813 and its crew, who are preparing their rations. The tactical sign is for Company D, as indicated by the small square aligning with the top of the vertical bar. The platoon number is 3. National Archives*

**Left:** *The following series of photographs represents various tanks and crews from the 2nd Battalion, 13th Armored Regiment in Tunisia in late November 1942. Here, crewmen from a Company D M3, registration number W-309132, are getting some of their on-vehicle equipment and effects in order, including a disassembled .30-caliber machine gun in the foreground. On the 75mm gun sponson is the company-specific tactical sign 1st Armored Division used for its tanks in the North Africa Campaign. The basic part of the sign was a vertical bar, to the right side of which was affixed a small square. When the square was along the center of the vertical bar, as seen on this tank, it signified, for purposes of identification, the 13th Armored Regiment, Company E. The small number to the right of the symbol was the platoon number: in this instance, 2nd Platoon. The photo was taken at the bivouac at Souk El Arba, Tunisia, on 23 November 1942. National Archives*

**Above:** *Members of 3rd Platoon, Company D, 2nd Battalion, 13th Armored Regiment, exude confidence and a high morale as they pose with 75mm rounds next to their M3 medium tank, W-309576, at Souk el Arba on 23 November 1942. From left to right, the first, fourth, and sixth tankers are holding 75mm M61 armor-piercing rounds with tracers. National Archives*

**Left Above:** *The crewmen of M3 W-309751 pose next to their tank at Souk El Arba, Tunisia, on 23 November 1942. Box-type oil-bath air cleaners are below the rear overhang of the upper hull. National Archives*

**Left:** *Lined up alongside M3 W-309731 at a bivouac, possibly at Souk El Arba on 23 November 1942, are the members of the crew, who were caught finishing up their personal cleaning when the photographer came to call. Note the teapot and the large Thermos container on the ground in front of the man to the left. National Archives*

**Above:** *The crewmen of M3 W-309592 of the 2nd Battalion, 13th Armored Regiment, photographed at Souk El Arba on 26 November 1942, exhibit a variety of clothing items, from the herringbone twill overalls on the man to the left, to the winter-combat tanker's jackets on the second and third men from left, to the V-neck sweater vest on the fourth man from left. The man to the right is wearing a herringbone twill jacket authorized in early 1941. The man to the left is wearing a cap, while the next two men to the right wear garrison caps. National Archives*

**Left Above:** *About 12 miles northeast of Souk El Arba, there was another bivouac of the 2nd Battalion, 13th Armored Regiment, on 23 November 1942: at Souk El Khemis, Tunisia. Holding a position there was the 2nd Platoon of Company D, including this M3, W-309508, and its crew. The man to the far right is Lt. Charles Davis, the vehicle commander. Note the small bracket welded to the grab handle above the side door, to hold the tow cable in place. Of interest is the helmet of the crewman holding the rifle with bayonet affixed: it is marked with a circle with a representation of the inverted-L tactical sign of Company D. National Archives*

**Left:** *Visible on the 75mm gun sponson of M3 registration number W-309503, assigned to the 2nd Battalion, 13th Armored Regiment at Souk El Arba on 23 November 1942, is the L-shaped tactical sign representing Company F. A collection of topographical maps is on the ground to the left. The recoil guard of the 75mm gun and the turret basket are visible through the side door. A nearly invisible detail is of interest: to the front of the squatting man with the light-colored shirt and sweater vest is a helmet marked with the Company F tactical sign on a circle. National Archives*

**Above:** *Parked to the front of several of the crewmen's pup tents is M3 W-309498 of the 2nd Battalion, 13th Armored Regiment. Although the tactical sign is not visible on the 75mm gun sponson, the crewman sitting to the left has the tactical sign of Company E marked on his helmet: a vertical bar with a small square jutting from the center of its right side. The white object resting on the fighting-compartment roof is the frame of the recoil guard of the 75mm gun. National Archives*

**Above:** *One of the more recognizable M3s of the North Africa Campaign was Kentucky, registration number W-309513, of the 3rd Platoon, Company D, 2nd Battalion, 13th Armored Regiment. The Kentucky nickname was on the left storage box, and on close inspection, it appears to have been applied with chalk. National Archives*

**Above:** *An inscription on a photo of an M3 crew following a battle in North Africa indicates that one of them was a 1st Lieutenant Curry. This evidently was Lt. James M. Curry, whose tank would be destroyed in battle near Tebourba, Tunisia, on 2 December 1942. National Archives*

**Above:** *Under the command of Lt. Col. Henry Gardiner, the 2nd Battalion, 13th Armored Regiment, had its first pitched battle with German panzer forces on 28 November 1942, at Djedeida, Tunisia. The battalion engaged with German forces in subsequent days and weeks, often suffering serious losses. Shown here is one of 2/13th Armor's M3 medium tanks after being shot up by Germans in Tunisia.*
*National Archives*

**Above:** *The same M3 depicted in the preceding photo is viewed from the front. An armor-piercing projectile, apparently an 88mm, penetrated the armor next to the driver's vision port. Two smaller-caliber rounds penetrated the glacis and the center section of the final-drive assembly. A number 4 is faintly visible on the glacis. National Archives*

**Right Above:** *A close-up view of a Medium Tank M3 knocked out by the Germans during fighting at Medjez El Bab, Tunisia, around 10 December 1942, keys in on a perforation in the front of the turret below the corner of the opening for the 37mm gun mount. The gun mount had been removed for salvage. The photo is so sharp, casting numbers are clearly visible on the antenna bracket and the armored fuel-filler cover. National Archives*

**Right:** *The same turret depicted in the preceding photo is viewed from the inside, showing the hole in the armor from an antitank round below the lower left corner of the opening for the 37mm gun mount. Some of the white paint has spalled off around the hole. National Archives*

**Above:** *Documentation is available on the status and condition of this Medium Tank M3 assigned to the 2nd Battalion, 13th Armored Regiment, photographed in a field five miles east of Souk El Khemis, Tunisia, on 17 December 1942. The registration number was W-309056, and the tank saw action from 29 November to 12 December 1942. The engine had logged 267 hours, and the mileage was 1,376 miles. Due to this hard use, the track blocks and the tires of the bogie wheels were worn out. National Archives*

**Above:** *Service in North Africa was particularly tough on the running gear of tanks. This photograph of Medium Tank M3 W-309478, serving with the 2nd Battalion, 13th Armored Regiment, was photographed 10 miles east of Souk El Khemis, Tunisia, on 17 December 1942, to document the extreme wear on the bogie wheels following 273 motor hours and 1,757 miles of driving. While the front bogie wheel is not sufficiently visible, the rubber tires have completely worn off all of the other bogie wheels except the rear one. The rubber treads also have worn off many of the track links. National Archives*

**Above:** *British Grant tanks are lined up at the U.S. Army Ordnance repair depot at Heliopolis, Egypt, in January 1943. Stacks of 75mm ammunition are to the fronts of the tanks, as well as storage boxes and bits of vehicular gear. National Archives*

**Above:** *This Grant tank at the Heliopolis repair depot received several penetrating hits in battle, including two on the rear of the left storage box and one on the right engine-access door. What appears to have been a non-penetrating hit was registered below the lower hinge of the left engine-access door. National Archives*

**Left:** *A British Grant tank is in a U.S. Army tank-repair depot in North Africa for refurbishment in January 1943. The shop was probably at Heliopolis, based on a comparison of the structure of the building with known photos of Heliopolis. A worker is visible in the turret where the 37mm gun mount has been removed. The right rear panel of the fighting compartment was removed so the 75mm gun could be extracted from the tank. This vehicle has the box-type oil-bath air filters on the rear of the hull, which were easier to service than the original air cleaners mounted inside the engine compartment. National Archives*

**Above:** *Two U.S. Army mechanics examine the center-right bogie assembly of a British Grant in a shop at the tank-repair depot at Heliopolis in January 1943. The census number on the sponson is T-24223, which indicates an early-production M3 completed by Pullman-Standard in September 1941. Inside the fighting compartment, the padding on the ceiling is hanging loose. Visible inside the side door are part of the instrument panel and the left side of the gun sponson. National Archives*

**Right:** *Two members of U.S. Army Ordnance are standing on a battle-damaged British Grant tank about to receive repairs at a U.S. depot in January 1943. The census number, T-24758, applies to a vehicle completed at the Pressed Steel Car plant in December 1941 under British Contract A-1795, which provided for 501 Grant tanks. National Archives*

**Right:** *U.S. Army Ordnance men are preparing to mount a new 75mm gun in a British Grant tank at a repair facility in North Africa in January 1943. Lying upright on the ground below the gun is the carriage and recoil-mechanism assembly. National Archives*

**Left:** *In a continuation of the preceding photo, the Ordnance troops have rolled the gantry crane to straddle the rear of the tank and are preparing to insert the new 75mm gun through the opening in the right rear of the fighting compartment. Because of the awkward method of changing guns, it took careful management of the chain hoist to perform the task without injury to crewmen or damage to the gun. National Archives*

**Left:** *A column of newly refurbished and repainted Grant and Sherman tanks is departing from an unidentified tank-repair depot in North Africa in January 1943. In the lead is Grant census number T-24739, completed by Pressed Steel Car in November 1941. Though the location of the base is not identified, it was likely Heliopolis, which carried the formal designation OMET 5 , "OMET" standing for Ordnance Middle East Tasks. National Archives*

**Above:** *Grant tanks were active participants in the British drive into Libya in early 1943, although their role would steadily diminish as Sherman tanks became more numerous during that final campaign of the war in North Africa. Shown here is a Grant with four crewmen in view on the tank as it passes through an intersection in the settlement of Tarhuna during the advance to Tripoli on 25 January 1943. The heavily weathered paintwork shows evidence of a mix of Light Stone and Green or Olive Drab coloration. Note the elevated barrel of a .30-caliber machine gun to the vehicle commander's right side, above the turret. Imperial War Museum*

**Above:** *As the tank crews of the 1st Armored Division gained battle experience in North Africa, they learned to camouflage their tanks to make the dark-toned Olive Drab paint less conspicuous. On these 1st AD M3 medium tanks operating in combat conditions near Sened, Tunisia, in early 1943, the crews have swabbed random stripes of mud over the OD paint to better make the tanks blend in with the terrain. The tank to the right is still showing large areas of OD paint, while the two M3s in the far left of the photo are exhibiting more of the mud color than the Olive Drab, giving them a very light overall tone. National Archives*

**Above:** *Four Medium Tanks M3 from the 1st Armored Division are crossing the desert in the middle distance during one of the several battles for Sened Station, Tunisia, in early 1943. The vehicles have mud camouflage, giving them a much lighter appearance than tanks with the usual Olive Drab camouflage paint. National Archives*

**Above:** *Two columns of M3 medium tanks, in the left and the right distance, are driving across the desert during one of the battles for Sened Station in early 1943. National Archives*

**Above:** *U.S. Army Medium Tank M3 W-309538 was knocked out during combat at Sened, Tunisia, as seen in a photo dated 3 February 1943. Among other damage, the right side door was blown off its hinges. Under high magnification, the closest tank on the right has a squiggly pattern of mud camouflage on the turret, with narrow squiggles of the original Olive Drab paint showing through.*
*National Archives*

**Above:** *During one of the battles for Sened in early 1943, this Medium Tank M3 was knocked out. Fire consumed the tank, turning the exterior paint a powdery gray and burning off the tires of the bogie wheels.*

**Above:** *At a road intersection in Tunisia, vehicles and troops that have evacuated the town of Telepte are in retreat on 15 February 1943. Entering the intersection is a Medium Tank M3, followed by another one. The tank on the left is a riveted-hull example with side doors and the long-barreled 75mm Gun M3, while the tank on the right has a welded hull with no side doors, and an M3 main gun. National Archives*

**Above:** *A U.S. 1st Armored Division Medium Tank M3 proceeds across the desert on the second day of the Battle of Kasserine Pass, the first large-scale battle between German and U.S. armor in the North Africa Campaign. The vehicle commander, standing in the cupola, is wearing an M1 steel helmet. National Archives*

**Above:** *Against a foreground of beaten-down prickly pear cactuses, three Medium Tanks M3 assigned to the 1st Armored Division drive across a plain near Kasserine Pass, Tunisia, on 20 February 1943. Camouflage netting and baggage is stowed on the engine deck of the tank to the left. During the Battle of Kasserine Pass, 19-24 February 1943, the Allied forces suffered losses of 183 tanks of all types, as well as approximately 300 killed in action, 3,000 wounded in action, and 3,000 missing in action.*
*National Archives*

**Above:** *British troops are checking over a newly refurbished Grant tank next to a stone tower at the tank-repair depot at Heliopolis, Egypt, on 25 March 1943. There are white recognition stars on dark-colored circles on the side of the turret and on the glacis of the tank. National Archives*

**Above:** *A riveted-hull M3 with the side doors eliminated is rolling along a street in Bizerte, Tunisia, on 8 May 1943, one day after the Allied forces captured the city. National Archives*

**Above:** *A Medium Tank M3 moves through recently captured Bizerte, Tunisia, while another M3 comes up on the left, on 8 May 1943. A pith helmet is lying on the right headlight brush guard of the tank to the right. On the turret, aft of the pistol port, is a large number 3, with white or light-colored outlining. On the sponson is a nickname written in large letters; it is indistinct but appears to be AFTER-EFFECT. National Archives*

**Above:** *This U.S. Army Medium Tank M3 chassis was used for tests to evaluate the armor protection against U.S. 57mm and 3-inch projectiles. Penetrating hits were registered at several places on the glacis, final-drive assembly, turret, cupola, and 75mm gun sponson. One hit, probably from a 57mm round, punched out the fairing for the two bow machine guns. Two evidently non-penetrating strikes were registered on the joint between the glacis and the top of the final-drive assembly; these are circled and numbered 1 and 2. National Archives*

but found none. The Australian 26th Brigade attacked the German observation post at Point 29 at midnight, the assault supported by artillery and 30 tanks of 40th Royal Tank Regiment. Point 29 was taken, although fighting continued in the area for a week as the Germans made repeated attempt to retake the position.

Relatively speaking the 26th was quiet, but on the 27th the fighting resumed in earnest near Outpost Woodcock and Outpost Snipe near Tel el Aqqaqir. At 23:00 the assault began, and the fighting was continuous throughout the day, and at 16:00 Rommel launched a counter attack, which the British were able to repel, but with terrible losses on both sides.

Over the next five days fighting continued, with the overwhelming British force essentially fighting a war of attrition against Rommel, who besides being vastly outnumbered in terms of tanks, was also desperately short on ammunition and fuel. The latter was so critical that fuel was being flown in, and rarely were there more than two day's supply. As an example of the type of war being waged, the 9th Armoured Brigade was ordered to attack toward Tel el Aqqaqir on 1 November. Lieutenant-General Bernard Freyberg of the 2nd New Zealand Division ordered Brigadier John Cecil Currie to carry this out, to which Currie objected, pointing out that the operation was better suited to infantry. Freyberg replied that General Montgomery "... was aware of the risk and has accepted the possibility

**Above:** *In a left view of the same M3, four glancing hits from 57mm projectiles are indicated on the forward armored panel of the upper hull. Two of these hits sheared off several rivets and screws, which then would have become ricocheting projectiles inside the tank. Other shell holes are on the turret and above the center track-support roller. National Archives*

**Above:** *At an unidentified site on 2 June 1943, a wrecker is towing a Medium Tank M3 off of the trailer of a Heavy Tank Retriever M19 while another M3 is on the trailer of an M19 to the right. The turret of the tank to the right is marked "301 ORD TANK SHOP," a reference to the 301st Ordnance Regiment. Note the extreme sag of the track on the M3 to the right and the fact that most of the rubber of the track shoes have worn off. National Archives*

**Above:** *An American M3 medium tank nicknamed SHILOH is burning on a battlefield in the North Africa Campaign; flames are erupting from the hull over the second-from-rear bogie wheel. On the 75mm gun sponson are a tactical sign in the shape of a tilted L and a platoon number, 3. Painted on the 75mm gun barrel is "JACK SHARKEY," while the 37mm gun barrel is marked "TOMMY LOUGHRAN." These are references to two professional boxers who fought each other in bouts twice in the 1930s.*
*National Archives*

of losing 100% casualties in 9th Armoured Brigade to make the break, but in view of the promise of immediate following through of the 1st Armoured Division, the risk was not considered as great as all that."

The 9th Armoured Brigade left the El Alamein station at 20:00 with 130; tanks these were of almost equal portions of Grant, Sherman and Crusader types. Of these, 36 failed before the Brigade reached the launch point. The attack began at 06:15, and when it was over Brigadier William Gentry of 6th New Zealand Brigade was inspecting the aftermath. He approached Brigadier Currie who was resting, asking, "Sorry to wake you John, but I'd like to know where your tanks are?" Motioning to the tanks around him, Currie replied, "There they are."

In response, Gentry said, "I don't mean your headquarters tanks, I mean your armoured regiments. Where are they?"

Again motioning with his arm, Currie repeated, "There are my armoured regiments, Bill."

The Brigade had lost all but 14 of its tanks. Rommel had lost a similar number, but the British had far greater reserves.

The Second Battle of El Alamein continued until 7 November, resulting in 1,139 German killed, 3,886 wounded, and 8,050 captured. The Italians lost 971 dead, 933 wounded and 15,552, lacking motorized transport to withdraw, were captured.

The Eighth Army had 2,350 men killed, 8,950 wounded and 2,260 missing. While El Alamein is frequently remembered as the combat debut of the Sherman, and many feel its role in that battle and the desert campaign thereafter was pivotal, that is only part of the story. Only 252 Shermans were ready for combat at the start of the battle, with other types, including the Grant, making up the bulk of the British armored force, and no more

**Above:** *Developed in North Africa, the Scorpion III, like this one, used a truck engine to drive a forwarded mounted reel, upon which chains were attached. These would beat the ground, detonating land mines. Although Scorpions were used in the Second Battle of El Alamein, those vehicles were Matilda-based, with the Grant-based Scorpion III through V variants improved models. David Fletcher*

**Above:** *A Scorpion IV comes ashore from an LCT in Sicily in 1943. The left lift arm of Scorpion IV was of an improved design compared to that of the prior Scorpions. David Fletcher*

**Above:** *This Scorpion IV is coming ashore with its flail rotor waterproofed with a tarpaulin. Less visible is the tarp waterproofing on the flail engine box. The improved left rotor support arm, compared to that of the Scorpion III, is clearly seen. Pat Ware, Warehouse Publications*

**Above:** *Moving along a street in Sicily is one of about 20 Scorpion IVs deployed there with the 41st Royal Tank Regiment which was renamed "The 1st Scorpion Regiment, Royal Armoured Corps" in May 1943. National Army Museum*

**Left:** *The only known Diesel-powered Scorpion is this experimental M3A5-based Scorpion V. Both flail arms on this vehicle are based on the left arm design used on the Scorpion IV. Production Scorpion V, of which there were only a handful, were based on the M4A4 Sherman. David Fletcher*

**Left:** *The flail mechanism of the Scorpion V was driven by two truck engines, the fuel supply for which was mounted atop the engine deck. In order to fit on the new Bailey Bridge, the width was reduced still further, to 11 ½-feet, and to do this flail engines were mounted on the tank engine deck. David Fletcher*

Shermans were delivered to the 8th Army until the African Campaign was over, at which time the M3 continued to outnumber the Shermans. The M3 truly held the line in the sand.

Following the North African campaign, a number of M3s were used in Iraq. A handful of these were shipped directly there from the United States, but most of almost 150 M3s in Iraq in the spring of 1943 were transferred there from North Africa. These tanks were assigned to the 31st Indian Armoured Division and the 7th Armoured Brigade.

April 1943 saw the only known combat use of the

Scorpion Mk III. This vehicle was based on a Grant with the 75mm gun removed and the mine flail apparatus installed. The flail operator was provided with a secure position inside the tank, taking up the space previously housing the 75mm gun. The similar Scorpion IV had a stronger left support arm, addressing a deficiency found in earlier models, and also was 12' 5" wide, a foot narrower than the Scorpion III. This allowed it to fit on Landing Craft, Tanks for amphibious assaults. A single Scorpion V was built, based on a M3A5 Grant and with the flail apparatus being powered by two truck engines, rather than the single engine used on previous models.

# US Use

Churchill learned of the fall of Tobruk while visiting Roosevelt at the White House in 21 June 1942. When asked by the President what could be done to help, Churchill replied, "Give us as many Sherman tanks as you can spare, and ship them to the Middle East as quickly as possible."

Roosevelt granted his wish, and in doing so stripped US armored units of the bulk of the Shermans, leaving the Americans to ride in M3 Lees.

Such was the case when plans were made for US armor to deploy to North Africa. The November 1942 US force included Combat Command B (CCB) of the 1st Armored Division, which included a single medium tank battalion, the 2nd Battalion of the 13th Armored Regiment (2/13th), Lt. Col. Hyman Bruss, commanding. Because the landing ships in use at the time could not accommodate the tanks, there arrival was delayed a few days until port facilities could be secured.

Moving toward the objectives of Tunis and Bizerta, the tanks were driven to Algeria; then moved by sea to Bone, with the road march resuming for two days. By the time they reached the forward area, they had driven 700 miles, and the tracks and suspensions showed this.

The first action of consequence that the medium tanks were involved in occurred on the 01:00 on

**Above:** *British Grant, Stuart, and Sherman tank hulls, stripped of their suspensions, turrets, engines and drive trains, and other components, are stacked in the U.S. Army's Camp Ataka Salvage Dump, in Egypt, on September 16, 1943. A Grant hull is at the bottom of the pile of Stuart hulls to the left, and several more Grant hulls are visible toward the middle of this assemblage. National Archives*

28 November 1942, when the tanks, carrying infantry from the British 5th Northamptonshire Regiment, attacked Djedeida. The tanks were those of Company D, plus one platoon from Company F, as well as the Headquarters tanks. Axis forces repelled the attack, knocking out many of the Lees.

The US combat for the next month consisted of a series of small but costly skirmishes, with the result being that CCB lost 84 M3 light tanks and 40 of the M3 medium tanks. In January 1943 the 2/13th advanced on Ousseltia Valley in a successful operation.

By February 1943 the rest of the 1st Armored Division had arrived in country, most of which were equipped with Shermans, the exception being the 3rd Battalion of the 13th Armored Regiment (3/13th), which like the 2/13th, was equipped with M3s.

When the Sherman-equipped 2nd Battalion of the 1st Armored Regiment was decimated on 15 February near Sidi bou Zid in the Faid Pass, the four surviving Shermans (44 were destroyed) fell back toward Sbeitla, forming a defensive line with the M3s of the 3/13th.

**Above:** *The M3A5 command tank of Maj. Gen. William Henry Evered Poole, Commander of the 6th South African Armoured Division is shown on the outskirts of Bologna on 21 April 1945. This tank has been equipped with Sherman-type suspension units and track, likely installed during the overhaul process that immediately preceded the conversion to command tank configuration. This tank has had both the 37mm and 75mm guns removed, and a 75mm barrel (probably a worn or damaged tube) installed in the turret as a false gun. This made the tank more closely resemble a Sherman, which by this point in the war had supplanted the M3 in combat use. David Fletcher*

Combat Command B, including the M3s of the 3/13th, was sent south to support a fighting withdrawal of the surviving Allied forces, arriving on 16 February. On the next day, Lt. Colonel Harry Gardiner's 2/13th, consisting of M3s supplemented with some M4s, all deployed in a concealed position, managed to ambush elements of the 21 Panzer Division. Achieving the element of surprise, Gardiner's men held their fire until the enemy was in close range. The opening barrage startled the Germans, knocked out five tanks and broke up the attack. The 2/13th continued to cover the US withdrawal through Kasserine Pass, during which time Gardiner's tank was knocked out, with him having to walk 30 miles to rejoin his troops.

The same battalion engaged the Germans again on 21 February, halting a German move toward Djebel el Hamra.

In May 1943 the 751st Tank Battalion supported the 34th Division in attacking Bizerte, marking the last U.S. use of the M3 as a combat tank in Europe or the Mediterranean.

Although the 1st Armored Division was supposed to have been equipped with Shermans by the end of March, at the end of the fighting in Tunisia 51 M3 mediums were still rostered. These tanks were turned over to Free French forces in Oran for driver training.

## 1st AD M3 tank status in Tunisia

| 3/3/43 | 3/9/43 | 3/12/43 | 3/22/43 | 3/26/43 | 5/43 |
|--------|--------|---------|---------|---------|------|
| 93 | 71 | 77 | 86 | 86 | 51 |

# Chapter 12
# The M3 in the Far East

## US

The only use of the M3-series Medium in the Pacific Theater by the US military was the deployment of the 193rd Medium Tank Battalion on Butaitar Island in the Gilberts in November 1943. The 15 tanks were used to support the 165th Infantry Regiment.

The M3A5s were Company A, and were landed on Yellow Beach by LCMs from the USS *Belle Grove*, LSD-2, on 20 November. Almost immediately, while driving through shallow water on the beach, two of the tanks drove into submerged shell holes and became mired. Worse, the water stalled the engines and disabled the radio equipment. One of these was the tank of Captain Robert S. Brown, who commanded Company A.

Soon thereafter, another tank knocked out a Japanese machine gun position with its 37mm gun.

A third tank was disabled when it hit a land mine, but the crew survived. A second machine gun nest was disabled by yet another tank. Moving west on Yellow Beach, two of the M3A5s, now under the direct control of Lt. Col. Harmon L. Edmondson, commander of the 193rd Tank Battalion, advanced directly to the south shore.

**Above:** *One day after the November 20, 1943, U.S. landings on Butaritari Atoll, in Makin Atoll, part of the Gilbert Islands, a Medium Tank M3A5 from the 193rd Tank Battalion is shelling Japanese forces on the opposite shore. In the background is another M3A5 that became mired during the preceding day's landings. On the engine deck of the M3 to the left is what appears to be the lower section of an air-inlet trunk of a deep-fording kit. The tracks are the T48 type, with chevron-shaped grousers built into the rubber blocks. National Archives*

**Above:** *In a photo taken at the same beach and date as the preceding photo, M3A5s are shelling Japanese troops on the King's Wharf, across Butaritari Lagoon. The tank in the foreground in the preceding photo is the one on the right in this one. The Butaritari operation was the only time the U.S. Army employed M3 medium tanks in combat operations in the Pacific Theater. National Archives*

**Above:** *Three Medium Tanks M3A5 on the tidal flats at Butaritari Lagoon are shelling two ship hulks lying alongside Ah Chong's Wharf in the lagoon on November 21, 1943. Smoke is pouring out of one of the hulks in the distance to the left of the leftmost tank. Japanese machine gunners were using these hulks as positions from which to fire on American troops. Finally, Navy planes were called in to finish off the hulks and the Japanese gunners. National Archives*

**Above:** *On November 24, 1943, one day after the U.S. victory on Butaritari Atoll, a U.S. Army M3, followed in the distance by another one, is being driven along a palm-lined road. Part of a number, apparently 19, is painted on the side of the turret, and a light-colored panel had been painted on the upper part of the glacis, with much of that paint having spalled off the Olive Drab base paint. National Archives*

**Above:** *An M3 Lee named 'Shrewsbury' of the 25th Dragoons, in the Ngakyedauk Pass in Burma during the second Arkan offensive in February 1944. National Army Museum*

**Above:** *A Lee tank of the 25th Dragoons, a British cavalry regiment, has paused near Fort White during the Burma Campaign. The cupola of this tank was removed, and a ring with a split hatch was installed in its place on the turret roof: a practice often done with Lee tanks in Asia. A storage bin has been added on to the sponson to the rear of the fighting compartment. Imperial War Museum*

**Above:** *Jolly crewmen pose in and on their Lee tank along the Mu River, near Chanta, Burma in January 1945. A wireless antenna is mounted in an unusual location, on the left fender. A roll of barbed wire, for defensive use when setting up bivouacs, is around the spare track section on the glacis. On the side of the turret are two smoke-grenade dischargers. Imperial War Museum*

Capt. Francis P. Leonard of Company F. , 2nd Battalion Landing Team, called for assistance, and five of the M3A5s moved across the island, spraying the trees with 37mm fire, seeking to eliminate machine gun nests and snipers. By 1230 hours this operation was complete, but an hour later a similar operation was undertaken by other M3A5s at the center of the island.

1st Platoon required support from the Lees in silencing fire from Japanese rifle pits and gun emplacements along the shore, but this objective was achieved by 1330.

Elsewhere, 3rd Platoon encountered a heavily fortified position that even the 75mm sponson gun

couldn't demolish, despite firing armor-piercing shells. Ultimately, Engineers silenced the position with a Bangalore torpedo.

## British

The British, on the other hand, put the M3 to considerably more use in the Far East. Burma had been a part of the Empire of India until 1937. In that year, the Burma Province was separated from British India, becoming a separate Crown Colony.

On 14 December 1941 the Japanese attacked Victoria Point, the first of a series of attacks and incursions into Burma. Japan believed Burma would be an easy conquest, in part due to the

**Above:** *A Grant tank speeds past a Dodge truck and a machine-gun carrier at a site in Burma in January 1945. For extra protection against frontal antitank fire, non-Grant tracks have been arrayed on the front of the hull. The vehicle commander is wearing what appears to be a U.S. Army tanker's helmet. Imperial War Museum*

friction between Burma and neighboring British Indian Empire. The Japanese saw the occupation of India as an easy way to cutoff the flow of supplies to China by severing the Burma Road. Japan made rapid advances in Burma, aided in some cases by Burmese who saw the Japanese as a liberating force that they believed would provide independence.

An alarmed Britain dispatched additional forces to India in order to both protect that part of the Empire as well as to prepare to retake Burma. Among the equipment sent to India were a number of M3 series Medium tanks, which were shipped directly from the factories in the US.

These shipments included 369 "Grant Gas," 10 "Grant Diesel," 515 "Lee Gas" and 2 "Lee Diesel" tanks in 1942. The first shipment consisted of 16 Grants and 8 Lees, which were shipped on 24 February 1942.

While some Indian armored units saw service in North Africa, it would be 1944 before the Indian M3 medium tanks saw combat in the Far East.

Initially the Medium Tank Regiments of the 50th Indian Tank Brigade, the 25th Dragoons and the 146th Regiment, Royal Armoured Corps (The Duke of Wellington Regiment) were equipped with Lee I tanks, as was the 254th Indian Tank Brigade.

The 25th Dragoons with their Lees took part in the second Arakan offensive along the coast of Burma in January 1944. The Japanese countered with the Ha-Go offensive in February, forcing the 7th Indian Infantry Division to take up a defensive position, which was supported by two squadrons of the Dragoons' Lees. Even more Lees arrived with the 5th Indian Infantry Division, which relieved the 7th. Soon thereafter, in what the British National Army Museum terms one of "Britain's Greatest Battles," the Grant Medium tanks were committed to battle in Burma as well.

On 29 March the Japanese advance cut the Imphal-Kohima road, nearly surrounding the British 17th Division, and pushing toward the British supply depot on the Imphal Plain. During early April, the British troops in Kohima and Imphal on the eastern frontier were surrounded.

**Above:** *The crew of a Lee tank strike a pose, gazing resolutely forward, during a pause at Ywathitgyi, Burma, in February 1945. A clear view is available of two smoke-grenade launchers, which are mounted on a bracket welded to the side of the turret. Imperial War Museum*

**Above:** *Three Lee tanks, part of a force supporting the 19th Indian Division, are preparing to resume the advance on Mandalay, Burma, on March 9 or 10, 1945. The Lee to the left has the nickname CENTURION and a large identification star painted on the side of the upper hull. A small insignia that appears to portray a lion is to the side of the driver's vision port on that tank. Tracks for extra protection have been installed on the fronts of the Lee to the left and the one to the right, but evidently not on the Lee in the background. Imperial War Museum*

**Above:** *Infantry of 19th Indian Division take cover behind a Lee tank nicknamed CALEDONIAN during the taking of Mandalay, 9-10 March 1945. Two spare track links are secured below the painted-on nickname, and three sections of tracks are arrayed on the front of the hull. Here again, a lion insignia is to the side of the driver's vision port. Imperial War Museum*

Lord Louis Mountbatten ordered the 2nd Division to march the 1,000 miles to Dimapur where it would join the 33rd Corps in an effort to relieve Kohima. The 2nd Division took with it A & B Squadrons of the 149th Regiment Royal Armoured Corps, which was equipped with 36 Grant I medium tanks. The British forces fought their way to Kohima, reaching the objective on 18 April.

However, the Japanese were not quick to acquiesce, and fighting in the Kohima continued until mid-May. During the fighting six of the Grants were lost.

The 33rd Corps along with the 2nd Division pressed on toward Imphal, where they broke through to the 4th Corps, which had been under

**Above:** *A Lee tank pushes forward along a dusty road during the advance south from Mandalay on March 20 1945. The War Department census number, T-25602, is faintly visible toward the rear of the sponson. A roughly painted recognition star is on the hull to the front of the side door. Two wireless antennas are on the left fender, a third antenna is visible to the right rear of the fighting compartment, and an ammunition box is strapped to the side of the driver's vision port. Imperial War Museum*

siege since 5 April. Near Tamu, during the push to Imphal, a column of A Squadron, 3rd Carabiniers (Prince of Wales's Dragoon Guards) were ambushed by 5 Japanese Type 95 tanks. One of the M3 Lees was knocked out with a hit to the fuel tank, but the remaining M3s, considerably better armed and armored that the Japanese tanks, quickly destroyed the Type 95s. The British casualties at Imphal were 12,500, with a further 4,000 at Kohima. Dead and missing Japanese, on the other hand, numbered 53,000.

By the time that the 146th Regiment, Royal Armoured Corps took part in the landing at Letpan in March 1945, the unit had a mixture of two Lee and 10 Grant tanks. This unopposed landing was likely the final combat use of the M3 medium in the Far East.

# Chapter 13
# The M3 in Australia

Japan had launched a full-scale invasion of China in 1937, and by 1941 held much of China's coast, as well as Indochina. In December 1941 the Japanese attacked US bases at Pearl Harbor, Wake Island, and the Philippines, as well as Commonwealth bases in Malaya, Singapore and Hong Kong.

Only an hour after the Japanese attack on Pearl Harbor, and two days prior to an official declaration of war, Australian Prime Minister John Curtin announced, "…from one hour ago, Australia has been at war with the Japanese Empire."

Faced with what at the time seemed like a steamroller of Japanese military successes, there were grave concerns that Australia would be invaded by the Japanese. Prime Minister Curtin in January 1942 requested "that adequate supplies of tanks should be diverted to Australia from the United Kingdom and American production at the earliest possible date. The immediate requirements are stated to be 775 Cruiser Tanks."

Thus British war planners gave priority to supplying Australia with tanks. Starting in April 1942 shipments of M3 Medium tanks from British orders began to arrive directly from the factories in the United States to Australia. Those shipments, which began with 54 tanks in April 1942, became a veritable flood with 757 of the M3 Mediums arriving by the end of the war.

**Above:** *Australian tankers are preparing a newly arrived Grant tank at a base in Victoria, Australia, on May 28, 1942. They appear to be cleaning the residue of sealant materials that have been removed from the guns. Evidence of that residue is visible around the various ports. Patton Museum*

**Above:** *The Australian crew of a Grant tank pose proudly with their vehicle at Victoria, Australia, on May 28, 1942. Note the sealant residue around the side door. The census number, T-23710, represented a Grant completed by Baldwin Locomotive in February 1942. The circles on the sponson and the turret represented C Squadron. Shipping stencils are present on the storage box. Patton Museum*

**Above:** *In a photo dated June 7, 1942, the insignia of the 1st Australian Armoured Division is on the right side of the rear plate of the upper hull of the closest vehicle in a column of Grant tanks. This vehicle, a welded-hull Grant, bears the British Army census number T23708, completed in February 1942 by Baldwin Locomotive. There also is an Australian Army registration number, 9144, on the left engine-access door. Patton Museum*

**Above:** *Nine Australian Grant tanks of the 1st Armoured Division are assembled on a parade ground prior to passing in review before Gen. Sir Thomas Blamey, commander-in-chief of Allied Land Forces, at Puckapunyal, Victoria, Australia, in late June 1942. Registration numbers are visible on the first three tanks: 9120, 10109, and 10117. The first three tanks have the number 61 above the registration*

**Above:** *Grant tanks with camouflage patterns painted on them are on Diamond T M20 tank transporters at Melbourne, Australia, during preparations for going on training maneuvers on September 7, 1942. These vehicles were assigned to the 1st Australian Armoured Division. Patton Museum*

**Above:** *A riveted-hull Grant from the same procession depicted in the preceding photo is viewed close-up. The British War Department number, T-23885, is in light-colored figures on a black or dark-colored background. The battle-axe insignia of the 1st Australian Armoured Division is on the left side of the final-drive assembly. Patton Museum*

The tanks included 259 Grant tanks with Diesel engines and 263 Grants with gasoline engines, as well as 255 M3 Lees, which began arriving 30 August 1942. These tanks included M3, M3A2, M3A3 and M3A5 models.

As mentioned, 259 of the tanks shipped to Australia were Diesel-powered, making that country the single largest user of the Diesel-powered Grant. It appears that all the Australian Grants, whether Diesel or gasoline-fueled, were originally armed with the short M2 75mm gun with counterweight on the barrel.

The initial deliveries of the M3 were used to outfit the 1st Australian Armoured Division. Through their service life, the vehicles were subjected to a

number of modifications, some drawn from the British experience in North Africa and others drawing on experiences closer to home, the fighting in Burma. Among these were an applique armor for the transmission housing, a locally-developed wading trunk, and anti-mine netting to protect the engine deck.

Ultimately, while taken on strength for combat units, the Australian use of the M3 was confined almost entirely to training and defense of Australia against a never-arriving Japanese attack. The exception were three M3A5 Grant tanks of the Australian 2/1st Armoured Brigade. These tanks were sent to Morotai, Dutch East Indies, and there modified by the installation of the US M1 dozer blade (intended for installation on the Sherman)

**Above:** *A crewman checks the turret hatch of Grant tank T-23891 of the 1st Australian Armoured Division prior to moving out for maneuvers, at Melbourne on September 7, 1942. A British census number is present but not entirely legible on the sponson. Patton Museum*

**Above:** *Tankers standing in front of a Grant tank confer over a chart at the annual Armored Fighting Vehicles School at Puckapunyal, Australia, in November 1942. The vehicle is painted in a camouflage pattern with a soft edge between the two colors. A white registration number is partially visible on the bottom of the glacis. In the background is the AFV School encampment. Patton Museum*

**Above:** *Recognizing the vulnerability of the three-piece final-drive assembly to enemy antitank weapons, the Australians experimented with applique armor to protect the final drive. They devised the cast-armor assembly shown installed here on a Diesel-powered, riveted-hull Grant tank. Painted white or a very light color, the casting was 44mm thick and was of sufficient strength to protect the final drive from Japanese antitank guns then in service. It is, however, doubtful that these castings saw extensive use on Australian Grants. Patton Museum*

**Above:** *A train transporting Grant tanks destined for the 1st Australian Armoured Division has just arrived at Morowa, Western Australia, on February 13, 1943. On the first two tanks, nicknames are painted in white on the 75mm gun sponsons but are illegible. Several of the tanks have round bridge-classification symbols with the number 24 on the fronts of the hulls. Patton Museum*

**Above:** *Crews of Grant tanks that have just arrived in Morowa, Western Australia, are preparing the vehicles for offloading from the flatcars. The British War Department number is visible on center of the final-drive assembly of the tank to the front: T-24887, which corresponds to a Grant completed by the Pressed Steel Car Company in February 1942. On this tank, note the two antenna mounts on the turret bustle and the additional antenna bracket on the left front of the fighting-compartment roof. Diamond symbols denoting a Headquarters vehicle are on the turret and the sponson. Patton Museum*

**Above:** *On the same date as the preceding two photos, February 13, 1942, a Grant tank nicknamed HERCULES being delivered for the 1st Australian Armoured Division is driving onto the trailer of a Diamond T M20 tank transporter at Morowa, Western Australia. Patton Museum*

**Above:** *Four Grant tanks are arriving on camouflage-painted Diamond T tank transporters at the base of the 1st Australian Armoured Division at Morowa on February 13, 1942. The turret of the first Grant has the diamond symbol of a vehicle assigned to Headquarters. Patton Museum*

**Above:** *Grant tanks from the Australian 2/10th Armoured Regiment are advancing in close formation during maneuvers near Mingenew, Western Australia, on February 25, 1943. The tanks are painted in varying camouflage patterns, with the one at the center having dark areas with a darker-colored edging. The 2/10th Armoured Regiment was part of the 2nd Armoured Brigade, 1st Armoured Division. Patton Museum*

**Above:** *On the same date and at the same location as the preceding photo, standing in the hatch of the turret of Grant British War Department number T-25094 is Lt. Col. R. E. Wade, commanding officer of the 2/10th Armoured Regiment, and to the left is Trooper P. D. Murtaugh. On the final-drive assembly are, left, the bridge-classification sign, and, right, the insignia of the 1st Armoured Division. Patton Museum*

**Above:** *Grant tank British War Department T-23833, from C Squadron, 2/9th Australian Armoured Regiment, is the subject of a tank-recovery demonstration at a training site in Queensland, Australia, on July 14, 1943. Above the registration is a circle tactical symbol, indicating C Squadron. Patton Museum*

**Above:** *During the same tank-recovery demonstration depicted in the preceding photograph, the Grant in the foreground has extracted T- 23833 from the mudhole in the center background using a tow cable. Another cable is visible to the left, presumably attached to another Grant. Note that the pistol port has been removed from the right side door of the Grant in the foreground. Patton Museum*

**Above:** *The Australians developed their own deep water fording kit for the M3 Medium tank, exhibited here on a M3A5 of the 4th Armoured Brigade. The vehicle was photographed in Southport, Queensland, in January 1944, wearing the 1942 Australian camouflage scheme of Khaki Green No. 3 and Light Stone No. 61. Patton Museum*

**Above:** *The nickname Curly is painted in script on the sponson of a Grant tank engaged in training exercises of 2/9th Armoured Squadron with 2/6th Infantry Battalion in the Watsonville area of Queensland, Australia, on April 28, 1944. Patton Museum*

**Above:** *In addition to General Grant tanks, Australia also received over 200 General Lee M3, including this one. General Lee shipments began in August, four months after shipments of General Grant. The Australians, like the British, disliked the American cupola, and their tanks lacked this feature, instead having a split hatch like that found on Grants. This is a late production M3 Lee, featuring the longer M3 75mm gun and no side doors. In the view of the Australians, who envisioned fighting in jungles, where the tank was apt to bog, the lack of side doors on these later M3s was a deficit. So strong was this feeling that they put together a plan to retrofit the side doors, although that modification program was never implemented. Patton Museum*

**Above:** *Late-production M3 T-26055, resplendent in the wavy camouflage scheme favored, shows off the open split-type commander's hatch typical of Australian Lee tanks. Patton Museum*

*Right: Grant tanks were not entirely retired from the service of the Australian Army after World War II. This example was photographed in a convoy of the 4th Australian Armoured Brigade as it moves out of its area en route to the Badiana Base Ordnance Depot in Victoria, Australia. This was in early 1946 at the time of the disbandment of the unit. Patton Museum*

were deployed to Balikpapan to support Australian Matildas there. One of the three tanks had its dozer blade removed, and although it went on a single patrol on 19 July 1945, neither its 37mm nor 75mm gun was fired – beginning and ending the deployment of Australia's Grant tanks.

While following the war the gasoline-powered vehicles were almost immediately declared obsolete, the Diesel-powered Australian M3s soldiered on for many years, the last one being

removed from service in October 1955. During this time, many of these tanks were refitted with later-type heavy-duty M4 suspension bogies, a process that had started before the end of the war.

Anecdotal accounts saying M3s were shipped from North Africa to Australia have circulated for years, however so far no documents have surfaced to support this; in fact all the documents located have contradicted this, indicating that the tanks were shipped directly from the US to Australia.

# Chapter 14

# The M3 in Soviet service

What the Germans called the Eastern Front was to prove Nazi Germany's most tenacious foe. Prior to the launch of Operation Barbarossa, the German invasion of Russia, on 22 June 1941, the two nations had a relationship that went well beyond cordial, in fact in November 1940 the Soviet Union had been invited to join the Axis, a possibility that was negotiated over two days.

Up until 22 June, Hitler's German forces had had unprecedented success, rolling through Poland, France and other nations with relative ease. Hitler forecast that victory over Russia would take only three months.

Initially, it looked like this would indeed be the case, with 3,300 Russian tanks claimed to have been captured by 27 June. It would be September before the Soviets rallied and began to hold the line against Germany; up to that point only the vast expanse of the nation prevented complete conquest.

With such tremendous losses in equipment, as well as facilities, the Russians turned abroad to aid in re-equipping their army.

While the Russians had been provided a considerable amount of information concerning the M2 Medium tank, counter to some published reports, the Soviets obtained none of that type.

In September 1941, Soviet emissaries saw press releases about the new M3, and by the following month had made the decision to purchase the M3, starting with an initial order for nine tanks.

The first four of these arrived in December. By that time, more examples had been ordered, and 24 more were delivered in January 1942.

**Above:** *A total of 1,386 U.S. Medium Tanks M3 were shipped to the Soviets under the Lend-Lease Program; of those, 410 were sunk en route to Russia, and 976 arrived intact. Here, four of these tanks have arrived by cargo ship in Murmansk, Russia, in 1942 and have been loaded on flatcars for shipment to a fighting front. Typically, sealant is on the doors and ports. The U.S. Army registration numbers have been painted over (or censored out).*

**Above:** *A Medium Tank M3 in Soviet service is observed from the front right. This is a riveted-hull, early-production example with no visible markings. The 75mm gun is the short-barreled M2 version, and no counterweights are present on the barrel of this gun or on the 37mm gun mount. Steve Zaloga collection*

**Right:** *The M3S Medium Tanks of the 192nd Tank Brigade were typically adorned with various patriotic or Communist party mottos, and this example is no exception. On the upper hull of this Lee has been written "The Banner of Lenin Forward to Victory!" and "For Stalin!" A red star with white outlining is on the side of the turret.*

**Above:** *Photos of Soviet M3 Lee tanks are not abundant, and those that exist often lack background information. This Lee tank is shown entering the city of Vyazma upon its liberation in March 1943. Grousers are visible on the tracks at varying intervals. Another Lee is coming up to the rear.*

One problem that cropped up early on was a lack of Russian-language documentation for the vehicles. Ultimately a Russian manual was compiled by Amtorg (Amerikanskaya Torgovlya), the Soviet trade agency in the US, but it was not a 100%-accurate translation of the American document.

Other issues came from R-975's requirement of 91-octane gasoline, not readily available in Russia. To address this, the Soviet's used their own idea of aviation gasoline, B-70 and B-78 (B=benzene) which were 70 and 78 octane rating respectively, and added to that their R-9 additive to boost the octane.

Lend-Lease shipments to the Soviet Union were handled under four "protocols," with each protocol covered a year ending 30 June. A protocol was a signed document binding the US, UK and Canada to furnish certain materials, including tanks. The details of these protocols were worked out in advance through high-level meetings that balanced the Soviet requests against production capacity and other nations' needs. On the U.S. end, each protocol had to be ratified by the State Department, the combined General Staffs, Army Service Forces and the Munitions Assignments Committee. The first protocol was signed on 1 October 1941 and covered the nine-month period ending 30 June 1942.

**Left:** *A knocked-out Soviet Lee tank has much graffiti written in German on the sponson, which, unfortunately, is not legible, although there are references to the cities of Altdamm and Stettin.*

**Right:** *Two German soldiers are inspecting a knocked-out Soviet Lee tank which had taken up position behind a stone wall before it met its demise. The explosion and fire that wracked the vehicle completely burned off the rubber of the tracks.*

After the attack on Pearl Harbor, the decision was made to use only Russian-flagged ships to transport Soviet Lend-Lease shipments in the Pacific, because at that time Japan was not at war with Russia. Most of the tonnage in the first half of 1942 went through Murmansk and Archangel.

President Roosevelt gave supplying the Russians the highest priority, writing to Donald M. Nelson, director of the War Production Board on 17 March 1942 that, "I wish that all material promised under the Protocol be released for shipment at the earliest possible date regardless of the effect of these shipments on any other part of our war program."

The initial shipments of tanks to the Soviet Union did not include any armor piercing projectiles for the 75mm cannon, leading Russian troops in the field to believe the big gun was intended for infantry support. AP rounds began to arrive in late April.

The trickle of tanks picked up pace as well, with 1,386 of the M3 Mediums ultimately being shipped to Russia. Only a handful came through Iran, the majority going to northern ports. In total, 945 of the tanks came from ships that docked, but an additional 12 were salvaged from a freighter which had been sunk near shore, raising the total number of M3 Mediums arriving in Russia to 957. Other

**Above:** *A German motorcycle trooper and a foot soldier are in the foreground of this view of a destroyed Soviet Lee tank that is still burning. The roof of the fighting compartment along with the turret were blown up when the tank exploded. To the side of the vehicle is a long section of its track.*

**Above:** *German troops, including two struggling to push a motorcycle over an embankment, are next to a destroyed Soviet Lee tank. Not much is left of the vehicle except for the wreckage of part of the hull, standing on its side, a section of track, and just beyond the motorcycle, a portion of the final drive and sprocket.*

ships and tanks were lost and not salvaged.

The first M3 to arrive, Chrysler-built W-304296, which arrived on 26 January 1942 was immediately shipped to the Russian tank school at Kazan, arriving there on 2 February. That same day, W-304293, also built by Chrysler, arrived in Russia. It was dispatched to the Scientific Institute for Armored Equipment (NIBT) proving ground near Kubinka on 18 February for evaluation. Interestingly, this tank survives, and is still there.

The evaluation concluded that the R-975 and its required high-octane gasoline would be a problem, and that a Diesel engine, in the form of the Guiberson radial, would be preferred. The height, bulk and slab-sided design were disliked, although it was noted that ten troops with submachine guns could join the crew in the fighting compartment. Except for the hull-mounted machine guns, the armament was praised, despite the lack, at that time, of armored piercing shells.

Although the relatively low top speed on-road was criticized, off-road mobility was praised with the exception of traversing of swamps.

In the field, the Soviets wisely chose in most instances to equip entire units with the M3, rather than creating units of mixed vehicles, which would have been a nightmare for maintenance as well as

training. The first combat units to be issued the M3 were the 114th and 192nd Tank Brigades.

The fulfilling of the Russian requests and the President's demands sometimes meant that shipments were less than ideal. For example, in June 1942 fifteen tanks arrived without cupolas, which were shipped separately.

Field service revealed some deficiencies in the M3, as it does with all military equipment. The rubber-padded track were well liked for their long life and relative quietness, however in winter conditions traction suffered. The riveted construction of the tank was notably hazardous to the crew. Perhaps equally hazardous were a couple of seemingly minor details. First, the inside of the tanks were painted, and that paint would burn. Also, a number of surfaces inside the tank were covered with a rubber padding to protect the crew from bumps and abrasions, and that padding as well would burn, and a rapidly-spreading fire brought with it the risk of an ammunition explosion.

In later years Soviet propaganda would label the M3 "coffin for six brothers" (since the Russians often did without radio operators), however the Lees filled a desperate need, and in the right hands could be brutally effective.

Between May 23 and May 25, an M3 commanded

**Above:** *In a photo apparently taken a short time after the preceding one, German troops are doing spade work next to the same destroyed Soviet Lee shown in the preceding photo. They may have been burying one of their own killed.*

**Above:** *A knocked-out or abandoned Soviet Lee tank in a village has extensive graffiti written on its sponson. The photo is not sufficiently clear to read the inscriptions, but it probably consists of German taunts. To the right is a destroyed German Horch Einheits Personen Kraftwagen 4x4 and another Lee.*

**Left:** *Wehrmacht troops are checking over a captured Soviet Lee tank. Several points of interest are visible in this photo. Residue of the sealant material placed over the various ports and the 37mm gun shield at the factory for shipment overseas is still visible as lighter-colored bands around those features. The left brush guard for the headlight is completely missing. The main gun is the long-barreled 75mm Gun M3, and the hull is riveted with the side doors deleted. The bogie wheels are solid spoked.*

**Above:** *In the aftermath of a battle on the steppes of the Eastern Front in the summer of 1943, a Soviet Medium Tank M3 smolders after being knocked out. Faintly visible on the sponson is written in Cyrillic the patriotic slogan, "A. Nevskiy," a reference to Prince Aleksandr Nevskiy, an important leader in Medieval Russia who continued to be popular in that country even during Communist rule. Steve Zaloga collection*

**Above:** *Chrysler-built M3 W-304850 was captured intact from the Soviets by the Germans who then shipped the vehicle to the German proving ground at Kummersdorf, where it was extensively evaluated in 1943. Tom Laemlein collection*

**Above:** *Such studies were not at all unusual, as all of the combatants closely studied examples of both their enemies' and their allies' vehicles that fell into their hands. Tom Laemlein collection*

by Lieutenant A.D. Mimotin destroyed 4 German tanks near Chepel. According to Soviet records, in another action on July 14, a force of 240 German tanks launched multiple attacks against the 2nd Company of the 230th Tank Regiment, equipped with 2 M3S (sredniy, or medium) and 5 M3 (M3L) Light tanks. The 230th turned back three attacks, claiming 17 German tanks in the process.

In another incident, one which is often cited as illustrating the weakness of the M3, Podpolkovnik Matvyey K. Akoponov's 245th Tank Regiment, equipped with 12 M3S and 27 M3L, were pitted against Panzer-Regiment Von Lauchert near Kursk in July, 1943. Von Lauchert had 200 of the new Panther tanks. Akoponov lost 16 of his American-made tanks, however the Soviets gave as good as they got, and knocked out 1 Tiger, 13 Panzer IIIs, 5 Panthers and 10 other German tanks that were not specified.

The true status of the M3 were revealed in a secret meeting that was held in Moscow between Brigadier General S.P. Spalding, US Army, and Lt. General I.U. Lebedev, Engineer Technical Service,

Deputy Chief of the Supreme Directorate of Army Corps, Soviet Army, on 22 June 1944 to discuss tanks.

In the minutes of the meeting, General Lebedev is quoted, "We have also used your medium M3. The Sherman has been in only a few operations so far, but it is much better than the M3. Mr. Harriman thought it was not necessary to have riflemen or sub-machine gun(ners) on the tanks. Actually, this is impossible on the M3....However, I wish to say again your tanks have been fighting very well."

Despite the Soviet preference for Diesel-powered tanks as explained previously in this volume, it is important to note that all the M3 Medium Tanks supplied directly to the Soviet Union by the United States were the basic M3 gasoline-powered versions; no M3A3s or M3A5s were shipped directly to Russia. Instead, the Soviets waited on the 6046 Diesel-powered M4A2.

By 1 June 1945 the Soviets had 102 M3s left, and several of those vehicles were still issued to combat units.

**Above:** *While the Russians had hoped to obtain M3 Medium tanks powered by the Guiberson radial Diesel, when that engine failed to achieve production status, they accepted the R-975-powered M3 instead. All Lees furnished to Russia by the United States utilized that power plant. Tom Laemlein collection*

A US M III Medium tank which had been
captured in Russia and sent to Hillerslieben Prov. Gd.

**Above:** *A photo of a Lee tank chassis captured by the Germans from the Soviets bears a typed label, "A US M III Medium tank which had been captured in Russia and sent to Hillerslieben Prov. Ground." This is a reference to Hillerleben Proving Grounds, in Germany. Markings were stenciled at various places on the hull, turret, and cupola, giving the armor thickness and slope in degrees. Military History Institute*

# Appendix

The following pages present data compiled principally from various period government or manufacturers' records. In a few rare cases the data from different period documents are not in agreement with each other. We have made no attempt at 'correcting' these official records with our interpretations; rather we leave that to the reader.

# M3 Series Serial and Registration Numbers

* Unless otherwise specified, all quantities given are M3
** plus 1 more T-25589
*** final 150 serial numberes not used, instead became M31 #1 through #149

## Rock Island Arsenal

| | Contract | Production Order | Mar-41 | May-41 | Jul-41 | Aug-41 |
|---|---|---|---|---|---|---|
| Quantity* | | | 1 M3 Riveted | 1 M3 Cast | 1 M3 Welded | 1 M3 Welded |
| Serial number | | | 2371 | 2372 | 2373 | 2374 |
| Registration Number | | | 304191 | 304192 | 304193 | 304194 |

## Pullman-Standard

| | Contract | Production Order | Jun-41 | Jul-41 | Aug-41 | Sep-41 | Oct-41 | Nov-41 | Dec-41 | Jan-42 | Feb-42 | Mar-42 | Apr-42 | May-42 | Jun-42 | Jul-42 |
|---|---|---|---|---|---|---|---|---|---|---|---|---|---|---|---|---|
| Quantity* | W-ORD-694 | A-1381 | | | 9 | 27 | 19 | 29 | 37 | 61 | 74 | 63 | 71 | 48 | 47 | 15 |
| Reg # start | | | | | T-24189 | T-24198 | T-24225 | T-24244 | T-24273 | T-24310 | T-24371 | T-24445 | T-24508 | T-24579 | T-24627 | T-24674 |
| Reg # end | | | | | T-24197 | T-24224 | T-24243 | T-24272 | T-24309 | T-24370 | T-24444 | T-24507 | T-24578 | T-24626 | T-24673 | T-24688 |

## Pressed Steel

| | Contract | Production Order | Jun-41 | Jul-41 | Aug-41 | Sep-41 | Oct-41 | Nov-41 | Dec-41 | Jan-42 | Feb-42 | Mar-42 | Apr-42 | May-42 | Jun-42 | Jul-42 |
|---|---|---|---|---|---|---|---|---|---|---|---|---|---|---|---|---|
| Quantity* | W-ORD-694 | A-1795 | | | 1 | 18 | 21 | 22 | 42 | 60 | 76 | 25 | 46 | | | |
| Quantity* | DA-W-271-ORD-698 | T-3751 | | | | | | | | | | | 49 | 40 | 67 | 33*** |
| Reg # start | W-ORD-694 | A-1795 | | | T-24689 | T-24690 | T-24708 | T-24729 | T-24751 | T-24793 | T-24853 | T-24929 | T-24954 | | | |
| Reg # end | W-ORD-694 | A-1795 | | | T-24689 | T-24707 | T-24728 | T-24750 | T-24792 | T-24852 | T-24928 | T-24953 | T-24999 | | | |
| Reg # start | DA-W-271-ORD-698 | T-3751 | | | | | | | | | | | T-25000 | T-25049 | T-25089 | T-25156 |
| Reg # end | DA-W-271-ORD-698 | T-3751 | | | | | | | | | | | T-25048 | T-25088 | T-25155 | T-25188 |

## Baldwin - British

| | Contract | Production Order | Jun-41 | Jul-41 | Aug-41 | Sep-41 | Oct-41 | Nov-41 | Dec-41 | Jan-42 | Feb-42 | Mar-42 | Apr-42 | May-42 | Jun-42 | Jul-42 |
|---|---|---|---|---|---|---|---|---|---|---|---|---|---|---|---|---|
| Quantity* | A-1960 | A-1960 | | | | | 9 | 18 | 57 | 62 M3<br>2 M3A2 | 56 M3<br>5 M3A5 | 9 M3<br>3 M3A2<br>12 M3A5 | 4 M3<br>88 M3A5 | 18 M3A3<br>105 M3A5 | 46 M3A3<br>97 M3A5 | 15 M3A3<br>74 M3A5 |
| Quantity* | W-ORD-694 | T-4155 | | | | 9 | 9 | 18 | 84 | 148 | 214 | 238 | 330 | 453 | 596 | 685 |
| Cummulative total | | | | | | | | | | | | | | | | |
| Construction Number start | | | | | | | 63226 | | | | | | | | | 63910 |
| Reg # start | | | | | | | T-23504 | T-23513 | T-23531 | T-23588 | T-23652 | T-23718 | T-23742 | T-23834 | T-23957 | T-24100 |
| Reg # end | | | | | | | T-23512 | T-23530 | T-23587 | T-23651 | T-23717 | T-23741 | T-23833 | T-23956 | T-24099 | T-24188 |

# Baldwin - US

| | Contract | Production Order | Jun-41 | Jul-41 | Aug-41 | Sep-41 | Oct-41 | Nov-41 | Dec-41 | Jan-42 | Feb-42 | Mar-42 | Apr-42 | May-42 | Jun-42 | Jul-42 | Aug-42 | Sep-42 | Oct-42 | Nov-42 | Dec-42 | |
|---|---|---|---|---|---|---|---|---|---|---|---|---|---|---|---|---|---|---|---|---|---|---|
| Quantity* | W-ORD-483 | T-693 | 2 | 2 | 12 | 8 | 15 | 20 | 21 | 3 M3 / 2 M3A2 / 1 M3A5 | 0 | 1 M3 / 1 M3A3 | 9 M3A5 | 1 M3A5 | 0 | 20 M3A3 / 41 M3A5 | 91 M3A3 / 62 M3A5 | 30 M3A3 / 28 M3A5 | 46 M3A3 / 28 M3A5 | 41 M3A3 / 39 M3A5 | 10 M3A3 / 1 M3A5 | |
| Cummulative total | | | 2 | 4 | 16 | 24 | 39 | 59 | 80 | 86 | 86 | 88 | 97 | 98 | 98 | 159 | 312 | 370 | 444 | 524 | 535 | to 1686 (1536)*** |
| SN Start | | | 1002 | 1004 | 1006 | 1018 | 1026 | 1041 | 1061 | 1082 | | 1088 | 1090 | 1099 | | 1100 | 1161 | 1314 | 1372 | 1446 | 1526 | |
| SN end | | | 1003 | 1005 | 1017 | 1025 | 1040 | 1060 | 1081 | 1087 | | 1089 | 1098 | 1099 | | 1160 | 1313 | 1371 | 1445 | 1525 | 1536 | |
| Construction Number start | | | 62541 | | | | | | | | | | | | | | | | | | | to 63225 |
| Reg # start | | | 305072 | 305074 | 305076 | 305088 | 305096 | 305111 | 305131 | 305152 | | 305158 | 305160 | 305169 | | 305170 | 305231 | 305384 | 305442 | 305516 | 305596 | |
| Reg # end | | | 305073 | 305075 | 305087 | 305095 | 305110 | 305130 | 305151 | 305157 | | 305159 | 305168 | 305169 | | 305230 | 305383 | 305441 | 305515 | 305595 | 305606 | |

# Alco

| | Contract | Production Order | Jun-41 | Jul-41 | Aug-41 | Sep-41 | Oct-41 | Nov-41 | Dec-41 | Jan-42 | Feb-42 | Mar-42 | Apr-42 | May-42 | Jun-42 | Jul-42 | Aug-42 |
|---|---|---|---|---|---|---|---|---|---|---|---|---|---|---|---|---|---|
| Quantity* | W-ORD-485 | T-749 | 8 | 17 | 8 | 45 | 37 | 26 | 83 | 47 | 4 M3 / 7 M3A1 | 30 M3 / 66 M3A1 | 20 M3 / 66 M3A1 | 28 M3 / 62 M3A1 | 7 M3 / 51 M3A1 | 4 M3 / 17 M3A1 | 21 M3 / 31 M3A1 |
| Cummulative Total | | | 8 | 25 | 33 | 78 | 115 | 141 | 224 | 271 | 282 | 378 | 464 | 554 | 612 | 633 | 685 |
| SN start | | | 1687 | 1695 | 1712 | 1720 | 1765 | 1802 | 1828 | 1911 | 1958 | 1969 | 2065 | 2151 | 2241 | 2299 | 2320 |
| SN end | | | 1694 | 1711 | 1719 | 1764 | 1801 | 1827 | 1910 | 1957 | 1968 | 2064 | 2150 | 2240 | 2298 | 2319 | 2371 |
| Reg # start | | | 305757 | 305765 | 305782 | 305790 | 305835 | 305872 | 305898 | 305981 | 306028 | 306039 | 306135 | 306221 | 306311 | 306369 | 306390 |
| Reg # end | | | 305764 | 305781 | 305789 | 305834 | 305871 | 305897 | 305980 | 306027 | 306038 | 306134 | 306220 | 306310 | 306368 | 306389 | 306441 |

# Chrysler

| | Contract | Production Order | Jun-41 | Jul-41 | Aug-41 | Sep-41 | Oct-41 | Nov-41 | Dec-41 | Jan-42 | Feb-42 | Mar-42 | Apr-42 | May-42 | Jun-42 | Jul-42 | Aug-42 |
|---|---|---|---|---|---|---|---|---|---|---|---|---|---|---|---|---|---|
| Quantity* | W-ORD-461 | T-519 | | 7 | 50 | 95 | 148 | 194 | 235 | 261 | 10 | | | | | | |
| Quantity* | W-ORD-461 | T-1473 | | | | | | | | 39 | 290 | 366 | 381 | 400 | 117 M3 / 33 M3A4 | | |
| Quantity* | W-ORD-461 | T-1506 | | | | | | | | | | | | | 144 M3 / 8 M3A4 | 317 M3 / 73 M3A4 | 26 M3 / 3 M3A4 |
| Quantity* | W-ORD-461 | T-2593 | | | | | | | | | | | | | 163 M3 / 18 M3A4 | | |
| Cummulative total | | | | 7 | 57 | 152 | 300 | 494 | 729 | 1029 | 1329 | 1695 | 2076 | 2476 | 2933 | 3323 | 3352 |
| SN start | W-ORD-461 | T-519 | | 2 | 9 | 59 | 154 | 302 | 496 | 731 | 992 | | | | | | |
| SN end | W-ORD-461 | T-519 | | 8 | 58 | 153 | 301 | 495 | 730 | 991 | 1001 | | | | | | |
| Reg # start | W-ORD-461 | T-519 | | 301000 | 301008 301026 | 301057 | 304224 | 304372 | 304566 | 304801 | 305062 | | | | | | |
| Reg # end | W-ORD-461 | T-519 | | 301007 | 301023 301056 | 301122 304223 | 304371 | 304565 | 304800 | 305061 | | | | | | | |
| Reg # start | W-ORD-461 | T-519 | | | 307044 | | | | | | | | | | | | |
| SN end | W-ORD-461 | T-519 | | | 307046 | 304195 | | | | | | | | | | | |
| SN start | W-ORD-461 | T-1473 | | | | | | | | 2372 | 2411 | 2701 | 3067 | 3448 | 3848 | | |
| SN end | W-ORD-461 | T-1473 | | | | | | | | 2410 | 2700 | 3066 | 3447 | 3847 | 3971 | | |
| Reg # start | W-ORD-461 | T-1506 | | | | | | | | 309007 | 309046 | 309336 | 309702 | 3010083 | 3010483 | 3010607 | |
| Reg # end | W-ORD-461 | T-1506 | | | | | | | | 309045 | 309335 | 309701 | 309999 3010000 | 3010482 | 3010606 | 3010758 | |
| SN start | W-ORD-461 | T-1506 | | | | | | | | 305071 | | | 3010082 | | 3972 | 4123 | 4695 |
| SN end | W-ORD-461 | T-1506 | | | | | | | | | | | | | 4124 | 4304 | 4723 |
| Reg # start | W-ORD-461 | T-2593 | | | | | | | | | | | | | 3028782 | 3028963 | 3058286 |
| Reg # end | W-ORD-461 | T-2593 | | | | | | | | | | | | | 3028962 | 3029081 | 3058314 |
| Reg # start | W-ORD-461 | T-2593 | | | | | | | | | | | | | 4304 | 4305 4694 | 4695 |
| Reg # end | W-ORD-461 | T-2593 | | | | | | | | | | | | | | 3058015 3058285 | |

**Above:** *In addition to the United Kingdom and USSR, Brazil was the only other recipient of Lend-Lease M3-series tanks. Beginning in August 1942, the South American nation received a mixture of M3A3 and M3A5 Diesel-powered tanks. Although the Brazilian Expeditionary Force deployed to Italy in 1944, they did not take the Lees with them. Some of these tanks were repowered with Continental radials in the 1950s, and a few were transferred to Paraguay by Brazil in the 1950s.  Steve Zaloga collection*

# M31

| Baldwin - US | Production Order | Contract | Oct-42 | Nov-42 | Dec-42 | Jan-43 | Feb-43 | Mar-43 | Apr-43 | May-43 | Jun-43 | Jul-43 | Aug-43 | Sep-43 | Oct-43 | Nov-43 | Dec-43 |
|---|---|---|---|---|---|---|---|---|---|---|---|---|---|---|---|---|---|
| Qty - Diesel | T-6876 | W-670-ORD-3243 | | 2 | 0 | 10 | 21 | 12 | 14 | 20 | 21 | 17 | 18 | | | 1 | |
| SN Start | | | | 1 | | 3 | 13 | 34 | 46 | 60 | 80 | 115 | 132 | | | | |
| SN end | | | | 2 | | 12 | 33 | 45 | 59 | 79 | 114 | 131 | 149 | | | | |
| Reg # start | | | | 4096598 | | 4096600 | 4096610 | 4906631 | 4096643 | 4096657 | 4096677 40103602 | 40103616 | 40103633 | | | 40103651 | |
| Reg # end | | | | 4096599 | | 4096609 | 4096630 | 4096642 | 4096656 | 4096676 | 4096697 40103615 | 40103632 | 40103650 | | | | |
| Qty - Gas* | T-4417 | W-670-ORD-3243 | 10 | 0 | 0 | 40 | 23 | 45 | 46 | 40 | 56 | 50 | 33 | 42 | 50 | 46 | 28 |
| SN Start | | | 151 | | | 161 | 201 | 224 | 269 | 315 | 355 | 411 | 461 | 494 | 536 | 586 | 632 |
| SN end | | | 160 | | | 200 | 223 | 268 | 314 | 354 | 410 | 460 | 493 | 535 | 585 | 631 | 659 |
| Reg # start | | | 40103652 | | | 40103662 | 40103702 | 40103725 | 40103770 | 40103816 | 40103856 | 40103912 | 40103962 | 40103995 | 40104037 | 40104087 | 40104133 |
| Reg # end | | | 40103661 | | | 40103701 | 40103724 | 40103769 | 40103815 | 40103855 | 40103911 | 40103961 | 40103994 | 40104036 | 40104086 | 40104132 | 40104160 |
| Qty-Diesel** | T-8871 | W-670-ORD-3243 | | | | | | | | | | | 40 | 49 | 40 | 16 | 1 |
| SN Start | | | | | | | | | | | | | 751 | 791 | 840 | 880 | 896 |
| SN end | | | | | | | | | | | | | 790 | 839 | 879 | 895 | |
| Reg # start | | | | | | | | | | | | | 40142501 | 40142541 | 40142590 | 40142630 | 40142646 |
| Reg # end | | | | | | | | | | | | | 40142540 | 40142589 | 40142629 | 40142645 | |

*Converted from used M3
** Converted from used Diesel for Soviet Lend-Lease

# MEDIUM TANK M3

## GENERAL DATA

*weight based on T48 or T51 track installed

| | |
|---|---|
| Quantity produced: | 3712 |
| Crew: | 6 or 7 men |
| Length: w/75mm Gun M2, w/o sandshields | 222 inches |
| Length: w/75mm Gun M3, w/o sandshields | 241 inches |
| Length: w/o gun. w/o sandshields | 222 inches |
| Gun Overhang: 75mm Gun M3 | 19 inches |
| Width: Over side doors | 107 inches |
| Height: Over cupola | 123 inches |
| Tread: | 83 inches |
| Ground Clearance: | 17 inches |
| Fire Height: 75mm gun | 69 inches |
| Turret Ring Diameter: (inside) | 54.5 inches |
| Weight, Combat Loaded: | 61,500 pounds* |
| Weight, Unstowed: | 57,400 pounds* |
| Power to Weight Ratio: Net | 11.1 hp/ton |
| Gross | 13.0 hp/ton |
| Ground Pressure: Zero penetration | 12.6 psi |

## ARMOR

| Type: | Hull, rolled homogeneous steel riveted assembly | |
|---|---|---|
| | Turret, cast homogeneous steel | |
| | Hull Thickness, actual | Angle w/Vertical |
| Front. Upper | 2.0 inches | 30 degrees |
| Middle | 1.5 inches | 53 degrees |
| Lower | 2.0 inches | 0 to 45 degrees |
| Sides | 1.5 inches | 0 degrees |
| Rear | 1.5 inches | 0 to 10 degrees |
| Top | 0.5 inches | 83 to 90 degrees |
| Floor, Front | 1.0 inches | 90 degrees |
| Rear | 0.5 inches | 90 degrees |
| | Turret Thickness: | |
| Front | 2.0 inches | 47 degrees |
| Sides | 2.0 inches | 5 degrees |
| Rear | 2.0 inches | 5 degrees |
| Top | 0.875 inches | 90 degrees |

## ARMAMENT

| | AMMUNITION | FIRE CONTROL EQUIPMENT | |
|---|---|---|---|
| | | Direct | Indirect |
| *Main:* | | | |
| 75mm Gun M2 or M3 in Mount M1 in right front of hull | 50 rounds 75mm | Periscope M1 with Telescope M21A1 | Gunner's Quadrant M1 |
| Traverse: Manual | 30 degrees (15 degrees L or R) | | |
| Elevation: Manual | +20 to -9 degrees | | |
| Firing Rate: (max) | 20 rounds/minute | | |
| Loading System: | Manual | | |
| Stabilizer System: | Elevation only | | |
| *Primary* | | | |
| 37mm Gun M5 or M6 in Mount M24 in turret | 178 rounds 37mm | Periscope M2 with Telescope M19A1 | |
| Traverse: Hydraulic and manual | 360 degrees | | |
| Traverse Rate: (max) | 20 seconds/360 degrees | | |
| Elevation: Manual | +60 to -7 degrees | | |
| Firing Rate: (max) | 30 rounds/minute | | |
| Loading System: | Manual | | |
| Stabilizer System: | Elevation only | | |
| *Secondary:* | | | |
| (1) .30-caliber MG M1919A4 in turret cupola | 9,200 rounds .30-caliber | | |
| (1) .30-caliber MG M1919A4 coaxial w/37mm gun in turret | | | |
| .30-caliber MG M1919A4 fixed in front plate* | | | |
| Provision for caliber (1) .45 caliber SMG M1928A1* | 1,200 rounds .45-caliber | | |
| 12 Hand grenades | | | |
| * (2) in early production vehicles | | | |

## ENGINE

| | |
|---|---|
| Make and Model: | Wright (Continental) R-975-EC 9-cylinder, 4 cycle. Air-cooled, radial, Magneto ignition |
| Displacement: | 973 cubic inches |
| Bore and Stroke: | 5 x 5.5 inches |
| Compression Ratio: | 6.3:1 |
| Net Horsepower (max): | 340 hp at 2400 rpm |
| Gross Horsepower (max): | 400 hp at 2400 rpm |
| Net Torque (max): | 800 ft-lb at 1800 rpm |
| Gross Torque (max): | 890 ft-lb at1 800 rpm |
| Weight: | 1137 lb, dry |
| Fuel: 92 octane gasoline | 175 gallons |
| Engine Oil: | 36 quarts |

## POWER TRAIN

| | | | | | | | |
|---|---|---|---|---|---|---|---|
| Clutch: | Dry disc. 2 or 3 plate | | | | | | |
| Transmission: | Synchromesh, 5 speeds forward, 1 reverse | | | | | | |
| Gear Ratios: | | 1st | 2nd | 3rd | 4th | 5th | Reverse |
| | | 7.56:1 | 3.11:1 | 1.78:1 | 1.11:1 | 0.73:1 | 5.65:1 |
| Steering: | Controlled differential | | | | | | |
| Bevel Gear Ratio:3.53:1 | | | | | | | |
| Steering Ratio: 1.515:1 | | | | | | | |
| Brakes: | Mechanical, external contracting | | | | | | |
| Final Drive: Herringbone gear | Gear Ratio: 2.84:1 | | | | | | |
| Drive Sprocket: | 13 teeth, mounted at front of vehicle | | | | | | |
| Pitch Diameter: | 25.038 inches | | | | | | |

## ELECTRICAL SYSTEM

Nominal Voltage: 24 volts DC
Main Generator: (1) 24 volts, .50 amperes, driven by power take-off from main engine
Auxiliary Generator: (1) 30 volts, 50 amperes, driven by the auxiliary engine
Battery: (2) 12-volt in series

## COMMUNICATIONS

*Early vehicles may be equipped with SCR-245

| Radio: | SCR-508 in left front sponson SCR-506* (command tanks only) in right rear sponson |
|---|---|
| Interphone: | (part of radio). 5 stations plus earphones for all crew members |

## RUNNING GEAR

| | |
|---|---|
| Suspension: | Vertical volute spring |
| | 12 wheels in 6 bogies (3 bogies/track) |
| Tire Size: | 20 x 9-inches |
| Return rollers: | 6 1 on top of each bogie |
| Idler: | 22 x 9-inches, adjustable, rear-mounted |
| Tracks: Outside guide | Type |
| Type: | (T41) Double pin. 16.0 inch width. smooth, rubber |
| | (T48) Double pin. 16.56 inch width. chevron, rubber |
| | (T49) Double pin. 16.56 inch width. parallel bar, steel |
| | (T51) Double pin. 16.56 inch width. smooth, rubber |
| Pitch: | 6 inches |
| Shoes per Vehicle: | 158 (79/track) |
| Ground Contact | 147 inches |

## VISION DEVICES

| | Direct | Indirect |
|---|---|---|
| Driver: | Hatch | Protectoscope (1) |
| Gunner (75): | None | Periscope M1 (1) |
| loader (75): | Hatch & Piistol port | Protectoscope (1) |
| Commander: | Hatch & vision slots (2) | Protectoscope (1) |
| Gunner (37): | None | Periscope M2 (1) |
| Loader (37): | Pistol port | Protectoscope (1) |

## FIRE PROTECTION

| |
|---|
| (2) 10 pound carbon dioxide. fixed |
| (2) 4 pound carbon dioxide, portable |

## PERFORMANCE

| | |
|---|---|
| Maximum Speed: Sustained. level road | 21 miles/hour |
| Short periods, level | 24 miles/hour |
| Maximum Grade: | 60 per cent |
| Maximum Trench: | 7.5 feet |
| Maximum Vertical Wall: | 24 inches |
| Maximum Fording Depth: | 40 inches |
| Minimum Turning Circle: (diameter) | 62 feet |
| Cruising Range: Roads | approx. 120 miles |

# MEDIUM TANK M3A1

## GENERAL DATA

*weight based on T48 or T51 track installed

| | |
|---|---|
| Quantity produced | 300 |
| Crew: | 6 or 7 men |
| Length: w/75mm Gun M2, w/o sandshields | 222 inches |
| Length: w/75mm Gun M3, w/o sandshields | 241 inches |
| Length: w/o gun. w/o sandshields | 222 inches |
| Gun Overhang: 75mm Gun M3 | 19 inches |
| Width: Over side doors | 107 inches |
| Height: Over cupola | 123 inches |
| Tread: | 83 inches |
| Ground Clearance: | 17 inches |
| Fire Height: 75mm gun | 69 inches |
| Turret Ring Diameter: (inside) | 54.5 inches |
| Weight, Combat Loaded: | 63,000 |
| Weight, Unstowed: | 58,900 |
| Power to Weight Ratio: Net | 10.8 hp/ton |
| Gross | 12.7 hp/ton |
| Ground Pressure: Zero penetration | 12.9 psi |

## ARMOR

| Type: | Upper Hull, cast homogeneous steel | |
|---|---|---|
| | Lower Hull, rolled homogeneous steel riveted assembly | |
| | Turret, cast homogeneous steel | |
| | Hull Thickness, actual | Angle w/Vertical |
| Front, Upper | 2.0 inches | 30 degrees |
| Middle | 1.5 inches | 53 degrees |
| Lower | 2.0 inches | 0 to 45 degrees |
| Sides | 1.5 inches | 0 degrees |
| Rear | 1.5 inches | 0 to 10 degrees |
| Top | 0.5 inches | 83 to 90 degrees |
| Floor, Front | 1.0 inches | 90 degrees |
| Rear | 0. 5 inches | 90 degrees |
| | Turret Thickness: | |
| Front | 2.0 inches | 47 degrees |
| Sides | 2.0 inches | 5 degrees |
| Rear | 2.0 inches | 5 degrees |
| Top | 0.875 inches | 90 degrees |

## ARMAMENT

| | AMMUNITION | FIRE CONTROL EQUIPMENT | |
|---|---|---|---|
| | | Direct | Indirect |
| *Main:* | | | |
| 75mm Gun M2 or M3 in Mount M1 in right front of hull | 50 rounds 75mm | Periscope M1 with Telescope M21A1 | Gunner's Quadrant M1 |
| Traverse: Manual | 30 degrees (15 degrees L or R) | | |
| Elevation: Manual | +20 to -9 degrees | | |
| Firing Rate: (max) | 20 rounds/minute | | |
| Loading System: | Manual | | |
| Stabilizer System: | Elevation only | | |
| *Primary* | | | |
| 37mm Gun M5 or M6 in Mount M24 in turret | 178 rounds 37mm | Periscope M2 with Telescope M19A1 | |
| Traverse: Hydraulic and manual | 360 degrees | | |
| Traverse Rate: (max) | 20 seconds/360 degrees | | |
| Elevation: Manual | +60 to -7 degrees | | |
| Firing Rate: (max) | 30 rounds/minute | | |
| Loading System: | Manual | | |
| Stabilizer System: | Elevation only | | |
| *Secondary:* | | | |
| (1) .30-caliber MG M1919A4 in turret cupola | 9,200 rounds .30-caliber | | |
| (1) .30-caliber MG M1919A4 coaxial w/37mm gun in turret | | | |
| (1) .30-caliber MG M1919A4 fixed in front plate* | | | |
| Provision for caliber (1) .45 caliber SMG M1928A1* | 1,200 rounds .45-caliber | | |
| 12 Hand grenades | | | |

* (2) in early production vehicles

## ENGINE

| | |
|---|---|
| Make and Model: | Wright (Continental) R975 EC 9 cylinder, 4 cycle. Air-cooled, radial, Magneto ignition |
| Displacement: | 973 cubic inches |
| Bore and Stroke: | 5 x 5.5 inches |
| Compression Ratio: | 6.3:1 |
| Net Horsepower (max): | 340 hp at 2400 rpm |
| Gross Horsepower (max): | 400 hp at 2400 rpm |
| Net Torque (max): | 800 ft-lb at 1800 rpm |
| Gross Torque (max): | 890 ft-lb at1 800 rpm |
| Weight: | 1137 lb, dry |
| Fuel: 92 octane gasoline | 175 gallons |
| Engine Oil: | 36 quarts |

## POWER TRAIN

| | | | | | | |
|---|---|---|---|---|---|---|
| Clutch: | Dry disc. 2 or 3 plate | | | | | |
| Transmission: | Synchromesh, 5 speeds forward. 1 reverse | | | | | |
| Gear Ratios: | | 1st | 2nd | 3rd | 4th | 5th | Reverse |
| | | 7.56:1 | 3.11:1 | 1.78:1 | 1.11:1 | 0.73:1 | 5.65:1 |
| Steering: | Controlled differential | | | | | |
| Bevel Gear Ratio:3.53:1 | | | | | | |
| Steering Ratio: 1.515:1 | | | | | | |
| Brakes: | Mechanical, external contracting | | | | | |
| Final Drive: Herringbone gear | Gear Ratio: 2.84:1 | | | | | |
| Drive Sprocket: | 13 teeth, mounted at front of vehicle | | | | | |
| Pitch Diameter: | 25.038 inches | | | | | |

## ELECTRICAL SYSTEM

Nominal Voltage: 24 volts DC
Main Generator: (1) 24 volts. .50 amperes, driven by power take-off from main engine
Auxiliary Generator: (1) 30 volts, 50 amperes, driven by the auxiliary engine
Battery: (2) 12-volt in series

## COMMUNICATIONS

*Early vehicles may be equipped with SCR-245

| Radio: | SCR-508 in left front sponson SCR-506* (command tanks only) in right rear sponson |
|---|---|
| Interphone: | (part of radio), 5 stations plus earphones for all crew members |

## VISION DEVICES

| | Direct | Indirect |
|---|---|---|
| Driver: | Hatch | Protectoscope (1) |
| Gunner (75): | None | Periscope M1 (1) |
| loader (75): | Hatch & Piistol port | Protectoscope (1) |
| Commander: | Hatch & vision slots (2) | Protectoscope (1) |
| Gunner (37): | None | Periscope M2 (1) |
| Loader (37): | Pistol port | Protectoscope (1) |

## RUNNING GEAR

| | |
|---|---|
| Suspension: | Vertical volute spring |
| | 12 wheels in 6 bogies (3 bogies/track) |
| Tire Size: | 20 x 9-inches |
| Return rollers: | 6 1 on top of each bogie |
| Idler: | 22 x 9-inches, adjustable, rear-mounted |
| Tracks: Outside guide | Type |
| | (T41) Double pin. 16.0 inch width. smooth, rubber |
| Type: | (T48) Double pin. 16.56 inch width. chevron, rubber |
| | (T49) Double pin, 16.56 inch width. parallel bar, steel |
| | (T51) Double pin. 16.56 inch width, smooth. rubber |
| Pitch: | 6 inches |
| Shoes per Vehicle: | 158 (79/track) |
| Ground Contact Length: | 147 inches |

## FIRE PROTECTION

| |
|---|
| (2) 10 pound carbon dioxide. fixed |
| (2) 4 pound carbon dioxide, portable |

## PERFORMANCE

| | |
|---|---|
| Maximum Speed: Sustained. level road | 21 miles/hour |
| Short periods, level | 24 miles/hour |
| Maximum Grade: | 60 per cent |
| Maximum Trench: | 7.5 feet |
| Maximum Vertical Wall: | 24 inches |
| Maximum Fording Depth: | 40 inches |
| Minimum Turning Circle: (diameter) | 62 feet |
| Cruising Range: Roads | approx. 120 miles |

# MEDIUM TANK M3A2

## GENERAL DATA

*weight based on T48 or T51 track installed

| | |
|---|---|
| Quantity produced: | 2 + 10 Grant I |
| Crew: | 6 or 7 men |
| Length: w/75mm Gun M2, w/o sandshields | 222 inches |
| Length: w/75mm Gun M3, w/o sandshields | 241 inches |
| Length: w/o gun, w/o sandshields | 222 inches |
| Gun Overhang: 75mm Gun M3 | 19 inches |
| Width: Over side doors | 107 inches |
| Height: Over cupola | 123 inches |
| Tread: | 83 inches |
| Ground Clearance: | 17 inches |
| Fire Height: 75mm gun | 69 inches |
| Turret Ring Diameter: (inside) | 54.5 inches |
| Weight, Combat Loaded: | 60,400 pounds* |
| Weight, Unstowed: | 56,300 pounds* |
| Power to Weight Ratio: Net | 11.3 hp/ton |
| Gross | 13.2 hp/ton |
| Ground Pressure: Zero penetration | 12.4 psi |

## ARMOR

| Type: | Hull, rolled homogeneous steel welded assembly | |
|---|---|---|
| | Turret, cast homogeneous steel | |
| | Hull Thickness, actual | Angle w/Vertical |
| Front, Upper | 2.0 inches | 30 degrees |
| Middle | 1.5 inches | 53 degrees |
| Lower | 2.0 inches | 0 to 45 degrees |
| Sides | 1.5 inches | 0 degrees |
| Rear | 1.5 inches | 0 to 10 degrees |
| Top | 0.5 inches | 83 to 90 degrees |
| Floor, Front | 1.0 inches | 90 degrees |
| Rear | 0.5 inches | 90 degrees |
| | Turret Thickness: | |
| Front | 2.0 inches | 47 degrees |
| Sides | 2.0 inches | 5 degrees |
| Rear | 2.0 inches | 5 degrees |
| Top | 0.875 inches | 90 degrees |

## ARMAMENT

* (2) in early production vehicles

| | AMMUNITION | FIRE CONTROL | |
|---|---|---|---|
| | | Direct | Indirect |
| Main: 75mm Gun M2 or M3 in Mount M1 in right front of hull | 50 rounds 75mm | Periscope M1 with | Gunner's |
| Traverse: Manual | 30 degrees (15 degrees L or R) | | |
| Elevation: Manual | +20 to -9 degrees | | |
| Firing Rate: (max) | 20 rounds/minute | | |
| Loading System: | Manual | | |
| Stabilizer System: | Elevation only | | |
| Primary 37mm Gun M5 or M6 in Mount M24 in turret | 178 rounds 37mm | Periscope M2 with | |
| Traverse: Hydraulic and manual | 360 degrees | | |
| Traverse Rate: (max) | 20 seconds/360 degrees | | |
| Elevation: Manual | +60 to -7 degrees | | |
| Firing Rate: (max) | 30 rounds/minute | | |
| Loading System: | Manual | | |
| Stabilizer System: | Elevation only | | |
| Secondary: | | | |
| (1) .30-caliber MG M1919A4 in turret cupola | 9,200 rounds .30 caliber | | |
| (1) .30-caliber MG M1919A4 coaxial w/37mm gun in turret | | | |
| (1) .30-caliber MG M1919A4 fixed in front plate* | | | |
| Provision for caliber (1) .45 caliber SMG M1928A1* | 1,200 rounds .45 caliber | | |
| 12 Hand grenades | | | |

# ENGINE

| | |
|---|---|
| Make and Model: | Wright (Continental) R975 EC 9 cylinder, 4 cycle. Air-cooled, radial, Magneto ignition |
| Displacement: | 973 cubic inches |
| Bore and Stroke: | 5 x 5.5 inches |
| Compression Ratio: | 6.3:1 |
| Net Horsepower (max): | 340 hp at 2400 rpm |
| Gross Horsepower (max): | 400 hp at 2400 rpm |
| Net Torque (max): | 800 ft-lb at 1800 rpm |
| Gross Torque (max): | 890 fl-lb at1 800 rpm |
| Weight: | 1137 lb, dry |
| Fuel: 92 octane gasoline | 175 gallons |
| Engine Oil: | 36 quarts |

# POWER TRAIN

| | |
|---|---|
| Clutch: | Dry disc. 2 or 3 plate |
| Transmission: | Synchromesh, 5 speeds forward. 1 reverse |

| Gear Ratios: | 1st | 2nd | 3rd | 4th | 5th | Reverse |
|---|---|---|---|---|---|---|
| | 7.56:1 | 3.11:1 | 1.78:1 | 1.11:1 | 0.73:1 | 5.65:1 |

| | |
|---|---|
| Steering: | Controlled differential |
| Bevel Gear Ratio:3.53:1 | |
| Steering Ratio: 1.515:1 | |
| Brakes: | Mechanical, external contracting |
| Final Drive: Herringbone gear | Gear Ratio: 2.84:1 |
| Drive Sprocket: | 13 teeth, mounted at front of vehicle |
| Pitch Diameter: | 25.038 inches |

# ELECTRICAL SYSTEM

Nominal Voltage: 24 volts DC

Main Generator: (1) 24 volts. .50 amperes, driven by power take-off from main engine

Auxiliary Generator: (1) 30 volts, 50 amperes, driven by the auxiliary engine

Battery: (2) 12-volt in series

# COMMUNICATIONS

*Early vehicles may be equipped with SCR-245

| Radio: | SCR-508 in left front sponson SCR-506* (command tanks only) in right rear sponson |
|---|---|
| Interphone: | (part of radio), 5 stations plus earphones for all crew members |

# RUNNING GEAR

| | |
|---|---|
| Suspension: | Vertical volute spring |
| | 12 wheels in 6 bogies (3 bogies/track) |
| Tire Size: | 20 x 9-inches |
| Return rollers: | 6 1 on top of each bogie |
| Idler: | 22 x 9-inches, adjustable, rear-mounted |
| Tracks: Outside guide | Type |
| Type: | (T41) Double pin. 16.0 inch width. smooth. rubber |
| | (T48) Double pin. 16.56 inch width. chevron, rubber |
| | (T49) Double pin, 16.56 inch width. parallel bar, steel |
| | (T51) Double pin, 16.56 inch width, smooth. rubber |
| Pitch: | 6 inches |
| Shoes per Vehicle: | 158 (79/track) |
| Ground Contact Length: | 147 inches |

# VISION DEVICES

| | Direct | Indirect |
|---|---|---|
| | | Hatch | Protectoscope (1) |
| Driver: | Hatch | Protectoscope (1) |
| Gunner (75): | None | Periscope M1 (1) |
| loader (75): | Hatch & Piistol port | Protectoscope (1) |
| Commander: | Hatch & vision slots (2) | Protectoscope (1) |
| Gunner (37): | None | Periscope M2 (1) |
| Loader (37): | Pistol port | Protectoscope (1) |

# FIRE PROTECTION

(2) 10 pound carbon dioxide. fixed

(2) 4 pound carbon dioxide, portable

# PERFORMANCE

| | |
|---|---|
| Maximum Speed: Sustained. level road | 21 miles/hour |
| Short periods, level | 24 miles/hour |
| Maximum Grade: | 60 per cent |
| Maximum Trench: | 7.5 feet |
| Maximum Vertical Wall: | 24 inches |
| Maximum Fording Depth: | 40 inches |
| Minimum Turning Circle: (diameter) | 62 feet |
| Cruising Range: Roads | approx. 120 miles |

461

# MEDIUM TANK M3A3

## GENERAL DATA

*weight based on T48 or T51 track installed

| | |
|---|---|
| Quantity produced: | 239 + 83 Grant II |
| Crew: | 6 or 7 men |
| Length: w/75mm Gun M2, w/o sandshields | 222 inches |
| Length: w/75mm Gun M3, w/o sandshields | 241 inches |
| Length: w/o gun. w/o sandshields | 222 inches |
| Gun Overhang: 75mm Gun M3 | 19 inches |
| Width: Over side doors | 107 inches |
| Height: Over cupola | 123 inches |
| Tread: | 83 inches |
| Ground Clearance: | 17 inches |
| Fire Height: 75mm gun | 69 inches |
| Turret Ring Diameter: (inside) | 54.5 inches |
| Weight, Combat Loaded: | 63,000 pounds* |
| Weight, Unstowed: | 59,000 pounds* |
| Power to Weight Ratio: Net | 11.9 hp/ton |
| Gross | 13.0 hp/ton |
| Ground Pressure: Zero penetration | 12.9 psi |

## ARMOR

| Type: | Hull, rolled homogeneous steel welded assembly | | |
|---|---|---|---|
| | Turret, cast homogeneous steel | | |
| | | Hull Thickness, actual | Angle w/Vertical |
| Front. Upper | | 2.0 inches | 30 degrees |
| Middle | | 1.5 inches | 53 degrees |
| Lower | | 2.0 inches | 0 to 45 degrees |
| Sides | | 1.5 inches | 0 degrees |
| Rear | | 1.5 inches | 0 to 10 degrees |
| Top | | 0.5 inches | 83 to 90 degrees |
| Floor, Front | | 1.0 inches | 90 degrees |
| Rear | | 0.5 inches | 90 degrees |
| | | Turret Thickness: | |
| Front | | 2.0 inches | 47 degrees |
| Sides | | 2.0 inches | 5 degrees |
| Rear | | 2.0 inches | 5 degrees |
| Top | | 0.875 inches | 90 degrees |

## ARMAMENT

* (2) in early production vehicles

| | | AMMUNITION | FIRE CONTROL EQUIPMENT | | |
|---|---|---|---|---|---|
| | | | Direct | | Indirect |
| *Main:* | | | | | |
| 75mm Gun M2 or M3 in Mount M1 in right front of hull | | 50 rounds 75mm | Periscope M1 with Telescope M21A1 | | Gunner's Quadrant M1 |
| Traverse: Manual | 30 degrees (15 degrees L or R) | | | | |
| Elevation: Manual | +20 to -9 degrees | | | | |
| Firing Rate: (max) | 20 rounds/minute | | | | |
| Loading System: | Manual | | | | |
| Stabilizer System: | Elevation only | | | | |
| *Primary* | | | | | |
| 37mm Gun M5 or M6 in Mount M24 in turret | | 178 rounds 37mm | Periscope M2 with Telescope M19A1 | | |
| Traverse: Hydraulic and manual | 360 degrees | | | | |
| Traverse Rate: (max) | 20 seconds/360 degrees | | | | |
| Elevation: Manual | +60 to -7 degrees | | | | |
| Firing Rate: (max) | 30 rounds/minute | | | | |
| Loading System: | Manual | | | | |
| Stabilizer System: | Elevation only | | | | |
| *Secondary:* | | | | | |
| (1) .30-caliber MG M1919A4 in turret cupola | | 9,200 rounds .30 caliber | | | |
| (1) .30-caliber MG M1919A4 coaxial w/37mm gun in turret | | | | | |
| (1) .30-caliber MG M1919A4 fixed in front plate* | | | | | |
| Provision for caliber (1) .45 caliber SMG M1928A1* | | 1,200 rounds .45 caliber | | | |
| 12 Hand grenades | | | | | |

# ENGINE

| | |
|---|---|
| Make and Model: | General Motors 6046, 12-cylinder, twin 6, liquid-cooled, compression-igniton |
| Displacement: | 850 cubic inches |
| Bore and Stroke: | 4.25 x 5 inches |
| Compression Ratio: | 16:01 |
| Net Horsepower (max): | 375 hp at 2100 rpm |
| Gross Horsepower (max): | 410 hp at 2900 rpm |
| Net Torque (max): | 885 ft-lb at 1900 rpm |
| Gross Torque (max): | 1000 fl-lb at 1400 rpm |
| Weight: | 5110 lb, dry |
| Fuel: 40 cetane Diesel | 148 gallons |
| Engine Oil: | 28 quarts |

# POWER TRAIN

| | |
|---|---|
| Clutch: | Dry disc. 2 or 3 plate |
| Transfer case: | Gear Ratio: 0.73:1 |
| Transmission: | Synchromesh, 5 speeds forward. 1 reverse |

| Gear Ratios: | 1st | 2nd | 3rd | 4th | 5th | Reverse |
|---|---|---|---|---|---|---|
| | 7.56:1 | 3.11:1 | 1.78:1 | 1.11:1 | 0.73:1 | 5.65:1 |

| | |
|---|---|
| Steering: | Controlled differential |
| Bevel Gear Ratio:3.53:1 | |
| Steering Ratio: 1.515:1 | |
| Brakes: | Mechanical, external contracting |
| Final Drive: Herringbone gear | Gear Ratio: 2.84:1 |
| Drive Sprocket: | 13 teeth, mounted at front of vehicle |
| Pitch Diameter: | 25.038 inches |

# ELECTRICAL SYSTEM

Nominal Voltage: 24 volts DC
Main Generator: (1) 24 volts, 50 amperes, driven by power take-off from main engine
Auxiliary Generator: (1) 30 volts, 50 amperes, driven by the auxiliary engine
Battery: (2) 12-volt in series

# COMMUNICATIONS

*Early vehicles may be equipped with SCR-245

| Radio: | SCR-508 in left front sponson SCR-506* (command tanks only) in right rear sponson |
|---|---|
| Interphone: | (part of radio), 5 stations plus earphones for all crew members |

# RUNNING GEAR

| | |
|---|---|
| Suspension: | Vertical volute spring |
| | 12 wheels in 6 bogies (3 bogies/track) |
| Tire Size: | 20 x 9-inches |
| Return rollers: | 6 1 on top of each bogie |
| Idler: | 22 x 9-inches, adjustable, rear-mounted |
| Tracks: Outside guide | Type |
| Type: | (T41) Double pin. 16.0 inch width. smooth, rubber |
| | (T48) Double pin. 16.56 inch width. chevron, rubber |
| | (T49) Double pin. 16.56 inch width. parallel bar, steel |
| | (T51) Double pin. 16.56 inch width. smooth, rubber |
| Pitch: | 6 inches |
| Shoes per Vehicle: | 158 (79/track) |
| Ground Contact Length: | 147 inches |

# VISION DEVICES

| Direct | Indirect |
|---|---|
| Hatch | Protectoscope (1) |
| None | Periscope M1 (1) |
| Hatch & Piistol port | Protectoscope (1) |
| Hatch & vision slots (2) | Protectoscope (1) |
| None | Periscope M2 (1) |
| Pistol port | Protectoscope (1) |

# FIRE PROTECTION

| | |
|---|---|
| (2) 10 pound carbon dioxide. fixed | |
| (2) 4 pound carbon dioxide, portable | |

# PERFORMANCE

| | |
|---|---|
| Maximum Speed: Sustained. level road | 21 miles/hour |
| Short periods, level | 24 miles/hour |
| Maximum Grade: | 60 per cent |
| Maximum Trench: | 7.5 feet |
| Maximum Vertical Wall: | 24 inches |
| Maximum Fording Depth: | 40 inches |
| Minimum Turning Circle: (diameter) | 62 feet |
| Cruising Range: Roads | approx. 150 miles |

# MEDIUM TANK M3A4

## GENERAL DATA

*weight based on T48 or T51 track installed

| | |
|---|---|
| Quantity produced | 109 |
| Crew: | 6 or 7 men |
| Length: w/75mm Gun M2, w/o sandshields | 242 inches |
| Length: w/75mm Gun M3, w/o sandshields | 261 inches |
| Length: w/o gun. w/o sandshields | 242 inches |
| Gun Overhang: 75mm Gun M3 | 19 inches |
| Width: Over side doors | 107 inches |
| Height: Over cupola | 123 inches |
| Tread: | 83 inches |
| Ground Clearance: | 17 inches |
| Fire Height: 75mm gun | 69 inches |
| Turret Ring Diameter: (inside) | 54.5 inches |
| Weight, Combat Loaded: | 64,000 |
| Weight, Unstowed: | 60,000 |
| Power to Weight Ratio: Net | 11.6 hp/ton |
| Gross | 13.3 hp/ton |
| Ground Pressure: Zero penetration | 12.1 psi |

## ARMOR

| Type: | Hull, rolled homogeneous steel riveted assembly | | |
|---|---|---|---|
| | Turret, cast homogeneous steel | | |
| | | Hull Thickness, actual | Angle w/Vertical |
| Front. Upper | | 2.0 inches | 30 degrees |
| Middle | | 1.5 inches | 53 degrees |
| Lower | | 2.0 inches | 0 to 45 degrees |
| Sides | | 1.5 inches | 0 degrees |
| Rear | | 1.5 inches | 0 to 20 degrees |
| Top | | 0.5 inches | 83 to 90 degrees |
| Floor, Front | | 1.0 inches | 90 degrees |
| Rear | | 0. 5 inches | 90 degrees |
| | | Turret Thickness: | |
| Front | | 2.0 inches | 47 degrees |
| Sides | | 2.0 inches | 5 degrees |
| Rear | | 2.0 inches | 5 degrees |
| Top | | 0.875 inches | 90 degrees |

## ARMAMENT

* (2) in early production vehicles

| | | AMMUNITION | FIRE CONTROL EQUIPMENT | |
|---|---|---|---|---|
| | | | Direct | Indirect |
| **Main:** | 75mm Gun M2 or M3 in Mount M1 in right front of hull | 50 rounds 75mm | Periscope M1 with Telescope M21A1 | Gunner's Quadrant M1 |
| Traverse: Manual | 30 degrees (15 degrees L or R) | | | |
| Elevation: Manual | +20 to -9 degrees | | | |
| Firing Rate: (max) | 20 rounds/minute | | | |
| Loading System: | Manual | | | |
| Stabilizer System: | Elevation only | | | |
| **Primary** | 37mm Gun M5 or M6 in Mount M24 in turret | 178 rounds 37mm | Periscope M2 with Telescope M19A1 | |
| Traverse: Hydraulic and manual | 360 degrees | | | |
| Traverse Rate: (max) | 20 seconds/360 degrees | | | |
| Elevation: Manual | +60 to -7 degrees | | | |
| Firing Rate: (max) | 30 rounds/minute | | | |
| Loading System: | Manual | | | |
| Stabilizer System: | Elevation only | | | |
| **Secondary:** | | | | |
| (1) .30-caliber MG M1919A4 in turret cupola | | 9,200 rounds .30 caliber | | |
| (1) .30-caliber MG M1919A4 coaxial w/37mm gun in turret | | | | |
| (1) .30-caliber MG M1919A4 fixed in front plate* | | | | |
| Provision for caliber (1) .45 caliber SMG M1928A1* | | 1,200 rounds .45 caliber | | |
| 12 Hand grenades | | | | |

464

# ENGINE

| | |
|---|---|
| Make and Model: | Chrysler A57, multibank, 4-cycle, liquid-cooled |
| Displacement: | 1253 cubic inches |
| Bore and Stroke: | 4.37 x 4.5 inches |
| Compression Ratio: | 6.2:1 |
| Net Horsepower (max): | 370 hp at 2400 rpm |
| Gross Horsepower (max): | 425 hp at 2850 rpm |
| Net Torque (max): | 1020 ft-lb at 1200 rpm |
| Gross Torque (max): | 1060 ft-lb at 1400 rpm |
| Weight: | 5400 lb, dry |
| Fuel: 80 octane gasoline | 160 gallons |
| Engine Oil: | 32 quarts |

# POWER TRAIN

| | |
|---|---|
| Clutch: | Dry disc, 2 or 3 plate |
| Transmission: | Synchromesh, 5 speeds forward, 1 reverse |

| Gear Ratios: | 1st | 2nd | 3rd | 4th | 5th | Reverse |
|---|---|---|---|---|---|---|
| | 7.56:1 | 3.11:1 | 1.78:1 | 1.11:1 | 0.73:1 | 5.65:1 |

| | |
|---|---|
| Steering: | Controlled differential |
| Bevel Gear Ratio:3.53:1 | |
| Steering Ratio: 1.515:1 | |
| Brakes: | Mechanical, external contracting |
| Final Drive: Herringbone gear | Gear Ratio: 2.84:1 |
| Drive Sprocket: | 13 teeth, mounted at front of vehicle |
| Pitch Diameter: | 25.038 inches |

# ELECTRICAL SYSTEM

| |
|---|
| Nominal Voltage: 24 volts DC |
| Main Generator: (1) 24 volts, 50 amperes, driven by power take-off from main engine |
| Auxiliary Generator: (1) 30 volts, 50 amperes, driven by the auxiliary engine |
| Battery: (2) 12-volt in series |

# COMMUNICATIONS

*Early vehicles may be equipped with SCR-245

| | |
|---|---|
| Radio: | SCR-508 in left front sponson SCR-506* (command tanks only) in right rear sponson |
| Interphone: | (part of radio), 5 stations plus earphones for all crew members |

*Early vehicles may be equipped with SCR 245

# RUNNING GEAR

| | |
|---|---|
| Suspension: | Vertical volute spring |
| | 12 wheels in 6 bogies (3 bogies/track) |
| Tire Size: | 20 x 9-inches |
| Return rollers: | 6 1 trailing each bogie |
| Idler: | 22 x 9-inches, adjustable, rear-mounted |
| Tracks: Outside guide | Type |
| | (T41) Double pin, 16.0 inch width, smooth, rubber |
| Type: | (T48) Double pin, 16.56 inch width, chevron, rubber |
| | (T49) Double pin, 16.56 inch width, parallel bar, steel |
| | (T51) Double pin, 16.56 inch width, smooth, rubber |
| Pitch: | 6 inches |
| Shoes per Vehicle: | 166 (83/track) |
| Ground Contact Length: | 160 inches |

# VISION DEVICES

| | Direct | Indirect |
|---|---|---|
| Driver: | Hatch | Protectoscope (1) |
| Gunner (75): | None | Periscope M1 (1) |
| loader (75): | Hatch & Piistol port | Protectoscope (1) |
| Commander: | Hatch & vision slots (2) | Protectoscope (1) |
| Gunner (37): | None | Periscope M2 (1) |
| Loader (37): | Pistol port | Protectoscope (1) |

# FIRE PROTECTION

| |
|---|
| (2) 10 pound carbon dioxide, fixed |
| (2) 4 pound carbon dioxide, portable |

# PERFORMANCE

| | |
|---|---|
| Maximum Speed: Sustained, level road | 20 miles/hour |
| Short periods, level | 25 miles/hour |
| Maximum Grade: | 60 per cent |
| Maximum Trench: | 8 feet |
| Maximum Vertical Wall: | 24 inches |
| Maximum Fording Depth: | 40 inches |
| Minimum Turning Circle: (diameter) | 70 feet |
| Cruising Range: Roads | approx. 100 miles |

# MEDIUM TANK M3A5

## GENERAL DATA

*weight based on T48 or T51 track installed

| | |
|---|---|
| Quantity produced | 210 + 381 Grant II |
| Crew: | 6 or 7 men |
| Length: w/75mm Gun M2, w/o sandshields | 222 inches |
| Length: w/75mm Gun M3, w/o sandshields | 241 inches |
| Length: w/o gun. w/o sandshields | 222 inches |
| Gun Overhang: 75mm Gun M3 | 19 inches |
| Width: Over side doors | 107 inches |
| Height: Over cupola | 123 inches |
| Tread: | 83 inches |
| Ground Clearance: | 17 inches |
| Fire Height: 75mm gun | 69 inches |
| Turret Ring Diameter: (inside) | 54.5 inches |
| Weight, Combat Loaded: | 64,000 pounds* |
| Weight, Unstowed: | 60,000 pounds* |
| Power to Weight Ratio: Net | 11.7 hp/ton |
| Gross | 12.8 hp/ton |
| Ground Pressure: Zero penetration | 13.1 psi |

## ARMOR

| Type: | Hull, rolled homogeneous steel riveted assembly | |
|---|---|---|
| | Turret, cast homogeneous steel | |
| | Hull Thickness, actual | Angle w/Vertical |
| Front. Upper | 2.0 inches | 30 degrees |
| Middle | 1.5 inches | 53 degrees |
| Lower | 2.0 inches | 0 to 45 degrees |
| Sides | 1.5 inches | 0 degrees |
| Rear | 1.5 inches | 0 to 10 degrees |
| Top | 0.5 inches | 83 to 90 degrees |
| Floor, Front | 1.0 inches | 90 degrees |
| Rear | 0.5 inches | 90 degrees |
| | Turret Thickness: | |
| Front | 2.0 inches | 47 degrees |
| Sides | 2.0 inches | 5 degrees |
| Rear | 2.0 inches | 5 degrees |
| Top | 0.875 inches | 90 degrees |

## ARMAMENT

* (2) in early production vehicles

| | | AMMUNITION | FIRE CONTROL EQUIPMENT | |
|---|---|---|---|---|
| | | | Direct | Indirect |
| Main: | 75mm Gun M2 or M3 in Mount M1 in right front of hull | 50 rounds 75mm | Periscope M1 with Telescope M21A1 | Gunner's Quadrant M1 |
| Traverse: Manual | 30 degrees (15 degrees L or R) | | | |
| Elevation: Manual | +20 to -9 degrees | | | |
| Firing Rate: (max) | 20 rounds/minute | | | |
| Loading System: | Manual | | | |
| Stabilizer System: | Elevation only | | | |
| Primary | 37mm Gun M5 or M6 in Mount M24 in turret | 178 rounds 37mm | Periscope M2 with Telescope M19A1 | |
| Traverse: Hydraulic and manual | 360 degrees | | | |
| Traverse Rate: (max) | 20 seconds/360 degrees | | | |
| Elevation: Manual | +60 to -7 degrees | | | |
| Firing Rate: (max) | 30 rounds/minute | | | |
| Loading System: | Manual | | | |
| Stabilizer System: | Elevation only | | | |
| Secondary: | | | | |
| (1) .30-caliber MG M1919A4 in turret cupola | | 9,200 rounds .30 caliber | | |
| (1) .30-caliber MG M1919A4 coaxial w/37mm gun in turret | | | | |
| (1) .30-caliber MG M1919A4 fixed in front plate* | | | | |
| Provision for caliber (1) .45 caliber SMG M1928A1* | | 1,200 rounds .45 caliber | | |
| 12 Hand grenades | | | | |

# ENGINE

| | |
|---|---|
| Make and Model: | General Motors 6046, 12-cylinder, twin 6, liquid-cooled, compression-igniton |
| Displacement: | 850 cubic inches |
| Bore and Stroke: | 4.25 x 5 inches |
| Compression Ratio: | 16:01 |
| Net Horsepower (max): | 375 hp at 2100 rpm |
| Gross Horsepower (max): | 410 hp at 2900 rpm |
| Net Torque (max): | 885 ft-lb at 1900 rpm |
| Gross Torque (max): | 1000 fl-lb at 1400 rpm |
| Weight: | 5110 lb. dry |
| Fuel: 40 cetane Diesel | 148 gallons |
| Engine Oil: | 28 quarts |

# POWER TRAIN

| | |
|---|---|
| Clutch: | Dry disc, 2 or 3 plate |
| Transfer case: | Gear Ratio: 0.73:1 |
| Transmission: | Synchromesh, 5 speeds forward, 1 reverse |

| Gear Ratios: | 1st | 2nd | 3rd | 4th | 5th | Reverse |
|---|---|---|---|---|---|---|
| | 7.56:1 | 3.11:1 | 1.78:1 | 1.11:1 | 0.73:1 | 5.65:1 |

| | |
|---|---|
| Steering: | Controlled differential |
| Bevel Gear Ratio:3.53:1 | |
| Steering Ratio: 1.515:1 | |
| Brakes: | Mechanical, external contracting |
| Final Drive: Herringbone gear | Gear Ratio: 2.84:1 |
| Drive Sprocket: | 13 teeth, mounted at front of vehicle |
| Pitch Diameter: | 25.038 inches |

# ELECTRICAL SYSTEM

Nominal Voltage: 24 volts DC
Main Generator: (1) 24 volts, 50 amperes, driven by power take-off from main engine
Auxiliary Generator: (1) 30 volts, 50 amperes, driven by the auxiliary engine
Battery: (2) 12-volt in series

# COMMUNICATIONS

*Early vehicles may be equipped with SCR-245

| Radio: | SCR-508 in left front sponson SCR-506* (command tanks only) in right rear sponson |
|---|---|
| Interphone: | (part of radio), 5 stations plus earphones for all crew members |

# RUNNING GEAR

| | |
|---|---|
| Suspension: | Vertical volute spring |
| | 12 wheels in 6 bogies (3 bogies/track) |
| Tire Size: | 20 x 9-inches |
| Return rollers: | 6 1 on top of each bogie |
| Idler: | 22 x 9-inches, adjustable, rear-mounted |
| Tracks: Outside guide | Type |
| | (T41) Double pin. 16.0 inch width. smooth, rubber |
| Type: | (T48) Double pin. 16.56 inch width. chevron, rubber |
| | (T49) Double pin. 16.56 inch width. parallel bar, steel |
| | (T51) Double pin. 16.56 inch width. smooth, rubber |
| Pitch: | 6 inches |
| Shoes per Vehicle: | 158 (79/track) |
| Ground Contact Length: | 147 inches |

# VISION DEVICES

| | Direct | Indirect |
|---|---|---|
| Driver: | Hatch | Protectoscope (1) |
| Gunner (75): | None | Periscope M1 (1) |
| loader (75): | Hatch & Piistol port | Protectoscope (1) |
| Commander: | Hatch & vision slots (2) | Protectoscope (1) |
| Gunner (37): | None | Periscope M2 (1) |
| Loader (37): | Pistol port | Protectoscope (1) |

# FIRE PROTECTION

(2) 10 pound carbon dioxide. fixed
(2) 4 pound carbon dioxide. portable

# PERFORMANCE

| | |
|---|---|
| Maximum Speed: Sustained. level road | 21 miles/hour |
| Short periods, level | 24 miles/hour |
| Maximum Grade: | 60 per cent |
| Maximum Trench: | 7.5 feet |
| Maximum Vertical Wall: | 24 inches |
| Maximum Fording Depth: | 40 inches |
| Minimum Turning Circle: (diameter) | 62 feet |
| Cruising Range: Roads | approx. 150 miles |

# CRUISER TANK GRANT I

## GENERAL DATA

*weight based on T48 or T51 track installed

| | |
|---|---|
| Quantity: | 1212 with riveted hull |
| Crew: | 6 men |
| Length: w/75mm Gun M2, w/o sandshields | 222 inches |
| Length: w/75mm Gun M3, w/o sandshields | 241 inches |
| Length: w/o gun. w/o sandshields | 222 inches |
| Gun Overhang: 75mm Gun M3 | 19 inches |
| Width: Over side doors | 107 inches |
| Height: Over turret periscope | 119 inches |
| Tread: | 83 inches |
| Ground Clearance: | 17 inches |
| Fire Height: 75mm gun | 69 inches |
| Turret Ring Diameter: (inside) | 54.5 inches |
| Weight, Combat Loaded: | 62,000 pounds* |
| Weight, Unstowed: | 58,000 pounds* |
| Power to Weight Ratio: Net | 11.0 hp/ton |
| Gross | 12.9 hp/ton |
| Ground Pressure: Zero penetration | 12.7 psi |

## ARMOR

| Type: | Hull, rolled homogeneous steel riveted assembly | |
|---|---|---|
| | Turret, cast homogeneous steel | |
| | Hull Thickness, actual | Angle w/Vertical |
| Front. Upper | 2.0 inches | 30 degrees |
| Middle | 1.5 inches | 53 degrees |
| Lower | 2.0 inches | 0 to 45 degrees |
| Sides | 1.5 inches | 0 degrees |
| Rear | 1.5 inches | 0 to I0 degrees |
| Top | 0.5 inches | 83 to 90 degrees |
| Floor, Front | 1.0 inches | 90 degrees |
| Rear | 0. 5 inches | 90 degrees |
| | Turret Thickness: | |
| Front | 3.0 inches | 47 degrees |
| Sides | 2.0 inches | 0 to 30 degrees |
| Rear | 2.0 inches | 0 degrees |
| Top | 1.25 inches | 80 to 90 degrees |

## ARMAMENT

* (2) in early production vehicles

| | AMMUNITION | FIRE CONTROL EQUIPMENT |
|---|---|---|
| | | Direct |
| **Main:** 75mm Gun M2 or M3 in Mount M1 in right front of hull | 65 rounds 75mm | Periscope M1 with Telescope M45 |
| Traverse: Manual | 30 degrees (15 degrees L or R) | |
| Elevation: Manual | +20 to -9 degrees | |
| Firing Rate: (max) | 20 rounds/minute | |
| Loading System: | Manual | |
| Stabilizer System: | Elevation only | |
| **Primary:** 37mm Gun M5 or M6 in Mount M24 in turret | 128 rounds 37mm | Periscope M2 with Telescope M40 |
| Traverse: Hydraulic and manual | 360 degrees | |
| Traverse Rate: (max) | 20 seconds/360 degrees | |
| Elevation: Manual | +60 to -7 degrees | |
| Firing Rate: (max) | 30 rounds/minute | |
| Loading System: | Manual | |
| Stabilizer System: | Elevation only | |
| **Secondary:** | | |
| (1) .30-caliber MG M1919A4 coaxial w/37mm gun in turret | 4,084 rounds .30-caliber | |
| (1) .30-caliber MG M1919A4 fixed in front plate* | | |
| Provision for caliber (2) .45 caliber SMG M1928A1 | 640 rounds .45 caliber | |
| (1) 2-inch Mortar Mk I (smoke) mounted in turret | 14 rounds | |

# ENGINE

| | |
|---|---|
| Make and Model: | Wright (Continental) R-975-EC 9 cylinder, 4 cycle. Air-cooled, radial, Magneto ignition |
| Displacement: | 973 cubic inches |
| Bore and Stroke: | 5 x 5.5 inches |
| Compression Ratio: | 6.3:1 |
| Net Horsepower (max): | 340 hp at 2400 rpm |
| Gross Horsepower (max): | 400 hp at 2400 rpm |
| Net Torque (max): | 800 ft-lb at 1800 rpm |
| Gross Torque (max): | 890 ft-lb at 1800 rpm |
| Weight: | 1137 lb, dry |
| Fuel: 92 octane gasoline | 175 gallons |
| Engine Oil: | 36 quarts |

# POWER TRAIN

| Clutch: | Dry disc. 2 or 3 plate | | | | | |
|---|---|---|---|---|---|---|
| Transmission: | Synchromesh, 5 speeds forward, 1 reverse | | | | | |
| GearRatios: | 1st | 2nd | 3rd | 4th | 5th | Reverse |
| | 7.56:1 | 3.11:1 | 1.78:1 | 1.11:1 | 0.73:1 | 5.65:1 |
| Steering: | Controlled differential | | | | | |
| Bevel Gear Ratio:3.53:1 | | | | | | |
| Steering Ratio: 1.515:1 | | | | | | |
| Brakes: | Mechanical, external contracting | | | | | |
| Final Drive: Herringbone gear | Gear Ratio: 2.84:1 | | | | | |
| Drive Sprocket: | 13 teeth, mounted at front of vehicle | | | | | |
| Pitch Diameter: | 25.038 inches | | | | | |

# ELECTRICAL SYSTEM

Nominal Voltage: 24 volts DC

| | |
|---|---|
| Main Generator: (1) 24 volts, ,50 amperes, driven by power take-off from main engine | |
| Auxiliary Generator: (1) 30 volts, 50 amperes, driven by the auxiliary engine | |
| Battery: (2) 12-volt in series | |

# COMMUNICATIONS

| | |
|---|---|
| Radio: | Wireless Set No. 19 mounted in turret rear |
| Interphone: | (part of radio), 5 stations plus earphones for all crew members |

# RUNNING GEAR

| | |
|---|---|
| Suspension: | Vertical volute spring |
| | 12 wheels in 6 bogies (3 bogies/track) |
| Tire Size: | 20 x 9-inches |
| Return rollers: | 6 1 on top of each bogie |
| Idler: | 22 x 9-inches, adjustable, rear-mounted |
| Tracks: Outside guide | Type |
| Type: | (WE 210) Double pin, 16.0 inch width, smooth rubber |
| | (T41) Double pin, 16.0 inch width, smooth, rubber |
| | (T48) Double pin, 16.56 inch width, chevron, rubber |
| | (T51) Double pin, 16.56 inch width, smooth, rubber |
| Pitch: | 6 inches |
| Shoes per Vehicle: | 158 (79/track) |
| Ground Contact Length: | 147 inches |

# VISION DEVICES

| | Direct | Indirect |
|---|---|---|
| Driver: | Hatch | Protectoscope (1) |
| Gunner (75): | None | Periscope M1 (1) |
| loader (75): | Hatch & Piistol port | Protectoscope (1) |
| Commander: | Hatch | Periscope, Vickers (1) |
| Gunner (37): | Pistol port | Periscope M2 (1) & Protectoscope (1) |
| Loader (37): | Pistol port | Protectoscope (1) |

# FIRE PROTECTION

| |
|---|
| (2) 10 pound carbon dioxide. fixed |
| (2) 4 pound carbon dioxide, portable |
| (2) Pyrene, portable |

# PERFORMANCE

| | |
|---|---|
| Maximum Speed: Sustained. level road | 21 miles/hour |
| Short periods. level | 24 miles/hour |
| Maximum Grade: | 60 per cent |
| Maximum Trench: | 7.5 feet |
| Maximum Vertical Wall: | 24 inches |
| Maximum Fording Depth: | 40 inches |
| Minimum Turning Circle: (diameter) | 62 feet |
| Cruising Range: Roads | approx. 120 miles |

# Lend-Lease shipments*

## M3, M3A2, M3A3, M3A5

| Total | British Empire | USSR | French Forces | China | Brazil | Canada |
|---|---|---|---|---|---|---|
| 4,377 | 2,887 | 1,386 | 0 | 0 | 104 | 0 |

- Information from "Lend-Lease Shipments World War II" 31 December 1946, Office, Chief of Finance, War Department

Breakdown of shipments by government from 11 March 1941 through 31 December 1944

**United Kingdom**
M3 2653
M3A3 49
M3A5 185

**Russia**
M3 1386
M3A3 0
M3A5 0

**Brazil**
M3A3 77
M3A5 23

# Monthly breakdown of Lend-Lease shipments

| | Prior to Dec-41 | Dec-41 | Jan-42 | Feb-42 | Mar-42 | Apr-42 | May-42 | Jun-42 | Jul-42 | Aug-42 | Sep-42 | Oct-42 | Nov-42 | Dec-42 | Jan-43 | Mar-43 |
|---|---|---|---|---|---|---|---|---|---|---|---|---|---|---|---|---|
| M3 UK | 59 | 195 | 256 | 285 | 359 | 406 | 406 | 807 | 34 | 0 | 0 | 0 | 0 | 0 | 0 | 252 |
| M3 USSR | 0 | 154 | 152 | 154 | 154 | 123 | 191 | 160 | 185 | 93 | 0 | 0 | 0 | 0 | 0 | 0 |
| M3 Brazil | 0 | 0 | 0 | 0 | 0 | 0 | 0 | 0 | 0 | 0 | 0 | 0 | 0 | 0 | 0 | 0 |
| M3A3 UK | 0 | 0 | 0 | 0 | 0 | 0 | 0 | 20 | 29 | 0 | 0 | 0 | 0 | 0 | 0 | 0 |
| M3A3 USSR | 0 | 0 | 0 | 0 | 0 | 0 | 0 | 0 | 0 | 0 | 0 | 0 | 0 | 0 | 0 | 0 |
| M3A3 Brazil | 0 | 0 | 0 | 0 | 0 | 0 | 0 | 0 | 5 | 10 | 15 | 23 | 22 | 0 | 2 | 0 |
| M3A5 UK | 0 | 0 | 0 | 0 | 0 | 0 | 0 | 125 | 60 | 0 | 0 | 0 | 0 | 0 | 0 | 0 |
| M3A5 USSR | 0 | 0 | 0 | 0 | 0 | 0 | 0 | 0 | 0 | 0 | 0 | 0 | 0 | 0 | 0 | 0 |
| M3A5 Brazil | 0 | 0 | 0 | 0 | 0 | 0 | 0 | 0 | 0 | 0 | 0 | 0 | 0 | 8 | 0 | 15 |

**M3 LEE GRANT**
The design, production and service of the M3 Lee Medium Tank,
the foundation of America's tank Industry.
Copyright © 2020 AFV Modeller Ltd

**Published by**
**AFV Modeller Publications**

Old Stables
East Moor
Stannington
Northumberland
NE61 6ES
England


Tel: 01670 823648

email: keith@afvmodeller.com

# www.afvmodeller.com

## ISBN 978-0-9935646-8-0

**Graphic Design** by Keith Colvin-Smith
**Cover Illustration and design** by David Parker